PRAISE FOR *WHAT TH*

T0013837

"I know of no other work that so elo[...] dogged search for a Nazi paper trail of evidence and a son's [...] iation with his family's Holocaust legacy. *What They Didn't Burn* is not only an engaging piece of rigorous research, but also a harrowing and heartwarming personal saga of discovery as well."

—SCOTT MILLER, author of *Refuge Denied,*
The St. Louis Passengers and the Holocaust

". . . A compelling blend of memoir and historical research, beautifully written. Laytner's deeply personal story is an important addition to Holocaust literature, but will also resonate as a historical detective story. Along the way, he ponders how do we know what we know about history, and the lives of those who made it or were brutalized by it? Are documents better evidence than memory? How does one understand the ethical (and unethical) choices made by victims and victimizers alike?"

—KENNETH S. STERN, director, Bard Center for the Study
of Hate, author of *The Conflict over The Conflict:*
The Israel/Palestine Campus Debate

"Mel Laytner's *What They Didn't Burn* offers the reader both an emotional account of a son retracing his father's traumatic experiences under Nazi persecution, and a gripping detective story of a savvy journalist uncovering 'what they didn't burn.' This beautifully written and deeply felt book, a powerful tribute to his father's fortitude, also serves as a reminder that the long shadow of the Nazi past stretches over generations."

—GABRIELLE ROBINSON, author of *Api's Berlin Diaries*

"Mel Laytner's book is remarkable . . . He puts his readers into every scene, astonishing us with surprises that allowed many Jews to survive, escaping the hideous concentration camps: Blechhammer, Auschwitz, Buchenwald, and others . . . Never forget the Holocaust. You will never forget Laytner's book as well."

—JOELLE SANDER, author of *Before Their Time: Four Generations*
of Teenage Mothers, awarded Best Book for Adults About
Children by the Braun Center for Holocaust Studies

WHAT
THEY
DIDN'T
BURN

....

Uncovering My Father's Holocaust Secrets

....

MEL LAYTNER

SPARKPRESS

Published by SparkPress, a BookSparks imprint,
A division of SparkPoint Studio, LLC
Phoenix, Arizona, USA, 85007
www.gosparkpress.com

Published 2021
Printed in the United States of America
Print ISBN: 978-1-68463-103-2

E-ISBN: 978-1-68463-104-9

Library of Congress Control Number: 2021908293

Interior design by Tabitha Lahr

To my children's children.
Never forget

But why do I talk of Death?
That Phantom of grisly bone,
I hardly fear its terrible shape,
It seems so like my own—
It seems so like my own,
Because of the fasts I keep;
Oh, God! that bread should be so dear
And flesh and blood so cheap!

—THOMAS HOOD, "The Song of the Shirt"
  [First published 16 December 1843.]

Contents

INTRODUCTION

··

They burned his younger sister and her two-year-old daughter. They burned his half-brothers and their families. They burned his uncles and their wives. They murdered the sister's husband. He probably wasn't burned but dumped into a shallow mass grave in the hills above a small village in western Poland.

When they couldn't burn any more people, they set about burning the records and documents to hide their sins. What they didn't burn was a paper trail that tracked the man's journey through ghettoes, slave labor, concentration camps, death marches, and more. They didn't burn the hidden records that revealed surprising and painful incidents he had never talked about—at least not to me, his son.

It's not that my father, Josef "Dolek" Lajtner, never told me stories about the war; he did, many of them. As a child, we'd snuggle together on the green living room armchair with the tassels—"Daddy's chair"—as he spoke of survival and escape from Hitler-and-the-Nazis, a phrase always uttered as a single malignant noun. The war was less than ten years past, my father's recollections fresh and detailed. His stories ended with the same moral: *So you see son, in the end it didn't matter if you had money or not, were smart or dumb. Life was worth nothing—absolutely nothing. You needed luck.*

Because of this reservoir of stories, I knew with the certainty of youth that I knew everything worth knowing about Hitler-and-the-Nazis—the camps, the struggle to survive, that life or death was a coin toss. I never felt a need or curiosity to explore beyond some popular war movies of the period. I never read memoirs by Elie Wiesel and Primo Levi or even The Diary of Anne Frank until well into my adult years, and only then because my daughters were assigned them for school and I felt obliged to know what they were talking about.

Only decades later, only after uncovering the documents they didn't burn, did I realize I had learned more about the Holocaust from Hollywood than from all of my father's stories.

After Dad's death, and especially after my mother's passing seven years later, I felt their stories fading like family snapshots in a shoebox. Our children may know who they are, intellectually. However, they will never speak Yiddish, the lingua franca of my parents' generation. They will never have a Grandpa Joe or a Grandma Helen as links to a world long gone. Something very important was being lost.

When my young daughters and nieces asked about the grandfather they had never met, I would recount Grandpa Joe stories that came to mind in the moment. I had been a reporter for some twenty years and prided myself on knowing how to spin a story. The children listened politely, asked a question or two, and reliably proclaimed the story "amazing." Yet doubts nagged: Did the story really stick? Would it be remembered, if at all, more as family fable than family fact? Though but one generation removed, was I one generation too far to recapture the poignant humanity, the essential truth of my father's calm, measured voice?

As a former journalist, I knew that relying on my memories of my father's remembered stories could never pass any sniff test of Reporting 101. Where was the corroboration, the proof, the facts?

The truth was, I had no facts, only memories of facts. I could tell my daughters no more because I knew no more. I had been repeating my father's vague vignettes in a vacuum.

Like my father, every Holocaust survivor has an amazing story. If they didn't, they wouldn't have survived. Yet if the stories sound too amazing, they risk being dismissed as exaggerations, or worse. How will their stories be remembered by future generations further and further removed from the war?

As I exhumed the documents they didn't burn from archives in Poland, Germany, France, Israel, and Washington, a gradual realization imposed a somber discipline I had not anticipated.

From the most unlikely of sources—the Nazis themselves—the documents corroborate not only a man's chronology but also the chronologies of his camp comrades, those who survived and those who did not.

These yellowing papers demanded respect. For mixing the warm memories of my father's stories with cold facts from these documents risked yielding a tepid brew that satisfied neither the soul nor the intellect. Still, I would have to resist the urge to dramatize the undramatic, insinuate significance into the insignificant, draw sharp conclusions from vague evidence, or, conversely, ignore hard evidence in favor of facts I might reasonably presume to improve the narrative.

Chapter 1

WEST 83RD STREET

The only time I heard anyone call my father a bastard was about a month after he died.

I was in an open-air café overlooking the Western Wall in the Old City of Jerusalem, sipping iced coffee and eating apple cake with Walter Spitzer, my father's old artist friend from the days before, during, and after "the camps."

Walter had flown in from Paris for business and had brought his daughter along to see the Holy Land. I was a reporter for NBC News and had returned from Dad's funeral in New York a couple of weeks earlier, still abraded and raw from his unexpected death.

Walter smiled when I pulled out my reporter's Sony cassette recorder.

To his daughter: "So he wants to know how his father survived."

To me: "I'll tell you how. Dolek was a bastard. A real bastard. You had to be if you wanted to live."

I was stunned, and it showed. This wasn't the quintessential type-B father of my childhood. That man was thoughtful and considerate, patient and gentle.

1

Walter cut off my stuttering protests with a laugh. "Dolek was a smuggler, a great smuggler—he smuggled everything."

In the forced labor camps, the Germans would appoint a Jew as *Judenälteste*, roughly the Jewish Elder or Senior Jew, charged with maintaining order inside the wire with his own staff. Walter said a German guard had caught my father with a bottle of schnapps he had just traded with a Pole. The guard dragged Dad to the *Judenälteste*. "The German tells him, 'Look, this is the man you are protecting—making business, black business, black-market business.'

"The *Judenälteste* screams at Dolek, 'You son of a bitch. I protect you and you do this to me?' And he punches your father, right-left-right. Knocks him down. Then he gives him a big shtup [kick] in his ass. 'Get out of my sight or I'll kill you.' He keeps kicking and screaming. Dolek crawls away on his hands and knees. And the SS man was happy to see this, a Jew beating another Jew."

Walter paused for a sip of iced coffee, but really for dramatic effect. "And that's how he saved your father's life."

"Saved?" I ask.

"Yes, of course. Otherwise the German would have killed Dolek like a fly. Is this not great? Fantastic, no?"

By now I'm a little off balance. My father never mentioned this incident. Evidently there was more to Dad's stories than he ever let on. What else didn't I know? I wanted to find out more. Why else bring my reporter's tape recorder to the meeting? But the wound of his sudden death was still too fresh, too painful. It would need to heal some before I began picking at those scabs. I put the Spitzer cassette into an old wooden humidor I used to store trinkets and memorabilia, promising myself I'd get back to it. It was a promise that took twenty years to keep.

Though Walter Spitzer couldn't have known it, he—more precisely, his art—had insidiously infected my life at a very young age.

As a child, our family lived in a rent-controlled apartment building next to a parking garage on West 83rd Street in

Manhattan. Friends from the old country would note with sly humor that my parents were the first "greenhorns" among them to move into a building with a functioning elevator.

The central hub of the apartment was a small square dining room with doorways or windows on three sides. That left only one wall large enough to hold art and only one piece of artwork on that wall, a dark brooding pastel that dominated the room. It was drawn by Walter Spitzer in 1946.

It was a ghetto scene of an old Hassidic Jew with his son. Each man has a yellow star on the breast of his dark frock coat. Each hugs a red prayer shawl bag under his arm. Glancing anxiously over their shoulders, in the distance they spy a jackbooted figure in paramilitary green with arms raised approaching an elderly Jewish couple. There is deep terror in the old man's eyes.

That drawing always hung on the most prominent wall in the most prominent room of every apartment in which we lived. It haunted me. It fascinated me. It was as much a part of my childhood reality as television. It catalyzed many a story on my father's knee.

Like Dad, his friends were all survivors and immigrants. Beryl worked in a grocery, Jack moved furniture, Charlie installed telephones, and Sam sold sheets and towels out of the back of his Oldsmobile in the days before credit cards were invented. My father was a presser of men's suits at a factory on Manhattan's far West Side.

They were modest men closing in on middle age. Shoulders rounded, faces creased, eyes searching, warily searching, even when they smiled. They spoke English with thick Polish accents, though none thicker than Dad's. They wore cheap brown suits and patterned shirts and ties knotted to the neck, even on Sundays.

Like his friends, Dad had married a tough Eastern European woman who had also survived the war, albeit with losses and, hence, had no tolerance for bullshit. Unlike his friends, though, he married a woman twelve years younger, Henci, a hot-tempered Magyar, a Hungarian, so very different in disposition than the retiring, cerebral father of childhood memory.

The friends sat around our red-and-gray Formica dining table with the chrome legs, chain-smoked Kents or Camels, sipped cold Ballantines from cans in summer or hot tea from steaming glasses in winter. They spoke in a lilting, singsong Yiddish. They talked of the old country and old acquaintances, of new lives and new families here in America.

On the Formica table there was always a white bakery box with cheese Danish and another full of rainbow cookies. With our parents egging us on, we kids picked out our favorites. Mine was the yellow cookie with the candied cherry on top.

There was much laughter and mirth in that small dining room. Once in a while, though, even a child of seven could detect a somber mood descend like the blue-gray cigarette smoke wafting over the table. Those men and women were their own support group long before the term was coined.

Conversation inevitably gave way to nickel-and-dime games of seven-card knock rummy for the women and more serious rounds of poker for the men, where pots could reach three, four, or even five dollars.

Except for Dad. He didn't play. When the red and blue Tally-Ho decks came out he quietly retired to another room with his *Reader's Digest* or Yiddish newspaper. When Mom berated him for this antisocial behavior, he'd mutter "I've gambled enough in my life" and end the debate.

We kids grew up fluent in Yiddish and the uniqueness of our parents' past. Like the faded blue numbers on Dad's arm, it was rarely discussed or acknowledged. Inside, we knew. Our parents were different not because of what they were—immigrants with accents—but who they were, survivors, the "S" always capitalized in our consciousness, the meaning self-evident. To me, this awareness was just there—a birthmark, not a birth defect.

Years went by. Families grew up. Friendships grew apart. When the old friends did meet, the suits fit better, the faces were fuller, the eyes more content, though the men still wore knotted neckties on Sundays.

Tzu mir, ales kimpt tze shpait, Dad would sigh, To me, everything comes too late. I never asked; I just assumed there would be time to question him at length and make sense of his stories. Then Dad suffered that fatal heart attack and it was too late for me, too. Joseph "Dolek" Laytner died at the age of seventy-three, four months before my brother and his wife could present him with his first grandchild.

By then I was a reporter in Jerusalem seven time zones away. The first call, my brother Alan says Dad suffered a heart attack and is resting in the cardiac unit at Mt. Sinai Hospital. *Dad? But Mom has the heart problems.* Alan's not sure if I should come home. *Bullshit.* I arrange to return immediately. The second call, after two hours: Dad's in bad shape. Come home quick. The third, about a lifetime later, from my Uncle Ari. "I'm sorry, boy. He's gone."

A gray numbness tasting of ash displaced the adrenalized dread of the past hours. I slumped into my wife Anat's embrace. *What do I do? How should I feel? How should I act?*

I remembered my father's last hug goodbye six months ago in the doorway of his apartment. He held me close and tight and sobbed, and I said, "Don't worry, Pop, we'll see each other next spring."

I remembered *Finita la commedia*. I was in high school and we were walking home after a condolence call to a neighbor. Holding his hand out, palm up, he announced, "One day you're here, a heart attack"—flipping the palm over—"and you're gone. *Finita la commedia*, the farce is over."

I remembered Dad telling me that before the war, a pious Jew in Europe would arrange to have a small sack of earth from Jerusalem placed in the casket so the head would rest for eternity on holy soil.

This is what I did after I remembered: I drove with Anat through the dark empty streets of Arab East Jerusalem, up a steep hill in the A'Tur neighborhood to the Mount of Olives cemetery. This is where Zachariah and Absalom and the righteous have been buried for three thousand years, a bona fide holy place where pilgrim buses line up during the day but where now, on this cool April night, the cemetery was pitch dark.

I told Anat to keep the car doors locked and the motor running because, even though it was safe, perfectly safe, you're always cautious about driving with yellow Israeli license plates at night into this isolated part of East Jerusalem.

I squeezed through a loosely chained fence, down terraced rows of flat limestone graves glowing pale white in the reflected starlight. From between tombstones, I scraped fistfuls of gravelly soil into a plastic sandwich baggie. Later, in the taxi to the airport for my 1:00 a.m. flight to New York, I smiled at the irony, that the head of my proudly agnostic father would rest on some of the holiest dirt in Judaism.

The funeral fell on a Sunday. The largest chapel in the Riverside Funeral Home on Amsterdam Avenue was packed to standing room with family, old friends, and many newer acquaintances who had known Joe only as the owner of a neighborhood candy store and then a linen shop for the last twenty-four years. Our parents' inner circle sat in rows close behind my mother, my brother Alan, and our wives.

My eulogy opened by noting that Dad was being buried on April 21, 1985, exactly forty years to the day that he had escaped a death march from a concentration camp in Germany. I often wonder about this coincidence.

At the cemetery, the grave was filled the traditional way—by friends and family taking turns with shovels—as Mom, Alan, and I stood by and watched. The hollow clunk of sod striking the pine coffin ricochets in my heart to this day. *Finita la commedia.*

The Orthodox religious traditions continued for the shiva,

the seven days of official mourning, at my parents' rent-controlled apartment. Mirrors had been covered immediately after Dad's death. We wore torn shirts to symbolize bereavement, sat on low stools to accept condolences, and ate only food brought by family and friends. At least ten adult males gathered early mornings and late afternoons so Alan and I could chant the *Kaddish*, the prayer for the departed, within a *minyan*, a religious quorum.

I stayed on in New York for another week. Alan and my father had been working together in the family business for many years now and had grown close—much closer than I ever could, two continents and a career away. I volunteered to go through Dad's clothes while Mom and Alan were out.

From the inside pocket of Dad's sports jacket, the one he had been wearing when he was rushed to the hospital, I pulled out a creased snapshot of Schlep, our German shepherd mutt who had died a few years earlier. Until that moment I had kept it pretty much together, acting the role of Eldest Son and Older Brother. Seeing the photo, I broke down and sobbed loud and long and pressed the gray herringbone to my face to inhale Dad's lingering smell.

We donated most of his clothes to charity. Alan and I split the silk ties. The shoes were especially tough. Every scuff, crease, and fold of the leather was uniquely our father's. I cannot remember how we disposed of them. I did keep, and still wear, the short navy-blue wool robe I had given Dad for Father's Day years before.

It was later that month that Walter Spitzer called my father a bastard.

....

After Mom died some years later, I laid claim to the Spitzer ghetto picture and, as the eldest son, became the designated repository of Dad's war stories including the oft-repeated family favorite about Dad and Bill Ball.

Both had been forced laborers at a giant oil refinery in Germany. Only Bill was a British POW who wore proper khakis and received food packages from the Canadian Red Cross. My father was a concentration camp inmate in striped pajamas on starvation rations.

Contact between POWs and Jews was strictly forbidden and stringently enforced. Bill Ball nevertheless did something truly extraordinary for my father. Under the Geneva Convention, POWs could write postcards home. Bill Ball used this privilege to instead send a postcard to my father's family in Brooklyn, where Dad's sister had immigrated many years before the war. Because of censorship, my father said the card could only say something like, "Doing as well as can be expected. My mate Joe is still with me." That postcard was the only word Dad's family had between 1939 and 1945 that he was alive.

As my daughters evolved into teenagers, they began asking questions: Where did this happen? Did Grandpa Joe meet Bill Ball after the war? What happened to the postcard? They said, "You ought to write about this." I thought, *Yeah, but it would have to be fiction because confirming the facts would be impossible.*

That suited me just fine. I'd been out of journalism for almost two decades. I was a father of three and lived a suburban life complete with dog, cockatiel, and a red Sears barbeque in the backyard. I had joined my brother in the family's expanding retail business and had prospered in an acceptable middle-class sort of way. I learned to like it well enough and it paid the bills a lot easier than the news business. Still, it never gave me the creative rush it did for my brother.

Bill Ball and the postcard story seemed a good way to get back to writing. All I needed was some context, some details about time and place. From among the trinkets and memorabilia in the old wooden humidor, I retrieved the Sony audio cassette marked Walter Spitzer, recorded twenty years earlier as we sipped iced coffee and ate apple cake in that open-air café, overlooking the Western Wall, in the Old City of Jerusalem.

Chapter 2

FINDING BILL BALL

M y search for Bill Ball begins with the name of the camp my father talked about. I turn to my computer and type, "Blechamer."

Google asks, "Did you mean blechhammer?" I frown. I click. Up comes the first ten of fifty-two thousand one hundred entries. I learn that Blechhammer was the name of twin refinery complexes each larger than New York's Central Park and built by some forty thousand workers. It was also the name of a nearby *Zwangsarbeitslager fur Juden,* a forced labor camp for Jews that supplied up to four thousand slave workers to the refinery.

On April 1, 1944, the camp came under the administrative control of the Auschwitz Concentration Camp, about thirty-five miles to the southeast. One website listed Blechhammer under its "Forgotten Camps" category. "The first 3,056 male prisoners of Blechhammer have tattoos of the Auschwitz numbers 176512 to 179567—"

I remember my father's tattoo was 177-something.

Ransacking old photo albums I find a snapshot with his left arm exposed. A magnifying glass reveals the faded blue numbers: 177904.

The site also says that two thousand British POWs worked at the refineries.

In less than five minutes, I've confirmed that my father had indeed been in Blechhammer and could have interacted with British POWs there.

I reach out to relatives around the country to ask if they recalled anything about a postcard from a British POW during the war. None do. Instead, I get intriguing tidbits about Dad.

An older cousin in Florida emails that the only story she remembers is "how he got a bag of diamonds from an old Belgian Jew, whom your dad took care of, giving him some extra bread & water since the man was dying of typhoid fever. He told your dad where he had buried a bag of diamonds & then died."

My father had mentioned diamonds in a couple of his stories, but I was too young to think of asking how he got them. I file the email away.

An unexpected lead comes from the keeper of our family tree, Cousin Avi in Los Angeles. "The US Holocaust Museum website has a link to an Auschwitz database of prisoner registrations," he writes. "Your dad's name shows up there (you probably know this) and his 'arrest' date is given as sometime in June 1943."

I didn't know. I had surfed the museum's website many times but found nothing of specific interest. I search it again, for hours. No luck. I reach out to researchers at the museum's Survivors' Registry. They sound dubious but agree to help.

I am also still looking for Bill Ball, the British POW. All I remember is Dad saying he was big and ruddy-faced and his name was Bill Ball . . . or was it Bill Bell? Maybe it was Bill Baird. Dad said he was a Scotsman. Or perhaps Australian . . . but he was definitely a POW. How hard can it be?

At least six POW subcamps fed labor to the Blechhammer refineries. POWs were shifted from one subcamp to another and rotated back to the main POW camp, Stalag VIIIB. More than one hundred thousand POWs passed through Stalag VIIIB during the war. Some were repatriated as part of prisoner exchanges. Tracking down a single POW will be a lot tougher than I had imagined.

On the internet, many POWs recounted their own captivity. Occasionally, one mentioned the Jewish prisoners. "We thought that all the Jews in Blechhammer were destroyed," said Ray Corbett from Scotland. "You could see them fading away as the weeks went by and then they would suddenly disappear. I would say virtually worked to death."

There are also firsthand stories from Jewish survivors of Blechhammer. Some recall incidents so similar to my father's stories that I imagine both men side by side witnessing the same event—the sickly-sweet smell of bodies incinerating in the camp's crematorium, or the hanging of a prisoner for some minor infraction of the rules.

The internet leads me to Yale University's Fortunoff Video Archive for Holocaust Testimonies. Of its four thousand four hundred survivor testimonials, I get only forty-three hits for Blechhammer on its online database. It's 2005, and the VHS tapes cannot be viewed online.

On a crisp, clear Friday in October, some two months into my quest, I am at Yale's majestically Gothic Sterling Memorial Library in New Haven when it opens to view six tapes on reserve.

I had picked the first tape because the online synopsis promises accounts of day-to-day life in Blechhammer. It was recorded in 1982 by Sigmund Walder, then a sixty-one-year-old wholesale jeweler in North Haven, Connecticut.

Tinted aviator glasses mask Sigmund Walder's eyes. Iron-gray hair brushes his temples and his then-fashionable sideburns. In clipped, German-accented English he recounts his family history in pedantic, mind-numbing detail. My eyes glazing over, I scan the three-page summary of the tape folded into the VHS box. At the last line of the last page is a notation: "Knows Walter Spitzer, artist in France."

I sit up straight, now fully engaged. *If this man knew Walter...*

One hour and twelve minutes into the tape, Sigmund reaches behind his chair and pulls out a portrait Walter drew of him in 1946. It's Sigmund during the war, emaciated and bedraggled in blue-and-gray striped inmate pajamas. My heart skips. I remember a similar portrait Walter did of my gaunt and hollow-eyed father. It was never displayed but remained wrapped in a closet. Somewhere between the apartment moves after my parents' deaths the drawing had disappeared.

Driving home, Friday evening traffic on I-95 South moves like a broken snake. I barely notice, or care. Could I have so easily stumbled on someone who knew Dad at Blechhammer? Was this man still alive?

It's still dark Sunday morning when I wake my computer and google "Sigmund Walder, North Haven, CT."

Four hours and hundreds of page views later, his name appears on a posting about a 2002 art exhibit in Sarasota, Florida, "The Last Expression: Art in Auschwitz." Walder had brought his Spitzer portrait to the exhibit. I quickly find a phone number for a Sigmund Walder in nearby Longboat Key.

The accented voice from the Yale videotape answers on the first ring.

"Hello?"

I identify myself and ask for Sigmund Walder.

"Speaking."

I say, "I've been researching Blechhammer and viewed your testimony at Yale, and in it you showed a painting by Walter Spitzer."

"Yes, Walter's a dear friend."

"My father was a very close friend of Walter's and—"

"Dolek Lajtner?"

My chest constricts like I've been stiff-armed. None but my father's "old country" friends knew him by his Polish nickname.

"Yes," I breathe.

"Well, yes, I knew him but let me think a moment. It's been sixty years since I last thought about that name."

I remind Sigmund that Dad was a welder.

"Yes, it's coming back to me now," he says, and tells me of another survivor, Mark Beck, who had been a welder at Blechhammer and now also lives in Longboat Key. "I bet Mark might have known your dad."

Sigmund also has been in regular touch with Walter Spitzer in France. I had assumed Walter, like my father, was long gone. The last time we had talked was two decades ago in that Jerusalem café.

Sigmund offers to phone Mark Beck for me. After we hang up, I sit there numb, staring at the telephone. When I started in journalism, my biggest technological challenge was finding a working pay phone. The first IBM PC was nine years away. Now, in just four hours, I have tracked down a man—not a celebrity or politico but the commonest of common citizens—over a gap of twenty-three years and more than a thousand miles.

Soon, Sigmund calls back. Mark Beck remembers my father as a fellow welder. Mark has phoned his cousin in Los Angeles who had also been at Blechhammer and remembers my father well.

I barely control my glee. What began as one possible lead to my father's past has now become four eyewitnesses—Sigmund, Mark Beck, Mark's cousin, and the still-alive Walter Spitzer.

For the next half hour, Sigmund talks about Blechhammer, the war, and survival in his slow, pedantic pace as I type notes into my computer. After immigrating to the United States, Sigmund avoided contact with other survivors and chose to live in suburban Connecticut instead of New York City, with its large Jewish population.

"I separated myself from this life," he says, "or even from the afterlife if you want, the postwar life, the post-Holocaust life, the post-concentration camp, and even the survivors, most of whom, or many of whom, remained in close contact with their own."

There were two synagogues in Sigmund's North Haven neighborhood, one whose membership was predominantly American born, the other made up of European refugee émigrés. "And when we decided to join the temple, we did not join this temple. We joined a temple of American Jews, who were born here."

Only decades later, outraged by revisionist historians who denied the Holocaust had ever happened, did Sigmund give testimony to Yale. He also became a trained volunteer and helped other survivors to do the same.

Sigmund asks why I'm chasing my father's stories now, twenty years after his death. I tell him about my search for this British POW named Bill Ball or Bill Bell, who could have been a Scot or a—

"No, Bill was Canadian," Sigmund says. "I knew him well. I remember the maple leaf on his uniform."

I tell Sigmund the postcard story.

"He was a great guy," Sigmund says. "He helped me a lot. He helped a lot of us."

"And this is Bill Ball?" I ask.

"Well, I don't remember his last name, if I ever knew it. We all knew him as Bill. He escaped," Sigmund says. "This was in late '44, in fall of '44. I remember the day like today. There was still some snow on the ground, the sun was shining, and we were walking to the worksite, and coming in the opposite direction were the two guys that I knew, and I believe one of them was Bill, in civilian clothes. We made eye contact . . . I made no motion whatsoever that I knew them."

After we hang up, I join my family for a late Sunday breakfast.

"I'm going to Florida," I announce.

"When?" my wife asks.

"Soon, very soon. These guys aren't going to be around forever."

....

Turns out, Sigmund Walder and Mark Beck barely knew my father, if at all.

They pick me up at Sarasota Airport, across the bay from Longboat Key on Florida's Gulf Coast. It's December and snowing in New York. Florida is bathed in warm sunshine.

I recognize Sigmund from the Yale video recorded twenty-three years earlier. At eighty-four, he is debonair in a navy-blue blazer and open-collar dress shirt, though his eyes are somewhat watery with age.

Standing next to him, Mark Beck looks solidly built for his eighty-four years—stocky, with a thick neck, sloped shoulders, and a widow's peak of thinning gray hair. His short-sleeved shirt reveals a line of blue numbers tattooed on the back of his left arm.

Mark clasps my hand in both of his. "You know a lot of the kids these days don't really want to know about what their parents endured—I mean the details. So the parents don't talk about it."

Mark's voice startles me. It could have been my father talking: same thick Polish accent, same deliberate cadence, like he was translating from Yiddish in his head before saying the words out loud in English.

Sigmund drives us to Longboat Key in a large Mercedes sedan. This surprises me. Most survivors I know, certainly all my parents' friends, would no more drive a German car than put their tongue on the third rail of the subway. I let the issue pass without question or comment.

We arrive at a restaurant overlooking one of Longboat Key's many marinas. It's a starched-white-tablecloth kind of place where busboys offer grated Parmesan and green olive oil to go with the warm focaccia. The food is good—so good that any talk of concentration camps or slave labor seems inappropriate. Only over coffee and dessert do I take out my digital recorder and ask my hosts how they knew my father.

Sigmund explains he had worked as an electrician in the refinery's *betriebskontrolle*, the operations control center, alongside Canadian POWs. This gave him virtually unlimited opportunities for black-market trading. However, Sigmund cannot recall any specific incident about my father.

Sigmund turns testy when I ask how he knew my father's name. "I believe now that your dad had contacts with us upstairs, which is why I know his name. How else would I know 'Dolek'? Come on!"

I turn to Mark Beck.

"I think I remember your dad when we carried cylinders [of acetylene and oxygen] we used for welding."

That's it.

I had steeled myself not to expect much. After all, I'm asking two octogenarians to recall encounters from sixty years ago. Yet I hoped for more than "I believe" and "I think."

They see my disappointment.

Mark leans in across the table. "Listen: In Blechhammer I never really focused on anybody. What somebody did was *his* business, not *my* business. My business was my brother and my father—and myself. Nobody cared about anybody else. And nobody cared about me. And you really didn't want to make any relationship because tomorrow the person was dead. Then you would grieve. It's no way—you were in a jungle—it's no way to live."

As Mark speaks, I flash back to something my father had told me: "The Germans treated us like workhorses, and like horses we wore blinders." He would cup his hands to the sides of his face. "You didn't look left, you didn't look right. You looked only in front, for your own needs."

Outside the restaurant's picture windows, white cabin cruisers and tall sailboats sway gently on their mooring lines. *How peaceful* . . . I had read about the fragility of memory, how dates and incidents fade with the passage of time. I was ready for that. This is different. What Mark is saying, and what my father tried to tell me, is that survival required you to lobotomize your psyche and excise the fellow on the next pallet. Sure, prisoners forged friendships and alliances to help and encourage one another. You just did not dare get too close. Survival was more a game of solitaire than of bridge. House rules were brutal. Winners got to play again tomorrow. Losers did not.

I turn back to my two elderly hosts. Sigmund and Mark couldn't know my father because they didn't need to know him. Each was playing his own hand of survival solitaire. This revelation is sobering. Assuming I even find other survivors who remember Dad, their recollections will be facile at best. Not because they forgot, but because they wanted not to know.

We drive to Sigmund's tenth-floor condo with panoramic views of the Gulf of Mexico. His wife of fifty-eight years, Jennie, brings out platters of biscuits and fruit, coffee and tea. Trying to explain that we had just eaten is pointless.

Sigmund disappears into his study and returns with a copy of Walter Spitzer's new autobiography, in French. Having only recently received it, he proudly shows me extensively underlined and annotated passages with names of fellow Blechhammer prisoners, including one in which Dolek Lajtner is saved by the Jewish head of the camp after being caught with a bottle of schnapps by a German guard.

Mark, meanwhile, phones his cousin in Los Angeles. Motek Kleiman is eighty-eight. As he hands me the phone, Mark boasts that Motek's memory is so reliable, archivists have used him to identify faces from family photo albums recovered after the war.

"Sure, I knew Dolek for forty years, even after the war," Motek tells me. "The Lajtners were a very prominent family, with many business interests and influence."

This is more like it. I know my grandfather, Abram Lajtner, and two of his brothers were metal craftsmen who became wealthy manufacturers supplying the region's booming coal and steel industries with fabricated metal products like chimney covers and vents. Grandpa also owned a roofing-paper factory. Motek tells me something I hadn't heard: Abram Lajtner was also a silent partner in a coal mine—silent because Jews were forbidden from owning Polish mines outright.

Motek had gone to high school with my father's youngest sister, Pola.

"She was a beautiful girl, a beautiful personality," he says. "She had long black hair and was very popular. I'd see Dolek from time to time when he came to pick her up at school."

"Were you friends?" I ask. "Did you hang out with her?"

Motek half laughs. "In the old country there was a lot of, uh, snobbism. We were of a different class, so to speak. We had our groups and they had their groups, and I would have been too shy to speak to a girl like that."

Motek's father had been a high-end women's couturier, with exclusive boutiques in two cities. "We were very comfortable and had a good life—two maids—but the Lajtners, you could say, were among the town's royalty."

The last time Motek saw Pola was in December 1939, three months into the war. "She was in our house. My father was making for her a fur coat, but the fur was on the inside so no one would see it. I believe she was planning to go to Russia, but I don't know if she ever made it."

She didn't. It would take me two more years to piece together Pola's story.

Motek and his wife immigrated to the United States in 1954, six years after my parents had arrived in New York.

"I telephoned your father from the airport," Motek says. "When he told me he was working in a clothing factory as a presser, I couldn't believe it. Dolek Lajtner a presser? How could this be?"

....

During the 1950s, my father was a finishing presser at Ripley Clothing, ironing out the last creases and wrinkles before the suits were bagged and shipped to 150 Ripley stores nationwide.

His day started at 5:30 a.m. The glow of streetlights leaked along the edges of the paper window shade into the small bedroom I shared with my parents. Dad would swat the Little Ben alarm clock into silence and swing his legs out of bed. He'd just sit there, bare feet on the wood floor, head bowed, for a full minute, maybe more. He'd then retrieve two elastic support socks, the flesh-colored kind without heels or toes, and pull them up over his varicose-veined calves.

I watched this daily ritual from my cot a few feet from my parents' bed. Often I'd follow Dad to the bathroom. We'd stand side by side, peeing into the toilet, suppressing giggles lest we wake Mom, who worked nights.

Dad washed birdbath style, splashing soapy water under his armpits and across the back of his thick neck. I watched in awe as he injected a Gillette Blue Blade into the safety razor, brushed foam on his face, and shaved with quick, definite strokes.

I wanted to shave, "just like you, Dad."

"Soon enough, son, soon enough." He laughed and daubed shaving cream on my nose.

For breakfast, Dad soft-boiled two eggs, buttered a slice of rye bread, and stirred milk and sugar into a glass of Nescafe Instant Coffee. He was out the door with the sunrise. I'd climb into my father's side of the bed, fidget some, and fall asleep snuggled up against Mom. She never stirred.

Dad once took me to the factory to show me where he worked, a grimy red brick building overlooking the Hudson River. He was not working that day because an iron had burned his arm. It was wrapped in white gauze stained yellow with salve. He held my hand as we rode up a rattling elevator without a safety gate or door. He led me past hissing machines and racks of suits being wheeled along dingy corridors.

He lifted me onto a long worktable with eight built-in ironing boards. The irons, much larger than Mom's at home, were tethered to the ceiling with springs and chains. Dad's fellow pressers looked a lot like him: warm smiles and bad teeth, rounded shoulders and thinning hair. Sweat glistened on shiny foreheads and stained their sleeveless T-shirts. Everyone spoke Yiddish, even Irish Red and the Puerto Rican brothers at the far end of the table.

It was piecework—you were paid for each suit you pressed. The Amalgamated Clothing Workers Union enforced a strict quota system. This prevented the bosses from overloading workers. It also meant you couldn't earn more than your union brother no matter how badly you needed the extra cash.

The garment business was seasonal, lengthy furloughs a fact of life. Even during the season, work was not always guaranteed. Dad could leave home at dawn and return by noon; not enough suits had been cut to keep the line busy. I remember my father sitting home for days on end reading his Yiddish newspapers.

This drove Mom crazy. She would yell and taunt him for being lazy, for not seeking a real job, for not pulling his weight to support us. Once she got started, I'd run to the bathroom and cringe until the shouting ceased. Dad might yell back some, but, for the most part, he just took it. We accepted that Mom would blow up suddenly and cool down just as fast.

After I had heard some of Dad's war stories, I once asked why he didn't seek work as a welder, the skill that saved his life in the war. He looked down at the floor. "The smell of acetylene," he said, "it brings back memories of the camps. I can't do it."

He apprenticed for a while with an uncle to learn the picture-framing business. The lessons ended abruptly when the uncle got scared Dad would become a competitor. Or that's how Mom liked to tell it.

A cigarette and newspaper stand at the Excelsior Hotel, across from the Hayden Planetarium, lasted a couple of months, as did another kiosk at a midtown office building.

My parents' most ambitious endeavor was manufacturing vinyl doilies that were as delicate as fine lace. That's how I was introduced to the Main Reading Room of the New York Public Library, with its glorious frescoed ceiling and gold-and-rose painted rosettes. Dad used the library to teach himself the chemistry of vinyl. Insecure with his English, he took me along to translate our needs to the reference librarians. I was about eleven years old at the time.

Mom had acquired several brass plates etched with different doily patterns from distant cousins in the plastics business. Using a painter's spatula, a vinyl paste was spread into the etchings much like grout on bathroom tiles. Dad heated the plates on our kitchen stove until the paste became plastic. Using dental picks, he teased the doilies from the molds and set them aside to cool.

Weeks of trial and error followed—getting the chemicals and consistency of the paste right, applying it just so to the plates, and developing the light touch needed to lift the finished doilies from the forms with dental picks without tearing them. Cooking vinyl was a challenge. Too soon, and he ended up with taffy-like glop. Too hot, and the stench of melting plastic filled our home. Dad rented a basement apartment in a tenement a few doors down and turned it into a workshop with long tables and drying racks. He used his dormant knowledge of iron and welding to design a stove with six-foot-long burners and precise gas valves.

Dad worked late into the night cooking up vinyl doilies. Mom bundled them six to a pack and sold them door-to-door to small stores and gift shops. The real goal was to sell custom-designed doilies for hotels and tourist venues. My first visit to the Statue of Liberty came when Dad took me along to help pitch the idea to the gift shop manager.

After some months, the back of Dad's neck and shoulders started breaking out in suppurating boils. The doctor said it might be an allergy or a reaction to something at work. Dad read up on PCB, a chemical suspected of causing cancer, and realized cooking vinyl without proper ventilation, protective clothing, or a face mask was a bad idea. Doing so in the basement of a residential apartment building on the Upper West Side of Manhattan also violated any number of zoning and health codes. A proper workspace, with proper equipment and ventilation, cost money. We had none. Dad returned to the tethered irons of the clothing factory.

I still have those brass plates delicately etched in doily patterns.

....

Around the time of my Florida trip, the news is full of Iranian president Mahmoud Ahmadinejad denying the Holocaust. "Some European countries insist on saying that Hitler killed millions of innocent Jews in furnaces," Ahmadinejad said. "We don't accept this claim."

I think of Sigmund Walder and Mark Beck, how these old and gray men had reopened their wounded memories for me. I asked Mark why he had never recorded his memories as had other survivors.

"Why should I?" he said. "The world really doesn't want to know—and I don't have to justify my survival."

Decades earlier, my father had told me much the same thing. I was about twelve years old and enthralled with *Mila 18*, Leon Uris's novel about the Warsaw Ghetto uprising. Enraged and in tears, I declared that the uprising would live on in history and people would remember that Jews fought back.

Dad shook his head. "Look son, the world wants to forget and those who hate us will hate us anyway."

I also think of my children, how unprepared they are to confront the world's greater and lesser Ahmadinejads. *Papa, you should have recorded your stories for the kids.* I blame myself. Until my hunt for Bill Ball, I did nothing to preserve my father's legacy except repeat some old stories that I never fully understood or appreciated.

Before Ahmadinejad, I airily dismissed the notion that

anyone could seriously deny the Holocaust. Now, my outrage is magnified by what I have learned these past few weeks—and by my impotence to do anything about it.

Two days after my return from Florida, a thin brown manila envelope arrives from the Holocaust Memorial Museum in Washington.

Inside is a copy of this document:

Konzentrationslager AUSCHWITZ. Art der Haft: Sch.Jude Gef. Nr.: 177904

Name und Vorname: L A J T N E R JOSEF Israel (478)
geb. 11.8.1911 zu: Bendsburg O.S.
Wohnort: Strzemieszyce, Lange Str 40. Kr. Bendsburg O.S.
Beruf: Elektroschweißer Rel.: mos.
Staatsangehörigkeit: ehem. Polen Stand: led.
Name der Eltern: Abram u. Fajgla geb. Istowska Rasse: jüd.
Wohnort: v. gest. M. mb.A.
Name der Ehefrau: — Rasse:
Wohnort:
Kinder: keine Alleiniger Ernährer der Familie oder der Eltern:
Vorbildung: 4 Kl. Volkssch.
Militärdienstzeit: — von — bis
Kriegsdienstzeit: — von — bis
Grösse: 169 Gestalt: schlank Gesicht: längl. Augen: braun
Nase: gradl. Mund: norm. Ohren: m.gr Zähne: 2 f
Haare: schwarz Sprache: poln. deutsch
Ansteckende Krankheit oder Gebrechen: keine
Besondere Kennzeichen: keine
Rentenempfänger: nein
Verhaftet am: 23.6.43 wo: Strzemieszyce
1. Mal eingeliefert: 1. April 1944 2. Mal eingeliefert:
Einweisende Dienststelle: RSHA
Grund:
Parteizugehörigkeit: keine von — bis
Welche Funktionen: keine
Mitglied v. Unterorganisationen: keine /
Kriminelle Vorstrafen: ang.keine
Politische Vorstrafen: ang.keine

Ich bin darauf hingewiesen worden, dass meine Bestrafung wegen intellektueller Urkundenfälschung erfolgt, wenn sich die obigen Angaben als falsch erweisen sollten.

Der Lagerkommandant

v. g. u.
Lajtner Israel Juf
11.8.1911
KL/42/4.43 500.000

No doubts. None at all. My father's calligraphic signature hugs the lower left corner. His tattoo number—177904—the upper right. It is my father's *Häftlingspersonalbogen*, the prisoner registration form, filled out when Blechhammer became a subcamp of Auschwitz on April 1, 1944.

Here was Dad's life, reduced to a single page. Born August 11, 1911. Five feet seven inches. Black hair and brown eyes. A long face, a straight nose, a "normal" mouth and "mid-sized" ears and missing two teeth. He had no infectious diseases or illnesses, belonged to no political party, collected no pension. He had presumably not committed any criminal violations or criminal political acts. While the "reason" for his arrest was blank, the top of the form noted "type of arrest: Jew."

In 1938, as part of the notorious Nuremberg racial laws, the Nazis adopted Law #174, which required all Jewish men to add "Israel" and all Jewish women to add "Sarah" to their names so they could be more readily identified as Jews. Sure enough, printed boldly on the form next to my father's name was "Israel."

Dad lied to the Nazis twice. He listed his mother's whereabouts as "unknown" even though she was alive and well in Brooklyn, where she had gone to visit her daughter the year before the war broke out. By April 1944, American bombers were pounding German cities. Announcing that his mother was in the United States would have ensured him a beating, or worse. He also claimed only a fourth-grade education. In fact, he had graduated public high school in Dabrowa. Diminishing his educational background had its advantages. Dad often told how Nazi guards took particular pleasure in humiliating "uppity" educated Jews.

His profession was listed as "electro-welder" and his address as 40 Louge Street in the hamlet of Strzemieszyce, pronounced Shtre-ma-shitz-eh. Consulting a map, I see it would have been about a ten-minute tram or bicycle ride from his hometown of Dabrowa, an industrial city in the Dabrowa Basin, known locally as Zaglebie, close to Germany in southwestern Poland.

How did Dad end up in Strzemieszyce? I remember stories about the family's big house in Dabrowa built by his father. He shared that house with his half brothers and sisters. Why wasn't he living at home?

I study the form as if it were a religious relic, a talisman from antiquity. Dad brought back no photographs or war souvenirs. He received no purple hearts, medals, or citations celebrating his survival. Here is a document—*a Nazi document*—that told more about my father at a specific time and place than he ever had.

Here is independent corroboration from the most unlikely source that he had been seized, enslaved, branded, and sentenced to the most notorious factory of death devised by man. No longer does his story depend on fading memories of a fading generation.

Well, now. This changes everything. If one such relic exists, might not others? What truths might they hold? What secrets might they reveal?

Chapter 3

OF DIAMONDS AND DOCUMENTS

The three documents that forever changed the way I think of my father arrived in a large white envelope with an Auschwitz return address.

After finding my father's Auschwitz registration form, I emailed the three concentration camps where I knew he had been a prisoner—Auschwitz, Gross-Rosen, and Buchenwald—and the International Tracing Service (ITS) at Bad Arolsen, Germany. With thirty million documents, the ITS is the largest archive in the world on the Nazi persecution and its victims.

I asked for anything they might have about Josef Lajtner, born August 11, 1911, with Auschwitz tattoo number 177904.

Gross-Rosen responded almost immediately, saying my father's name was on a list of prisoners sent to Buchenwald in February 1945. Auschwitz replied a few weeks later asking for more details. An ITS form letter advised it would take at least a year before my queries were answered because of the backlog of requests. Buchenwald never acknowledged my emails.

Fall begat winter and by the time winter begat spring, my queries had become a distant memory. Now, six months later, here's this thin white envelope from the Auschwitz-Birkenau

State Museum in Poland sitting among the day's bills and brochures on the foyer table.

I hold my breath and pull out a packet of papers held together
with a large white clip. On top, an academic article about Blechhammer. I'd already read it. I exhale. Next, a copy of my father's
Auschwitz registration. It's the same form that had triggered my
queries in the first place. *Six months for this?* I gulp down my
rising frustration.

Behind the registration form are copies of three half-sheets
of paper in German. I glance through all three, then study each
one again, slowly.

"Holy shit."

"What?" my wife says. I slump against the foyer table. "What?
What?"

The first is little more than a scrap of paper with an elaborate
heading, a single typed sentence, and two lines of scrawled German:

PAŃSTWOWE MUZEUM

Konz.Lager Auschwitz III   Arb.Lager Blechhammer,
  Kommandantur/ Abt.II   den 19.1o.1944.

Dienstnotiz für die Abteilung III
in M o n o w i t z.

        Die Häftlinge Nr. 177904 - 178o89 - 178582
und 178921 sind an einer Strafsache beteiligt.

⌘ Unterscharführer

It lists four prisoner numbers, starting with my father's—
177904—who "partook in a criminal act." The hand-written
sentence reads, "The civilian acted with my consent and brought
the diamond here." It was signed by an SS sergeant.

This was the only document of three with a date, October 19, 1944, which I assume applies to all of them. I'm wrong. The date and handwritten scrawl will have very different implications.

It is my father's familiar signature on the bottom of the second document that triggers my expletive. It's titled "Interrogation Statement."

This is the translation:

I n t e r r o g a t i o n   P r o t o c o l

```
Here presents the Jewish prisoner Nr.
177904, L a j t n e r Josef, born 8/11/11 in
Bendsburg, from work kommando 27 (Building
408), when questioned, and cautioned to be
truthful, the following statements.
To the matter: I first became acquainted
with H o l i s c h RD. a.W. (Division III
DVL) in the year 1941 in Dabrowa. Fall
of 1943 I met him here in the work area.
```

I greeted him and asked for bread. He
brought me bread several times. Over the
course of time this may have occurred 5 or
6 times. At one of these visits I handed
Holisch 15 diamonds that he was supposed
to sell for me. He gave me 500 Rm for them
over the course of time. Yet the diamonds
had a value of about 1500 Rm. I do not
have further items of value such as money
in my possession. I have said the truth
and have nothing more to add.

V. G. U. [Read, Approved, and Signed]
Josef Lajtner

Main interrogation file is found at
Gestapo in Heydebreck

A signed confession? Fifteen diamonds? Dad never spoke of this, nor of any Pole named Holisch who had given him food.

I dig out the email my cousin in Florida had sent months earlier, about the old Belgian Jew dying of typhoid fever. Dad had given him bread and water. Before the old man died, he told Dad where he had buried a bag of diamonds.

Dad had mentioned diamonds only in passing. Like when he pulled his back carrying sacks of potatoes. "The pain was so bad, I could hardly breathe," he said. He went to the *Revier*, the infirmary, and bribed the orderly with "a very small diamond." That bought him daily liniment massages for a week until he could stand straight. The point of that story was not the bribe but the risk: The Gestapo would show up at the Revier unannounced and ship everyone to the gas chambers at Auschwitz. He then repeated the moral of so many of his stories: *So you see son, in the end it didn't matter if you had money or not, were smart or dumb. Life was worth nothing—absolutely nothing. You needed luck.*

So there was that.

But fifteen diamonds? Dad was more deeply involved in the black-market smuggling than he had ever let on. Smuggling diamonds under the nose of the SS? How could this be the same quiet, unassuming man who wouldn't play cards because he didn't like to gamble?

The third document—simply titled "*M E L D U N G*," or "*R E P O R T*"—leaves me stunned and shaken.

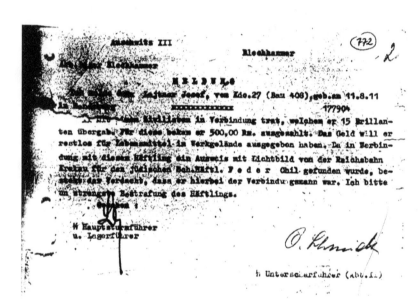

This is the translation:

R E P O R T

```
I am reporting Lajtner Josef, from
order 27(Building 408), born 8/11/11 in
Bendsburg. xxxxxxxxxxx    177904
He associated with a civilian, whom he
gave 15 diamonds. For these he received
500 Reichsmark. He was to have spent the
entire sum of money on nourishment in
```

the work area. In connection with this
prisoner, a picture identification card of
the Reich/National Railroad Krakau for the
Jewish prisoner F e d e r Chil was found.
Thus, the suspicion was aroused that he,
therein, was the contact person. I ask for
the strictest punishment of the prisoner.

....

I once asked my father why he didn't simply run away and escape like in the movies. I was a kid and wanted—no, needed—him to be a hero, to know that he had not accepted his fate like some sheep.

Dad took a deep breath and sighed, like how was he going to explain this to a ten-year-old? It wasn't that easy, he said. Blechhammer was in Germany, not Poland. He wore blue-and-gray striped pajamas, his head was shaved, and his left arm was tattooed with numbers. Assuming he had managed to get across the nearby border to Poland, chances were Polish peasants would turn him in for the reward.

"But I'll tell you something—I did try to escape," he said.

"Really?"

"You remember Charlie Feder?"

Sure. Charlie was an old family friend with frizzy hair and piercing blue eyes who installed telephones in the 1950s, back when AT&T was still known as Ma Bell.

At the refinery construction site, Charlie had met a Polish Christian friend from before the war who had contacts with the Polish underground. For his part, Dad was on good terms with some English POWs. He had traded with the English many times. He would get a bottle of vodka from Polish workers and swap it for English Player's cigarettes or tins of sardines or maybe a bar of chocolate from their Red Cross packages.

"Did you eat the chocolate?" I once asked.

"Nah. It was too valuable. For a bar of chocolate, the soup *Kapo* [the prisoner trustee] would double my portion for a week, and serve it from the bottom where there might be a piece of turnip or horse meat."

This time Dad wanted something very different from his British friends. The POWs had a camera and agreed to take head shots of Dad and Charlie.

Charlie gave the photos to his Polish friend who smuggled them to the underground. At a secret forgery shop, the photos were to be made into ID cards for the national railway. The phony cards would then be smuggled back to the refinery via Charlie's friend. Charlie and my father would use them to escape, dressed in civilian clothes bought from Polish workers at the worksite.

The plan was foiled by the Nazi Secret Police.

"The Gestapo raided the forgery shop," my father said. "They found the card with Charlie Feder's photo. But they never found my picture or any card."

He thought about this for a long moment. "Why my picture wasn't found? I don't know. Charlie always swore he gave them my picture too." Even today, I'm not sure my father completely believed his old friend Charlie Feder.

The Gestapo traced the forged card back to Blechhammer and arrested Charlie. Under torture, Charlie implicated my father.

"But I act stupid—completely ignorant—and they have no proof. They sent Charlie off to be gassed in Auschwitz. How he escaped death is another story, his story . . ."

That's where my father's account of attempted escape ended.

To a ten-year-old, it sounded, well, weird. That the Nazis would spare my father's life just because they couldn't prove something? Hard to grasp as a child, hard to explain as an adult. I had all but forgotten that story. I had never told it to my daughters or nieces.

Amazing stories abound in survivor testimonials. If I had doubts believing Dad's story, how would my children, who had never met their grandfather, accept it? How would future generations regard survivor stories like these?

With this Nazi document as confirmation, no longer would Dad's story of attempted escape be an improbable family tale. It was now bona fide history.

Rereading the documents now, it's obvious why the Germans would connect the forged railway cards with the diamonds. Why else would English POWs risk their secret camera for two Jewish prisoners? Why else would the Polish underground even consider helping? You needed more than luck to get POWs and Poles to take such risks.

The Germans had come to the same conclusion.

Over the following weeks, I research and read and speak to historians and survivors. None offer any credible explanation of why my father was allowed to live.

Mark Beck, the survivor from Longboat Key, offers the simplest answer: The SS had been bribed to keep my father alive.

"They were all corrupt," he says. "They didn't want to kill the golden goose. Either that, or someone bribed them. Maybe the *Judenälteste*. Someone was protecting your dad."

Chapter 4

PARIS, AUSCHWITZ, AND MOM

··

That June, two months after receiving the diamond docu-ments, I stop over in Paris to meet Walter Spitzer on my way to Poland.

It's been twenty-one years since Walter had told me about the German guard and the bottle of schnapps, and how the Jewish head of the camp had beaten my father in front of the German because otherwise the SS man "would have killed Dolek like a fly."

Now, I recall that story to Walter, again with a recorder running. Only this time, we're sipping *vin rouge ordinaire* in a noisy bistro around the corner from his Paris studio. Reliably gregarious and voluble, Walter turns quiet as he dons reading glasses and scans the diamond documents.

I say, "When you told me that story about the *Judenälteste* and my father, you said it involved a bottle of schnapps. . . ."

"Yes, that's what Dolek told me."

"Sure it wasn't diamonds?"

"He told me he was beaten because of schnapps."

"Did my father ever talk to you about diamonds?"

Walter shakes his head. "Not a word. Not even in the forty years since the war."

"Well, he only mentioned them to me once," I say, "in the context of how you needed luck more than money to survive and—"

Walter silences me with his hand on my arm. He leans in and looks closely into my eyes. "Dolek survived because he was smart. Maybe it exists, this luck. But with diamonds, you can improve your luck. Oh yes! You better help your luck."

Walter agrees with Mark Beck that the SS had let my father live for their own self-interests; they hoped to get more diamonds.

"If they hang Dolek, the source would die," Walter says. "They were not stupid. To kill? It was very easy for them to kill. But they were in business, too."

We stare into our half-empty glasses of red wine, thinking our own thoughts, oblivious to the clamor of the crowded bistro.

Why would Dad keep the diamonds secret from a close friend, even after forty years? Who was this man?

....

The middle-aged taxi driver outside the Krakow airport terminal looks me over with ice-blue eyes, checking out my clothes, my luggage, my face. I know he's assessing more than my tip potential. I know he's pegged me as a *Zyd*, a Jew.

I'm uneasy being here and it's not just the record heat wave baking Poland. While contemporary Polish historiography stresses cases where Poles risked their lives saving Jews, the country has a long history of violent anti-Semitism before, during, and after the war.

"American?" the cabbie asks.

"Yes."

"New York City?" *New Yawrk Zitty?*

"Yes."

"You know Greenpoint? *Grin-point?*"

"Well, I know it's a Polish neighborhood in Brooklyn," I say.

"Yes! I have brother."

In fact, the Poles I will meet in the coming days, especially the younger generation, are always helpful and courteous. Most glance aside an awkward moment when they learn the scope of my "project." They politely never ask many questions; I politely never offer many details. Our parents' collective history is left unspoken. But it's there.

Is it wrong to admit that I never thought much whether Dad would have approved of this trip? I believe he would have, though perhaps with a grimace. I'd like to think he'd allow that was then and this is now.

Besides, I tell myself, I'm not here seeking moral vindication. I'm here to interview officials at the Auschwitz Museum about the diamond documents, research my family's fate immediately after Germany's invasion, and, if possible, find my father's childhood home in Dabrowa, a grimy mining and steel center about an hour's drive northwest of Krakow.

To that end, I've brought copies from a 1929 Polish business directory listing my grandfather Abram's roofing-paper factory and listings from a 1930s Dabrowa phone book with his home address and phone number.

Both the business directory and phone book came from Jeff Cymbler, a New York attorney who had been tracing his own family's roots in the region for many years, amassing an impressive archive of artifacts and documents along the way.

I had told Jeff my plans included visiting Auschwitz, about thirty-five minutes from Krakow. "Bring someone with you," he said. "Auschwitz can be difficult, especially for people like us. It is not a place you want to be on your own."

He need not have worried. When my brother Alan heard of my plans, he insisted on coming along, partly for the same reasons I'm here and partly, I think, to watch over me. Of the two of us, Alan inherited our father's broad forehead and angular features as well as our grandfather's business sense. He is dependable and sharp. I am relieved to have him with me even though, because of work, he can only be here for the first two days.

Alan is flying in from New York. We were to meet up at Krakow airport but my flight from Paris is more than two hours late. I trawl the crowded arrival hall for twenty minutes, my rolling luggage like a drift net behind me, snagging bench corners and baby carriages in its wake. No Alan. He must have gone on to the hotel.

So now I am very alone in a very warm Fiat taxi with asthmatic air conditioning that does little but white out the noise of surrounding traffic.

In my hand is the internet printout for the Wilga Hotel, just five minutes from Krakow's old Jewish quarter of Kazimierz. The photo shows a modern three-story building with clean vertical lines and large picture windows overlooking the Vistula River. At seventy-six dollars a night, it's a bargain.

My first surprise is that Alan has not checked in. He should have landed hours ago. The clerk checks with the airline. Alan's flight from New York had been delayed four hours. The second surprise is the superheated tsunami of hot air that hits me when I open the door to my room. I search for an air conditioner switch. No luck. The clerk informs me the rooms are not air conditioned. Nor are there fans.

I strip off my sodden shirt and pants, pull out my laptop, and search the internet for an air-conditioned hotel in Krakow. That's how Alan finds me, room door wide open, in my black Jockeys, dripping sweat onto my laptop.

We check out of the Wilga, forfeiting one night's fee and, cashing in some hefty frequent-flier points, check into one of those terribly overpriced, albeit wonderfully air-conditioned, Western corporate expense-account hotels.

At 7:30 the next morning, we meet Zdzislaw Les in the hotel lobby. He's the owner of the Jarden Jewish bookstore and will be our translator, driver, and guide.

Tall, lean, balding, with a close-cropped salt-and-pepper beard, more like Sean Connery in his mature period than my idea of a bookstore owner. A ready smile softens the deep-set eyes and heavy brows.

"How do you pronounce your name?" I ask.

"ZGEE-swav Lesh."

"Zgeez-wav?" Alan asks.

"No, ZGEE-swav."

"ZiGee-swav?" I ask.

"Why don't you just call me 'Les'?"

"Works for me."

Les leads us to a very new and very shiny jet-black Chevrolet Impala with tinted windows, about as out of place on Krakow's worn streets as a Testarossa at a Walmart. *Not the car of your typical bookstore owner,* I think. We soon learn there's nothing typical about Les, and while he may look like Sean Connery, his manner is more Peter Falk's Columbo, the television detective famous for his well-timed, "Oh, and just one more thing . . ." Les uses a similar technique to charm recalcitrant Polish bureaucrats. There'll be many of those too.

Les pulls out a couple of gold-and-red foil-wrapped candies from the car's center console. "Have a Kopiko?" he offers. Sometimes it is the insignificant that punctuates our memories. So it is with these sweet "Kopiko Cappuccino" candies, made in Thailand. Les, a smoker, uses them as surrogate cigarettes when escorting nonsmoking clients. Every twenty minutes or so, he offers up a Kopiko from the car's console. Les does not believe in stopping for lunch. Those candies will be my only sustenance during long hours of travel ahead.

The road out of Krakow is a modern four-lane highway through wide rolling hills in earth browns and lush greens, terrain that has proved ideal for Poland's many invaders over the centuries, be they on horseback or in tanks. Speeding past squat stucco farmhouses with steeply pitched roofs, we could be driving through rural Pennsylvania were it not for the large ornate churches dominating many hilltops.

We ask Les, who is not Jewish, how he came to open the first Jewish bookstore since the war in Krakow, a city with virtually no Jews. The bookstore is in the old Jewish quarter of Kazimierz, which, Les explains, was at the time a derelict slum. Many properties were in a legal limbo because their owners of record, the Jews, were no more. Young artists and students were moving in because rents were cheap.

One day, Les walked into the Jarden Palace, one of the oldest buildings in the quarter. A bookshop occupied two small rooms to the right of the lobby entrance.

"This bookshop, in which sat two boring women, sold crime stories and poor literature," Les says, "and on one shelf in a corner was written 'Judaica.' Ten titles! And I asked these ladies, 'Do you know where you are? What this neighborhood was?' They had no idea!"

"Can you imagine that?" Les says, eyebrows arched in disbelief. "In Poland, 10 percent of the population, some three million people, just disappeared—and no one talked about it. It was a scandal."

Les took over the bookstore and began stocking its shelves with volumes about Poland's vanished Jewish community.

That was 1992.

The next year, Steven Spielberg released *Schindler's List*, his epic movie about the Holocaust that had been partly filmed in Kazimierz. Tourists began showing up at the bookstore asking for directions to the Schindler sites—the ghetto, the concentration camp, the factory. "So we made a few hundred copies of a map and sold them," Les says. The Jarden bookstore began offering organized tours, and itself became a must-stop landmark on many tourist maps.

Les's eyes twinkle. "Really, I was not so smart. I was absolutely lucky—but lucky is good too."

Large tour companies soon arrived, flooding hotels with slick flyers offering *Schindler's List* tours of Krakow and Kazimierz, with an optional half-day trip to the Auschwitz death camp.

As tourism flourished, development followed. The old Jewish quarter became hip. On one narrow street, the facades of abandoned Jewish shops were rebuilt, complete with awnings and Yiddish signs, as the entrance to a Jewish-themed (though non-kosher) restaurant. Trendy bars with blue neon lights and techno music rub up against restored Jewish synagogues that are little more than anthropological exhibits about an extinct community. In one restored synagogue/museum, Les opened a branch of the Jarden bookstore and gift shop. Only one synagogue still functions as a house of prayer, and regularly only during the tourist season. There are not enough Jews in Krakow to support it full-time.

As the revival took hold, a tiny Festival of Jewish Culture and Klezmer Music grew to a large annual event attracting performers from as far as Israel and the United States. The audience is overwhelmingly Polish Catholic. "Among certain circles," Les says, "it has become fashionable to hint at your Jewish roots."

This is not my father's Poland. I try to reconcile conflicting emotions. Intellectually, I applaud a new generation of Poles working to maintain the memory of the now-vanished Jewish population. Emotionally, not so sure. There is the undeniable commercialization of a historic tragedy. Which came first: the desire to salvage history or the desire to cash in on tourist dollars? The restored synagogues, museums, monuments, and memorials have been renovated tastefully and are indeed informative. So does it matter? *Is this how Native Americans feel when they visit Wounded Knee?*

Les has taken visitors like us to Auschwitz many times. We park away from the tourist buses at an isolated lot, outside the gates of Auschwitz I, the original concentration camp that had been converted from a Polish army barracks. Its long red brick buildings form a militarily neat, spacious grid. The main museum, auditoriums, offices, and archives are located here.

Important as it is historically, Auschwitz has also become the key tourist destination in the Krakow region, with 2.32 million visitors in 2019. By comparison, the Wieliczka Salt Mine, a breathtaking labyrinth of tunnels, salt sculptures, and glowing caverns, received 1.86 million visitors while the most popular castle in Poland, the Wawel in Krakow, about 1.9 million.

We head directly to Prisoner Block 23, inside the camp's main gates, beneath the infamous sign, *Arbeit Macht Frei*, Work Sets You Free. Early in the war, Block 23 warehoused Soviet prisoners of war and, after 1944, women prisoners. The day of our visit, it's the research department where Franciszek Piper, a senior historian and head of research, has his offices.

Early in his career, Piper wrote the definitive study of Blechhammer. The more I research the camp, the more obvious it is that nearly everything in print and online about it either quotes, misquotes, or paraphrases Piper's original work.

Piper is not without controversy. He's largely responsible for the downward revision of the number of Jews murdered at Auschwitz, from 4 million to 1.1 million. That revision, now accepted by most Holocaust historians, inadvertently provided ammunition to Holocaust deniers. They gleefully used Piper's research as "proof" that the Holocaust was a gross exaggeration, despite strenuous protests by Piper himself. He noted that most of Poland's three million Jews were already dead by the time the Auschwitz gas chambers opened for business in the spring of 1942.

I show Piper the diamond documents. As he reads, his eyes bulge behind oversized reading glasses as thick as Coke bottles. "This was a very dangerous situation for your father," he tells me. "By 1944, you know, the SS were hanging people at Blechhammer for a lot less."

Neither Piper nor any of the other historians at Auschwitz can explain how my father escaped death.

I also meet with Dr. Piotr Setkiewicz, at the time the museum's Director of Archives, whose offices are in Block 24. During the war, Block 24 housed a brothel, a perk for cooperative Polish political prisoners though used mostly by the *Kapos*, the prisoner trustees. I thank Setkiewicz for the diamond documents his department had provided and ask, might there be anything else about my father?

Setkiewicz smiles sadly, shaking his head. "You don't understand. Every year, we get thousands of requests from all over the world asking for something—anything—about a loved one who ended here in Auschwitz. Unfortunately, most of the time we have nothing to offer."

Of the more than 1.3 million prisoners estimated to have passed through Auschwitz and its forty-four subcamps, Setkiewicz says the museum has about three hundred "punishment reports" of the kind that outline my father's arrest for dealing in diamonds.

Of the three hundred, perhaps fifty involve Blechhammer.

"And of those fifty," he says, "you have three about your father."

I ask the archivists if they could identify any of the other prisoners from the numbers listed on that first cryptic document with only tattoo numbers but no names. All they could find is that one of the numbers belonged to a Martin Izsak, a Jew from Romania. The name means nothing to me.

We leave Block 24 and enter the visitors' center, a cavernous brick structure that had served as the prisoner intake building during the war. Tour groups platooned by nationality organize themselves in a large central hall. There's a bookstore, a cafeteria, and an auditorium for special presentations. Along one long wall, posters of past Auschwitz exhibits are offered for sale. The posters are all graphically powerful and stark. I cannot help but wonder who would hang a poster of Auschwitz in their room?

From the central hall, we head for the converted barracks that make up the permanent exhibit. A long glass display case in Block 4 is piled deep and high with human hair. A museum guidebook says when Soviet soldiers liberated Auschwitz, they found more than 7.7 tons of human hair. It's being allowed to disintegrate into dust naturally. Today, almost two tons of hair is on display. In another block, a jungle of twisted, intertwined eyeglasses. In Block 5, we see the stacks of artificial limbs and crutches. Elsewhere, there are thousands of men's, women's, and baby shoes and high piles of empty, battered suitcases, many marked with the names of their owners.

Outside in the warm sunshine, tour groups are guided to key sites arranged almost like stations of the cross—the Group Gallows, the execution wall near Block 11. It was in the basement of Block 11 that Zyklon B gas was first "tested" on six hundred Russian POWs.

Les drives us the mile and a half to Auschwitz Birkenau, or Auschwitz II, the death factory.

No photo, video, or words prepare me for the sheer vastness of Auschwitz Birkenau. It is the same take-my-breath-away awe I had the first time I peered over the Grand Canyon, though this context is very different. Standing atop the wall of the main gate, the camp's 350 acres seem to spread endlessly in all directions. The camp had housed some three hundred prisoner barracks, warehouses, processing centers—and four industrial-size gas chambers.

Most of the prisoner blocks are little more than rubble-strewn lots. Several of those still standing have been preserved close to their original state—long rows of triple-tiered shelves that slept five prisoners on each. We eavesdrop on a tour guide explaining that inmates fought each other for a higher shelf because diarrhea flows down.

We follow the railroad tracks from the main gate into the center of Birkenau. It's a very long fifteen-minute walk under the oppressive July sun. There are no shaded kiosks, no water fountains. The only concessions to tourism are some toilets and the multilingual signage.

The tracks terminate at a broad ramp flanked on either side by the remains of Crematories II and III a short distance away. These rail tracks had originally terminated outside the camp. They were extended in May 1944 to speed the "processing" of some four hundred thousand Hungarian Jews.

My grandfather, Moritz Grosz, and my mother, Henci, were two of them.

....

While Dad shared many stories about his experiences, Mom was silent, other than to say that she and her father arrived at Auschwitz Birkenau late on the eve of the Jewish holiday of Shavuot. That would have made it Saturday night, May 27, 1944.

She talked of cold spotlights, barking dogs, and screaming guards, of clubs and whips, tumult and chaos, of thousands of men, women, and children pushing, stumbling, falling off the cattle cars, of the terror of the next moment.

Mom did not want to leave her father's side, but he sent her back to the cattle car to retrieve his prayer shawl bag. She turned around and he was gone.

Researchers have deconstructed the Hungarian liquidation based on transport lists and arrival logs. Of the 148 train transports from Hungary over about ten weeks, nine came from Oradea, where my mother and grandfather had lived. Based on the logged departures, and knowing the date of arrival, it's likely Mom and Grandpa were on Transport 40.

Each trainload carried about three thousand people. The number and the arrival times were coordinated to match the capacities of Crematoria II, III, IV, and V. These were custom-built factories of death, unlike the first gas chambers at Auschwitz that had been adapted from existing structures.

Crematoria II and III, closest to the rail ramp, were identical in construction. They each had five groups of ovens with three doors on each oven—fifteen portals in all—and were designed to incinerate about fifteen hundred bodies in twenty-four hours. Crematoria IV and V were each designed to process about seven hundred fifty.

Logs show that five trains disgorged 15,850 Hungarian Jews at the Auschwitz ramp that Saturday. Some 6,734 men and women were selected for work; the remaining 9,116, including my grandfather, were sent to the gas chambers. Though this number is significantly higher than the stated capacities of the four crematoria combined, Auschwitz *Kommandant* Rudolf Höss confirmed, "The highest total figure of people gassed and cremated in twenty-four hours was slightly more than nine thousand." Writing from his prison cell awaiting execution for war crimes, Höss said this was during the Hungarian operation when five transports arrived within twenty-four hours because of a screwup in scheduling. Based on the transport logs, I could find where this happened only once—on May 27.

Just three days later, SS army photographers recorded the "processing" of another transport of Hungarian Jews. Those 197 photos were found after the war and published in 1980 as *The Auschwitz Album*. They are the only photographic record of the entire *selektion* process. The photos show the sorting of men and women assigned to labor. They also show the elderly, the ill, and mothers and children awaiting the gas chamber. Any photo you might see of selections in Auschwitz are from this book.

Of the 3,148 men, women, and children on Transport 40 from Oradea, an analysis suggests some 2,038 were sent directly to the gas chamber, while 528 men and 561 women were selected for work. With the arrival of thousands of Hungarian prisoners daily, the normal procedure of tattooing prisoners broke down and many Hungarian Jews, including Henci Grosz, were never branded with a number. Henci, then twenty, was assigned to Lager BIIc, a women's section of the camp designated for Hungarian prisoners. By June 1944, twenty thousand Hungarian women were held in BIIc. Henci was placed in Block 16.

Today, nothing remains of Block 16 except the concrete outline of the barracks, a pile of red bricks, and memory.

....

In our family, it was Mom who clawed us out of the dead-end poverty of piecework.

Henci was slim and pretty, with auburn hair and large brown eyes that could dance with laughter or fire bolts of malice, depending on her mood of the moment.

Among my earliest memories was taking the train with Dad to visit Mom at the Bedford Hills Sanatorium north of New York City. She spent nearly a year there being treated for tuberculosis, a disease suffered by many survivors of the camps.

The women Mom met in the tuberculosis ward—Rose, Ann, Lee, Lucie, and Hannah—were all survivors and became lifelong friends. They were the core of the knock rummy get-togethers. They summered together in the same bungalow colonies in the Catskill Mountains, known back then as the "Jewish Alps," and watched each other's children grow up.

I was about three years old when one day Mom was gone, and Grandma Felicia had moved in with us. Grandma spoke less English than Dad, even though she had lived in the United States since 1938. Still, I was relatively fortunate. Many of my childhood friends bounced around the New York City foster care system for months or years until their mothers returned from the tuberculosis ward.

After Mom came home, she started working part-time nights at the Barton's Bonbonniere flagship store on Broadway. On her off nights, she raised and lowered hems for a local tailor while we watched TV on the old black-and-white DuMont. She was soon promoted to night shift manager at Barton's and then assistant store manager working days.

She took classes in English, learned Gregg and Pitman shorthand, and became a 55-words-per-minute touch typist. Already fluent in six languages—Hungarian, Romanian, German, French,

Yiddish, and English—she quickly picked up Spanish. She landed a job at a lawyer's office but soon quit, hinting the lawyer was a *mooser*, a liar.

She then became a shift manager at Galil, a store that sold Israeli gifts and chocolates.

"I was never asked to leave a job; I was always asked to stay" was both her mantra and a life lesson for Alan and me.

By comparison, Dad always seemed tired and old. His teeth looked like misshapen corn kernels. He had a paunch and varicose veins. His thinning widow's peak rivaled Jack Nicholson's. He did nothing to improve his English, though he read English-language newspapers and magazines with no problem.

In early 1961, my parents' best friends, Rose and Jack, bought a candy store, the old-fashioned kind with a newspaper stand out front and a soda fountain in the back. Jack had moved furniture for a living until a hernia made him find other work. The candy store gave them an unheard-of level of financial stability. So when Mom heard that a candy store a block up from Galil on Broadway was for sale, she rushed over after work to meet the owner, Sam Kirsch.

The store was all of ten feet wide and thirty feet deep. Kirsch hadn't updated the décor since the 1940s, if ever. The oak-strip flooring was pocked and rutted. Dark mahogany-stained shelves with glass doors lined one wall. The front display case boasted boxes of Dutch Masters and White Owl cigars. While the money was in selling cigarettes, the heart of the store—the soda fountain—was in back, behind a scuffed black Formica counter and five chrome swivel stools with green vinyl seats that had been repeatedly patched with gaffer's tape.

After the brief tour, Mom pulled out a five-dollar bill.

What's this? Kirsch asked.

"I tell him, 'This is my deposit. I'll give you another fifty dollars next month,'" she loved to recall. "Kirsch stared at me like I was meshugah."

Kirsch let himself be persuaded and, because Mom could never qualify for a bank loan, agreed to be paid out over the next year or two.

Problem was, Mom did all this without partnering much with Dad. The contract was signed only by her—Dad was not on the lease. By then, the vinyl doily venture had failed and he was splitting his time between pickup shifts at the clothing factory and the unemployment line. With no real alternative, he reluctantly put on a white apron.

Dolek and Henci, struggling immigrants, became Joe and Helen, neighborhood candy store owners.

By 7:00 a.m., Joe was serving coffee and selling newspapers to the subway commuters. Helen came down after packing Alan and me off to school. After the lunch-hour rush, he'd take a break for a meal and a nap and relieve Helen by 4:00 p.m. so she could prepare dinner. Our family ate most meals in shifts for years. The store closed at 11:00 p.m. weekdays and midnight on Saturdays. On Sundays, Joe stayed open until the weekend newspapers that had been delivered the night before were sold out.

A small Coke cost six cents; an ice cream cone, a dime; an egg cream, twelve cents. Instead of a cash register, we had a black plastic tray with sections for pennies, nickels, dimes, and quarters and a longer section for one-dollar bills. Five-dollar bills went under the tray. Joe viewed any larger denomination with suspicion and, after careful inspection, folded the bill into his front trouser pocket.

There was no refrigeration. Every couple of days, the iceman would deliver a large slab on his shoulder. It was placed in an insulated cooler with the cans and bottles of soft drinks. Chunks were chipped off with ice picks for the Coke and Canada Dry machines and for customers who insisted on ice in their fountain drinks.

We did, however, have a deep freezer. It held vats of Sealtest ice cream. We offered eight flavors and chocolate, butterscotch, strawberry, coffee, and vanilla syrups, plus candied cashews, marshmallow sauce, and embalmed maraschino cherries.

The possibilities dazzled me. I was as happy as . . . a kid in a candy store. Perpetually underweight and skinny, I was encouraged to eat as much ice cream as I wanted, as often as I wanted, in any combination I wanted. After a week, I couldn't look at ice cream.

For Joe, the best part of the store was the racks of newspapers and magazines. Back then, New York had seven English and two Yiddish daily newspapers. He read them all. He also brought home everything from *Time, Newsweek,* and *U.S. News & World Report* to *Scientific American, Argosy, National Geographic,* and *Reader's Digest.* He regularly pointed out articles he thought would interest me. For my part, I became the best-read aficionado of DC, Marvel, and Archie comic books in my school. The rule was never to crease the bindings so they could be returned to the shelves for sale.

When I started high school, I was expected to help out. I learned the art of egg creams and of scooping frozen ice cream without spraining a wrist. At fourteen, I could brew perfect pots of Bunn drip coffee and learned to schmooze with customers.

High school also marked a distinct shift in my relationship with my father. With their limited English, my parents could not help much with my reading or spelling in elementary school. While Mom tried to help with math, she could never explain it to where I got it. As her frustration grew, so did the decibels until I was in tears. Only in high school, when I began studying history and current events, did my father become the go-to resource. There was nothing he did not know about history or geography. He had instant recall of names, dates, places, events, and their interconnections. While he might not have been able to work out physics formulas, he could discuss the significance of the latest theories behind them. Not coincidentally, the only subjects in which I excelled were advanced placement history and economics.

A vacancy opened in an apartment building around the corner. We moved from West 83rd Street next to the parking garage to a rent-controlled two-bedroom on West 81st. Though only a seven-minute walk apart, the two buildings could have been in different time zones. Instead of a plumbing supply warehouse, we now looked out on All Angels Church. Instead of a broken buzzer, we now had a part-time doorman.

We had crossed into the working middle class. The candy store paid for Joe's new teeth and varicose vein surgery. Still, for my brother and me, City College, with its free tuition, would be our first and only option.

For Helen, being her own boss was liberating despite the six-and-a-half-day workweeks. A natural raconteur, she loved schmoozing with customers, especially in a foreign language. Looking back, it was as if her command of languages proved, at least to herself, that she was as cosmopolitan and cultured as any of her well-heeled West End Avenue customers. She considered her customers her friends. She would argue baseball with neighborhood doormen as easily as she chatted about last night's performance of the City Opera with Beverly Sills, the renowned opera soprano. The actor Eli Wallach was also a regular and would lift the eyeglasses off Joe's face to read the newspapers.

At one point, Helen offered to help Walter Spitzer break into the New York art market by hosting a show of his work in our apartment. She assured Walter that her dear friends from the candy store were sure to snap up his paintings. Joe was hesitant but went along because once Helen made up her mind, there was no point in trying to dissuade her. I was fourteen or fifteen at the time and helped rearrange the living room furniture to better show off Spitzer's watercolors, oils, and lithographs. Helen ordered in trays of kosher hot and cold hors d'oeuvres and put out a couple bottles of liquor and an array of soft drinks.

After ninety minutes, it was clear no one was coming. Only Ilsa, with whom Helen chatted in German, phoned in an excuse.

The humiliation was palpable. Yet Helen didn't explode in righteous fury and Joe refrained from saying "I told you so." They quietly rewrapped the Spitzer art in cardboard and twine and moved back the furniture. The hot hors d'oeuvres were tossed; I snacked on the cold ones for days. They never mentioned this incident again, at least not in my presence.

The next time Ilsa came into the candy store, Helen brushed off the snub like it didn't matter. I knew better. Helen was infamous for recalling slights and keeping grudges, for years. She just had too much pride to let her hurt show.

As for Joe, he never liked the candy store despite the financial security it provided. He resented wearing chocolate-stained aprons. He resented patronizing customers who treated his heavy accent like a mental defect. He resented being called Joe, as in "Joe, can you warm up this coffee?" or "Joe, can you add a little more seltzer to the egg cream?"

Then there was Mr. Korn, who lived in the same white-gloved Riverside Drive co-op as Eli Wallach. Korn boasted of selling his Seventh Avenue garment business rather than letting the unions in. Joe, an old union man, for the most part kept quiet and let Korn opine endlessly.

Once Korn said something about the Amazon being the world's longest river. The store was crowded and we all were busy serving customers.

"You mean the widest," Joe said.

"Whaddya mean?" Korn asked.

"The Amazon is the world's widest river. The Nile is the longest."

"Longest, widest—what difference does it make?"

"Well, just that you said longest and—"

"Whaddya know anyway? You're just a greenhorn," Korn said. "If you're so smart, why are you in a candy store?"

My cheeks burned. Helen caught my eye for a nanosecond and turned on Korn. "And you're an ignoramus and a fool. You can take yourself and your opinions out of here."

"You can't talk to me like that. I'm a paying customer—"

"And I'm the greenhorn who owns this store. Now get out."

Korn looked to his fellow customers for support. "Can you believe this?"

Everyone stared into their coffee cups and Cokes and said nothing.

Korn sputtered some, swore he'd never come back, and stormed out.

Conversation resumed, like in every cowboy movie where the piano starts up again after the barroom brawl and the patrons go back to their drinking.

Through it all, Joe had said nothing. He was sullen for the rest of the day, his face drawn and pale, eyes often staring into the middle distance.

"Ignore him—he's nothing but a *nar* [a fool]," Helen said in Yiddish. It was the only time I can remember her trying to comfort Joe. "He's not worth it. Don't let him bother you."

But it did.

Chapter 5

FINDING PILSUDSKIEGO 3

We drive to Dabrowa-Gornicza the next morning to find the house built by my grandfather, Abram Lajtner, in the late 1800s.

My Uncle Icia, in an unpublished memoir, described the house as "a solid brick building. He [Abram] kept the apartment upstairs while renting the downstairs out to a rich bachelor. Three sides of the house faced the street, while the fourth side faced his shop. The complex occupied several square blocks and was surrounded by a very high cement wall with large gates."

We know the house itself was standing as late as 1987. That year my father's sister, Aunt Dorothy, having been diagnosed with leukemia, returned to Poland with her son Avi to visit the childhood home she had not seen since immigrating to the United States in 1932.

When she had lived there, the address had been Pilsudskiego 3, named after General Jozef Pilsudski, the father of modern Poland. When the Communists came to power after the war, they had discouraged symbols of Polish nationalism and renamed the street. With the help of a patient taxi driver, Aunt Dorothy and Avi found it—the street was now Swierczeskiego, after a Polish Communist general assassinated by Ukrainian nationalists in 1947.

As my cousin Avi snapped pictures, some local women gathered, curious about these visitors with their American clothes and fancy Japanese cameras.

"Do you know whose house this was?" my aunt asked in Polish.

It was the Lajtner house, one said.

"Well, I'm a Lajtner," Aunt Dorothy declared, the subtext being, *Yes, we are still alive!* The Polish women could only gape.

Aunt Dorothy loved telling that story.

I brought copies of snapshots Avi had taken that day. They show a worn though imposing building with badly peeling brown stucco that revealed patches of red brick. The most prominent architectural detail is a second-floor balcony of green filigreed iron hanging off the angled corner of the house.

When I once asked my father about life before the war, he'd replied with his heavy, cosmic sigh. "How can I explain it? It was a whole world—Jewish schools and theaters and Yiddish newspapers and benevolent societies. An entire culture. And it disappeared just like that"—*snap!*—"Vanished, like it never existed."

Dad had never wanted to return to Poland. For him, it was a dead subject.

One cousin, Adek, did return after the war. He claimed to be the only surviving Lajtner—and thus heir to the Lajtner properties. He won control of a number of them. When his cousins learned of this years later, it sparked quite a family scandal. They sued Adek in the Polish courts. Neither my father nor Aunt Dorothy had involved themselves in the lawsuit. In any event, Adek prevailed. The courts ruled too much time had passed to challenge his ownership.

I remember meeting Cousin Adek at a family get-together when I was about eleven or twelve years old. He was hard to forget. He had a tracheotomy and spoke through a battery-enhanced tube, the victim of throat cancer.

Now, with the Communists out of power, Polish nationalism was back in. Les had consulted maps before our arrival and easily found the street we were seeking, Pilsudskiego.

Because it's on the way, we first drive to Koscielna 13, where Grandfather Abram's roofing factory had stood. The black Chevy slowly climbs the steep, twisting street and stops opposite number 13—two stories of heavily patched gray stucco with a beat-up doorway in peeling green paint. Adjacent is a large fenced-in yard strewn with junk. This *could* have been a factory eighty years ago, though not a very big one.

I pull out my video camera while Alan mans the digital, snapping pictures from up the street, down the street, across the street. A heavy blonde woman leans out a second-floor window, her ponderous bosom resting on the sill. She calls down. Les tells her what we're doing. Though I do not understand a word of Polish, she's clearly agitated.

"She says this house and land have been in her husband's family for many generations," Les translates.

"That can't be," I say, waving my copy of the 1929 Polish business directory. "See, right here, 'Koscielna 13, roofing-paper factory, A. Lajtner.'"

Les translates to the woman. She becomes more agitated and disappears from the window. "She says she is calling her husband," Les says.

A few minutes later, a tiny car speeds up the hill out of which steps a huge man drenched in sweat. I place myself strategically behind Les and Alan. Les speaks. The man replies. Les tilts his head, two fingers tapping his lip in Columbo contemplation. "He says this land was always in his family, and the yard was used to grow grapes for wine."

"Then let him explain the business directory," I say, waving it in my hands. Les shows it to the man. He slowly shakes his big blond head and speaks softly, pointing down the hill toward central Dabrowa.

"A-ha, a-ha." Les nods and smiles. "He says in the old days, this was an independent village and Dabrowa a small town. Only after the war, Dabrowa grew into a city and swallowed up all of these surrounding little villages." Not only that, just about every village and town in Roman Catholic Poland has a street named Koscielna, which means Church Street.

Alan and I look at each other, smile weakly and, cameras in hand, get in the car. Les drives down the hill toward central Dabrowa in awkward silence.

"Have a Kopiko?" Les offers.

Some consolation prize. What an idiot I was to think we could just drive up after sixty years and find Grandpa's—

My dark thoughts are interrupted by Alan's uncontrolled giggling.

"Did you see the look on the woman's face?" he asks. "We were her worst nightmare. 'Here come the Jews to reclaim their property!'" We all laugh heartily. Buoyant, I crush the Kopiko in my teeth.

Once we reach Dabrowa, we quickly find Pilsudskiego. It's a major commercial thoroughfare with trams, buses, and choking traffic. We begin looking for No. 3 but something's clearly wrong. The street number sequence makes no sense. By the time we reach the lower numbers, we're out of the city altogether.

I pull out Aunt Dorothy's photographs from 1987. The street pictured is much smaller, with many trees and little traffic. Even twenty years later, the change could not be this dramatic.

Les stops a policeman. "He says many streets were renamed after the Communists fell. But maybe not to their old names." On to Dabrowa City Hall.

In a city where the architecture is mostly worn, old, and stained brown with decades of coal dust, the Dabrowa City Hall is a shock—a semi-spherical spacecraft of brushed steel and reflective glass perched atop a terraced parking lot.

Inside, however, it's déjà vu. I'm back in the Department of

Motor Vehicles on Centre Street in New York City circa 1970—bureaucratic green walls, electronic number signs, and long lines of morose citizenry awaiting the favor of bored clerks. Only here the clerks are mostly stout Polish ladies of a certain age, all sporting the same short hair bobs.

We find our way to the city planning office where the clerks are younger—too young to remember the Communist era. None have any idea how to find a street once named after a Communist general.

The supervisor appears. She's the only person in the office with the institutional memory of Dabrowa under Communist rule. She sizes Alan and me up with intelligent blue eyes behind wire-framed glasses as Les explains our dilemma. She studies Aunt Dorothy's photographs but, with a shrug, says, "*Przepraszamy, nie.*" Sorry, no.

Brow furrowed, Les taps his nose with two fingers. Sounding apologetic, he asks a question. The supervisor thinks a moment and nods. *Tak.* Yes.

As if struck by a brilliant idea, Les asks another question. The supervisor smiles broadly—*Tak, Tak*—and orders the younger clerks to pull table-sized clear-plastic map overlays from flat file drawers spread around the office. Aligning the maps one over another, she studies them for long minutes hunched over the large counter, occasionally glancing at Cousin Avi's snapshots.

"Ah-hah!" she says, stabbing a finger at some squiggly lines: a diagram of a house with a distinctive angled corner and a large enclosed courtyard.

The street once named for the father of modern Poland and then for an assassinated Communist general had been renamed yet again. It is now Augustynika, after Father Gregory Augustynik, the moving force behind the construction of the Basilica in Dabrowa. This makes a lot of sense in a resurgent Catholic Poland proud of its Polish Pope, John Paul II.

....

The black Chevrolet pulls up to the house of my father and grandfather. Les silences the engine. Alan and I stare out the car's tinted windows, unable to move.

It's a house, just an old house. But it's Dad's house . . . Which window was his room? And Aunt Dorothy's? And Aunt Pola's. Guess I'll never know. Now don't get emotional, not here in front Alan and Les. This is no different than seeing our old apartment building on West 83rd Street. Because it's just an old, worn house. But it's Dad's house . . .

Augustynika 3 is swathed in grimy cement stucco, chipped and peeling. A third floor had been added to part of the house sometime after the war. The filigreed iron balcony had been hacked off that distinctive angled corner of the second floor, leaving a stub of metal and a rotting wooden platform.

I gag at the stench of stale urine inside the hallway. Mailboxes are broken and bent. Generations of graffiti compete for space. Out back, the skeletons of two cars rust in a corner of the large yard.

Four shirtless young men with shaved heads emerge from a doorway. They're lean and muscular and as sweaty and grimy as coal miners in the July heat. Spotting us, they stop. They stare. I glance at Alan, a third-degree black belt, and know he's mentally sizing up which one he'll take out first, and how. Les walks over and chats quietly with the group. The leader looks at us, smirks, then leads the others away.

As we reconnoiter the building, two older women, each sporting different tints of red hair, approach us, *curious about these visitors with their American clothes and fancy Japanese cameras.*

"Do you know whose house this was?" Alan asks, with Les translating.

"It's the Lajtner house," says the stouter of the two.

"We are Lajtners," I say, consciously parroting Aunt Dorothy's defiant declaration. *So much for not seeking moral vindication.*

The woman smiles and speaks rapidly to Les. "She says that about twenty years ago, an older woman came with a young man and also said she was a Lajtner and this had been her house."

Alan and I turn to each other, stunned. We had not told Les of Aunt Dorothy's encounter nineteen years earlier. *What are the odds? Who would believe me?*

Les is still translating. "She says many years before a man came around and demanded money from everyone for rent."

"What man?" I ask.

"She says he had a hole in his throat and spoke through a pipe." So Cousin Adek had also gotten control of Grandpa's house. Because Dad and Aunt Dorothy had stayed out of the family drama, it never occurred to me that Adek had also gone after Abram Lajtner's properties. I wonder now if Dad and Aunt Dorothy had known this, would they have remained passive and stayed out of the lawsuit? One thing for sure, Dad never wanted to come back here. So why do I feel angry? Why should I care? Yet I do care. Adek had lied. He was not the last Lajtner and by so lying, he also denied my father's survival.

On a whim, I ask the women if they know where Koscielna Street used to be. They point to the street directly in front us, running perpendicular into Augustynika. A few blocks away, we can see the towering spires of Our Lady of Angels, the Basilica built largely under the direction of Father Gregory Augustynik.

The women can tell us no more about the house's current ownership. They direct us to the local public housing office at the end of the street that once was Koscielna. There, the administrator passes around cold drinks and cigarettes and orders copies of court papers dating back to the 1960s, after Adek had died of throat cancer. The municipality had billed the absentee landlord for repairs and renovations over several decades, tacking on interest to the compounding property tax arrears. One document shows that Adek's appointed trustee had petitioned the courts to give up his responsibilities in 1979, essentially walking away from the house. The property appears to be in a legal limbo. The city has done almost nothing to maintain it since the mid-1970s.

With the information in the court papers, we return to the city planning office where the helpful supervisor calls up the current tax records on her computer. As of 2006, Abram Lajtner was the owner of record of Augustynika 3. This makes no sense, as my grandfather died in 1931.

My "ah-ha" moment would come only years later, in an email from a cousin: "Don't you know that Adek's Hebrew name was Abraham and he used it in the courts to claim the Lajtner properties?"

Chapter 6

ROOTING THROUGH THE ROOTS

··

The next day, Les drives us to Bedzin, the town where my father was born and from where the Lajtners had originated. He has arranged for us to meet with a town official who, Les says, has been helpful in the past.

Before the war, Bedzin had been a sophisticated, bustling commercial center of forty-eight thousand, about 45 percent Jewish. It was comfortable, established, and safe. But for the sharp-elbowed, the bold, the entrepreneurial, the future was Dabrowa, a soot-stained boomtown and the heart of Poland's burgeoning coal and steel industries. So many holes were dug for coal under Dabrowa, locals joked the town was in danger of collapsing into itself.

My great-grandfather, Izyk Jehuda Lajtner, moved his family to Dabrowa around 1890, after Poland's Russian Czarist rulers eased residency restrictions that had barred Jews from living in certain areas.

Only a few miles separate Bedzin from Dabrowa, mere minutes apart by car. Les stops at the old Jewish cemetery on the outskirts of town. He pulls the Chevy to the side of the road and nods toward a heavily wooded hill. "It's up there."

Amid the deep shadows of the trees, I stumble on a jagged rock sticking up from the dirt. I glance down and my stomach heaves. The rock is a slab of a tombstone, the Hebrew letters clearly legible. As our eyes grow accustomed to the dim light, the hillside emerges strewn with upturned headstones, most smashed, others remarkably intact. Alan and I pick our way among the gravestones snapping photos, trying to make out the names chiseled in Yiddish.

The cemetery was established in 1831 to handle the surge of deaths from a cholera outbreak. Most of the 800 headstones are shattered or toppled. About 250 are intact, though deteriorating. The Bedzin municipality has reserved the area as a Jewish necropolis. Some headstones have been moved to a local museum. There are no gates, walls, or fences. Occasionally visitors like us stop by. So do vandals.

We drive on to Bedzin in silence. We're not the first visitors Les has escorted to this cemetery. He understands our need for reflection. "Have a Kopiko," he says.

We arrive at Bedzin City Hall for our meeting with the official, a tall and lean man in his thirties with a thin pencil mustache and warm smile. I return the smile and shake hands, but my head, my heart, and my gut are still in that broken cemetery.

The official leads us through a rabbit's warren of back-office cubicles and corridors and through a set of nondescript doors. We emerge into a large wood-paneled chamber with a red Oriental rug on the floor and a crystal chandelier hanging from the ceiling. A crimson banner emblazoned with a medieval eagle, Poland's national symbol, is draped behind an oversized mahogany desk.

"What is this place?" I ask.

"This is where they marry people," Les says.

The official has prepared for our meeting. He produces three inch-thick packs of square index cards with the birth, marriage, and death records, respectively, of all the Lajtners in Bedzin. Each card references a more complete entry in large ledgers.

I recall Dad once telling me that the Lajtner clan in Bedzin had "numbered more than seventy souls." Most of the names on the cards mean nothing to me. Seeing them here, spread out in neat rows on this mahogany desk, in this wood-paneled chamber where nuptials are performed, strikes me as ironic—and obscene.

Was Gabriel Lajtner or Juta Lajtner or Alter Lajtner family? I'll never know. If we were related, how so? I'll never know. Did my extended family get swallowed whole by the Holocaust? Probably—but I'll never know.

I willfully set these thoughts aside. Instead, Alan and I shuffle through the stacks like kids with baseball cards and pull out the ones with names we recognize, like the birth of our father and the card referencing our grandparents' marriage. The official then brings out the corresponding ledgers with Abram Lajtner's signature at the bottom of both, memorializing the birth of his ninth child and, three years earlier, his marriage to my grandmother Felicia.

....

Fajgla Rozia Mstowska was born in 1888, one of seven surviving children of eleven. Her father, Abraham, was an impoverished tailor. Her younger brother, Icia, recalled in his memoir that his family often depended on the charity of neighbors to eat. They lived in a one-street hamlet directly across from the huge smokestacks of an iron-smelting complex.

"Sometimes we would see flames shooting up from the high smokestacks, which in a few minutes gave way to thick smoke," Icia wrote. "Soot covered the roofs of the small houses and seeped in through doors and windows. It was a very unhealthful area to live in."

Poland in the early 1900s was wracked by severe recession, general strikes, and bloody clashes between Polish nationalists and Russian Cossack troops. Thousands were killed. In a spillover of the 1905 Russian Revolution, Russian Cossack troops crushed a sit-in strike at a nearby foundry, killing seventy-eight workers and wounding nearly two hundred others.

Even amid such unrest, Fajgla, or Felicia in English, then just sixteen, would travel by train across the border to the German city of Katowitz to buy children's clothing, dragging little Icia with her. "She would dress me heavily in the children's clothing," Icia wrote, "and this enabled her to pass the German-Russian border without paying import taxes. At home she sold these items to girlfriends and their Polish families."

On one such trip in 1907, Felicia caught the eye of Abram Lajtner, already a wealthy industrialist and businessman. Old sepia photographs show a compact man with a clipped Charlie Chaplain mustache. In one photo, he is in a dark three-piece suit with a stout cane in hand. He stares directly into the camera, the very image of self-confidence and success. At thirty-nine, Abram had already buried two wives and was estranged from his third.

Felicia was eighteen and, being a girl from an impoverished family, had received no formal education. Aside from reading Hebrew prayers, she was probably barely literate. They began to see more of each other. Abram bought her gifts and took her to expensive restaurants in Katowitz. He would call at her humble house with his two-horse carriage and driver, wait patiently for her to get ready, and drive her back to his mansion.

"My sister, coming from a poor home as she did, was greatly impressed by this lavish home," Icia wrote. "He courted her seriously and promised her a life of luxury and wealth if she consented to marry him."

Family lore passed on by Aunt Dorothy had it that Abram was something of a "ladies' man" who took extended business trips to Vienna, Prague, and Karlsbad where, Dorothy suspected, he might seek the favors of "certain ladies." This is not the image of Grandpa Abram passed down to me by my father. When I was a child, Dad spoke of Abram as secular and modern, very much the patriarch of the extended Lajtner clan, a tough businessman but honorable.

Nevertheless, reviewing the family tree hints at controversy if not outright scandal: Abram was courting Felicia while his estranged third wife, Ziesla, was pregnant. Their daughter, Natka, was born on March 2, 1908, nearly three weeks *after* Abram and Felicia wed on February 19. Genealogical records show that Natka's birth was only registered in 1928. Natka was raised only by Abram. The story behind this strange timeline is buried along with my ancestors.

Felicia was only about six years older than Abram's eldest son by his first marriage. This would become a source of tension in the years ahead.

"In her new rich home she felt herself the lady of a mansion and managed the place well, directing the cook and maid servant," Icia wrote. "Perhaps she consented to the marriage thinking that she could in this way assist her poor parents and alleviate their food shortage. Unfortunately, her husband was not the picture of generosity she had hoped for, and my parents' lot was not much improved."

Faced with grinding poverty, anti-Semitic discrimination, and no prospects, Felicia's parents, her three brothers and sister all immigrated to America in the decades bracketing World War I. They were part of the largest Jewish migration in history—2.5 million Jews—who moved to the United States from Poland and Russia.

Unlike the Mstowskas, the Lajtner brothers were third generation metal craftsmen who had forged success and wealth with their own calloused hands.

According to Icia, Abram won the contract for all sheet metal works as well as the contract to repair the roofs of the iron smelting complex, which was owned by foreigners.

One of Abram's younger brothers, Mortka-Hirsch, became so successful from iron foundries and real estate that he was among the first in the area to own a private automobile. A third brother, Bernard, also owned a large metal workshop and was partners in a tannery with his in-laws. Only a fourth Lajtner brother, Anschel, sought his fortune overseas and ended up in Canada.

In addition to his metalworking, Abram's roofing business expanded apace with Dabrowa's growth. According to Icia, the house on Pilsudskiego Street played a key role in winning a particularly lucrative contract.

As the story went, Abram had rented the ground-floor apartment to a young Polish aristocrat who was a trustee and treasurer for the new Lady of Angels, the basilica then being built down the street under the guidance of Father Gregory Augustynik. As treasurer, the Pole was charged with safekeeping the gold coins collected by the faithful and stored in a large vase. During the summer, the vase was hidden in the dormant tiled heating stove of the apartment.

"One year he decided to move to a more modern house," Icia wrote, "and in the moving process, forgot to check the tiled stove where lay the vase containing the accumulated gold treasure." When Abram's workers later found the vase, Abram "promptly notified the gentleman-trustee about it. Out of gratitude for his honesty, the aristocrat obtained the roofing contract for Mr. Lajtner, a Jew, instead of a Christian contractor." It was just one more feather in his already-stuffed cap—and a part of the good fortune that was visited upon all of the Lajtners in that era.

Into this family of growing wealth and privilege my father was born on August 11, 1911. His sister Doba, later called Dorothy, arrived two years later. Two years after that came Pola, the spoiled baby of the family.

World War I destroyed the two great empires that had partitioned Poland: Austria-Hungary in the west and Czarist Russia in the east, which fell to the Communist Revolution. President Woodrow Wilson had made an independent Poland one of his Fourteen Points, the document that became the basis for the League of Nations. In a series of border wars that lasted until 1922, the Polish leader, General Jozef Pilsudski, carved out a country from former German- and Russian-controlled provinces. The result was a polyethnic, polyglot nation where 22 percent of Poland's population were ethnic minorities—Germans, Ukrainians, Jews, Lithuanians, and Roma. Squeezed between larger and more powerful neighbors, Russia and Germany, Pilsudski knew he needed the support of the League of Nations and Wilson for his fledgling country. To that end, he signed treaties granting full citizenship to its ethnic minorities, including the Jews.

Under Pilsudski's rule, anti-Semitism was kept in check though it was never far from the surface. Polish ultranationalists rejected the very notion that Jews were Poles any more than the Ukrainians or Roma were Poles, and they resented being forced to grant them citizenship to win League of Nation and American support.

In 1925, when my father was about fifteen, rumors swept Dabrowa that Jews were using the blood of kidnapped Christian children for religious rituals. Several prominent Jews were arrested. In the past, blood libels like this had triggered pogroms, officially sanctioned riots. This time, a police investigation dismissed the accusations as fabrications and dropped all charges.

My father grew up into this new, modern Poland. He attended public high school and excelled in history and, especially, geography. "Your dad knew more about geography than the teacher," Aunt Dorothy had told me. "Once he corrected the teacher in front of the class, which was just not done. The teacher slapped him hard across his face and sent him home. Our father was not pleased."

From the few stories I had heard, Dad was a bit of a hellion. Like when he dipped the ponytail of the girl sitting in front of him into the inkwell of his desk. More seriously, Aunt Dorothy said, he once tied together the waist-long braids of several Polish girls and pushed them down a flight of stairs.

"It wasn't really a flight of stairs," he had told me, "just two or three steps."

As he grew into adulthood, my father became an accomplished horseman but also something of a dandy who enjoyed good clothes, theater, parties, and loved to dance. I remember being surprised when I saw him glide effortlessly around the dance floor with Mom at family functions. This from a man who showed no interest at home in music of any kind.

Wealthy Jews like the Lajtners were the exception. Most, like Grandma Felicia's family, were dirt poor. Illiteracy was widespread. The vast majority of Poland's Jews lived in small villages and towns. Their first language was Yiddish, and they rejected assimilation. In larger towns and cities, many working- and middle-class Jews integrated into Poland's social and political life while seeking to maintain their Jewish identity to a greater or lesser degree. Aware of their minority status, Jews in my father's region ran their own slates in municipal elections in the three sister cities—Dabrowa, Bedzin, and Sosnowiec—with some success. At the same time, Zionism, which advocated a return to the ancient Jewish homeland of Israel, attracted thousands of younger-generation Jews. Socialism and Communism, with their promises of equality in a classless society, attracted thousands more.

During these same years, a number of virulently anti-Semitic publications emerged, railing against Jewish influence in the economic and social life of the country. Now, however, Jewish groups could sue for slander—and win.

In the fall of 1930, Felicia sailed to the United States to visit her parents, brothers, and sister, whom she hadn't seen since they had emigrated in the years surrounding World War I. She remained in New York for more than six months despite entreaties from Abram to return home.

On the first night of Passover, April 1, 1931, a one-sentence telegram arrived from Poland: "Abram Lajtner is dead."

....

In 2006, the Dabrowa Registrar of Vital Statistics occupies a small, square room lined floor-to-ceiling with bookshelves and gray metal desks buried under stacks of computer printouts. About a half-dozen young women hunch before glowing green IBM computer screens. "California Dreamin'" by The Mamas & The Papas plays somewhere on a radio.

Inside a battered green metal cabinet, the kind where the doors always rattle, piled helter-skelter are a number of over-sized ledgers that record more than a century's worth of Jewish births, marriages, and deaths. The Jewish ledgers are segregated from those of their Christian Polish neighbors, a carryover from when such records were the domain of parish churches and local synagogues.

The ledgers themselves are on the verge of crumbling, the handwritten entries on the yellowing pages fading into oblivion. To the young women behind the glowing terminals, the ledgers may have been nothing more than curiosities. To me, they are irreplaceable records of a vanished community. That Dabrowa City Hall permits them to quietly disintegrate seems part of the conspiracy of silence to which Les had alluded to ignore uncomfortable truths about the city's history.

So it doesn't help when the office manager refuses to let us photocopy the entry of Grandpa Abram's death in 1931, citing "privacy issues."

Alan's anger needs no translation. "Privacy? Just whose 'privacy' are we violating?"

The louder we get, the more intransigent the office manager becomes. She forbids me from photographing the page with my digital camera.

The best I can do is scribble Les's off-the-cuff translation onto the back of a manila envelope I have with me:

"In Dabrowa-Gornicza on the 1st of April 1931 at 9 a.m. appeared at the registrar's office one witness, Israel Froiman, a shoemaker, forty years old, and a second witness, Josef Prezeroivich, and they proclaimed that in Dabrowa-Gornicza, Pilsudskiego 3, Abram Lajtner (died) on 31 March at 1 o'clock at night. Abram Lajtner, 61 years old, a trader, son of Izyk and Perla, born Strzegowski, and married to Fagla-Roza, born Mstowska."

Later I spot a mistake: Grandpa was sixty-three when he died of complications from pneumonia.

Les hustles us to our next stop, the Office of Deeds and Real Estate. "When we go inside, maybe is better I talk," he says. I nod, still seething at the office manager's bloody-mindedness that I can't help but think may have been anti-Semitism.

A clerk is dispatched to the basement and returns with a long ledger with a black marbleized cover like a child's composition book. It is the "Land Book" for Property Number 106.

This office manager also forbids us from photocopying the book, again citing "privacy issues." Speaking softly, Les cajoles her into letting me photograph a number of pages with my digital camera.

Hands trembling, we open Land Book 106. Entries before World War I, when Poland was part of Czarist Russia, are in flowing Russian Cyrillic. After the war, from 1918 on, the writing is in Polish.

The earliest entry is the record of a mortgage taken out by Abram in 1899 on the house built on land purchased by my great-grandfather, Izyk Jehuda Lajtner, in 1891. Most entries deal with taxes owed, taxes paid, and the recording and releasing of liens when the house was used as collateral for business loans.

Abram Lajtner's death in 1931 splintered the family. Abram's sons by his first two marriages, led by Wolf, then thirty, inherited all of Abram's businesses. Felicia received no provisions for support or income. My father, nineteen at the time, and his two younger sisters each received the equivalent of several thousand dollars, a considerable sum in those days, but it was kept in trust until they reached the age of majority.

Felicia was also cut out of any ownership share of Pilsudskiego 3, though she was allowed to live there for the rest of her life. In round numbers, Abram's three sons from his second marriage were awarded a 72 percent share of the house while my father and his two sisters received about 18 percent. A half brother (from Abram's first wife) and Natka, (the half sister from Abram's third wife), shared the remaining 10 percent. Land Book 106 chronicles this bitter dispute in entries running from 1931 into 1936. The house itself was subdivided, with some rooms going to Felicia and her three children and others to Wolf and his brothers.

By this time, the political landscape in Poland had also changed. The Great Depression of the 1930s devastated Poland's economy. After the death of Jozef Pilsudski in 1935, several ultranationalist parties vied for power, each trying to outdo the other in blaming the Jews for Poland's troubles. Reflecting rising Nazi anti-Semitism in neighboring Germany, they pushed for a national boycott and confiscation of Jewish businesses. Jews were subjected to increasing discrimination and restrictions in the legal and medical professions and in universities. Riots killed seventy-nine Jews and injured five hundred others between 1935 and 1937.

With rising anti-Semitism at home, and Hitler's Nazi Germany threatening war next door, my father persuaded Felicia to visit her family in the United States in 1938. She never returned.

The last entry in Land Book 106 before the war is dated June 19, 1939.

Barely ten weeks later, the Nazi invasion of Poland rendered all of our family's petty feuds forever irrelevant.

Chapter 7

THE 800-POUND GORILLA

B y the time I return from Poland, any pretensions that my project is a mere diversion from work are just that, pretensions. What started out as a curious exercise in Journalism 101 had become, well, if not obsession then something close to it.

Some friends, children of survivors themselves, suggest that our parents' trauma has indelibly defined us and that my "project" is my way of working out "issues."

I have a hard time with this. To this day, I wince at postings on Holocaust-related websites that wallow in the pain of the past as if it were the present, as if we, the children of survivors, deserve a merit badge for the suffering of our parents. I sometimes want to scream: Enough already. Get a life. Move on.

"Can I mention the 800-pound gorilla in the room?" my friend Karen asks.

"You mean, why have I spent years chasing down my father's stories?"

"Well, can you explain it?"

I can't, not completely. Not then. Not now.

Growing up, I saw my father as unspectacularly ordinary. From earliest awareness, I knew he and Mom had survived

Hitler-and-the-Nazis—but so had everyone else in our small circle. Nothing special there. My Jewish elementary school never had formal classes about the Holocaust. If it did, I don't remember any, not even vaguely.

My real education about what it meant to be a Jew came courtesy of my neighbors, Richie and Barbara, and their friends at the Holy Trinity School.

Richie was my best friend. He had two older sisters, Barbara and Diane. All three strongly favored their mother, with strawberry blond hair, fair skin, and freckles. I'd visit Richie's walk-up apartment, and he and Barbara were regulars at ours. Our mothers fed us Drake's Devil Dogs and milk from glass bottles. This was the 1950s. There was little fear of drugs or sick crimes against children. West 83rd Street was a safe place, strongly Irish Catholic, down to the bar on the corner of Amsterdam Avenue.

Richie and his sisters attended the Holy Trinity Catholic School farther down West 83rd Street. I went to a small Orthodox Jewish day school a few streets away where it was de rigueur for boys to wear large skullcaps in public as well as in school. The dual secular and religious curriculum meant I finished classes at 4:30 p.m. By then, Richie and his friends were playing stickball in the street or pitching pennies against stoops.

The school bus dropped me off on the corner of Amsterdam Avenue and I walked the half block home. One afternoon soon after I began first grade, Barbara, who must have been about eight years old, stopped me to ask about the black skullcap on my head. I told her I was Jewish, and Jews wore skullcaps as a sign of respect for God.

"Com'ere," she said, "I gotta secret for ya."

I leaned closer. "The Jews killed God," she whispered—and spat into my ear.

Shocked, I remember thinking, maybe even blurting, *That's impossible! We invented God.*

From that day until we moved out six years later, every time

I saw Richie and his buddies they'd chase after me, calling me "Jew boy" and "kike." During those years, I'd often come home with clothes disheveled and blood dripping from my nose or lip.

Mom would get hysterical and scream to run away from those *vilde chayas*, those wild beasts. Dad looked pained and said little.

The very thought of running scalded. For even in elementary school, awareness of tiny, heroic Israel beating back the surrounding Arab armies was part of my consciousness. Mom proudly spoke of her younger brother, Ari. As a seventeen-year-old during the war, Ari smuggled himself from Romania to Palestine, lied about his age, and joined the British Army. He fought with Montgomery's forces in Italy and Germany. Repatriated to Palestine after the war, he fought in Israel's War of Independence in 1948. During the 1956 Sinai campaign, he swam in the Suez Canal even though, officially, Israel never reached that waterway.

Photos showed a Hollywood-handsome man with a dazzling smile and laughing eyes. Tall, good-looking, and a real warrior... he was everything my father wasn't. Uncle Ari became my childhood hero years before I met him and was a role model for life.

I learned to run fast but also to stand my ground and fight. Though I was skinny, underweight, and short for my age, Richie never took me on one-on-one. He never came closer than yelling distance. Nor did any of his friends. We were children and the fights never got much beyond fists or throwing garbage. Still, I stopped going outside to play. I stayed indoors all week and met up with school friends only on weekends. I also replaced that black skullcap with a brown faux-leather hat with earflaps.

So it wasn't my parents' Holocaust trauma that sensitized me to anti-Semitism, what it meant to be a minority, or an outsider looking in. I had learned those lessons courtesy of Richie, Barbara, and their friends on West 83rd Street.

In graduate school, a classmate asked to talk to me about an article she was researching about, essentially, the psychological damage suffered by children of Holocaust survivors. I bristled at her very premise. I accused her of first coming to conclusions and then cherry-picking evidence to prove them. This was akin to an archer who fires the arrow into the tree, then draws the bullseye around it.

That classmate was Helen Epstein, and her groundbreaking book, *Children of the Holocaust*, is one of the defining works on the subject. So what do I know? The opening paragraph sets much of its tone:

> *For years it lay in an iron box buried so deep inside me that I was never sure just what it was. I carried slippery combustible things more secret than sex and more dangerous than any shadow or ghost . . . The safe world fell away and I saw things I knew no little girl should see. Blood and shattered glass. Piles of skeletons and blackened barbed wire with bits of flesh struck to it the way flies stick to walls after they are swatted dead. Hills of suitcases, mountains of children's shoes. Whips, pistols, boots, knives and needles . . . The 7th Avenue Local (subway) became a cattle car on its way to Poland.*

I never suffered such terrors growing up. I assumed none of my friends had, either. When I informally polled several whether they felt the Holocaust had defined their lives, I was stunned.

"Oh absolutely," Karen said. "My mother used to tell us, 'You think you're safe, but you're not. You think because you live in a big city, you're safe. I lived in a big city and I thought so, too. But you're not safe.'" Karen said this had an impact on the way she grew up, fear insinuating itself in her daily life.

Another friend, Andre, said, "A large part of who I am and my outlook on the world is defined by the fact that my parents were in concentration camps. My wife notices it. I'm the kind of person who keeps the shades drawn in the house—it's an outlook on life."

Andre said that looking back, he could now see that growing up in a house where his parents suffered from "some form of PTSD was part of my cultural environmental upbringing."

I called Eli, a family friend so close that we knew each other's parents nearly as well as our own. He said that, growing up, he most resented the role assigned to Jews, often by fellow Jews, of victimization. "I didn't want my parents to define themselves as being victims or being defined as a victim—your whole life is not being a victim."

I ask, "Did you ever tell that to your mom?"

"No, I didn't tell her that."

When I asked the question again but changed the word from "defined" by the Holocaust to "affected" by it, all my friends agreed that it was a more accurate term—how could it not affect us? They rejected, however, the notion that they were "damaged" by it, which is a central thrust of Helen Epstein's book.

Eli said, "I think of it, in a way, like growing up speaking a foreign language, the whole environment, how you talk, how you relate. The Holocaust for us was like growing up speaking a foreign language. Not good or bad, but it's the basis for how you grow up."

"The term 'damaged' troubles me," Andre said. "Show me a thousand adults and there'll be a percentage of us 'damaged' in some way. If not the Holocaust, it might be other types of 'damage.'"

Several times in her book, Helen Epstein points out that many children of survivors are named after relatives who died in the Holocaust, and thus we carry a significant psychological burden. I never felt that way. My Hebrew named is Moshe, after my maternal grandfather who was gassed in Auschwitz. When I thought about it, which was never, I saw being named after Grandpa Moshe as normal familial continuity and not a commemoration of his death. I never viewed it as full of dark portent. I saw it as being just the same as my brother, Alan, whose Hebrew name is Abraham, after our paternal grandfather

Abram who died prosperous in 1931. Naming a child after a grandparent or relative is a tradition old and rich, certainly not limited to Jews. Being psychologically burdened because of a name doesn't seem to fit, at least not me.

Then again, my brother Alan has zero doubt that our parents' trauma had also traumatized us.

"How so?" I asked.

"Don't you remember the screaming matches so loud the police once came?"

I remembered loud arguments over money, or the lack of it, but not the police showing up at our front door.

"You mean you don't remember grabbing the dog and pulling me out of the apartment, saying we're going for a walk, just to get away from the screaming?"

No, I had no memory of that, either.

"And the time you camped out on the hallway floor to keep them apart?"

No, I didn't remember anything like that.

Alan was incredulous. I was baffled. Clearly, I had repressed some painful childhood memories.

In my mind's eye, my father never screamed or yelled. Mom was the shouter, the disciplinarian. Dad would reason, cajole, negotiate. No, that's not right. When I reach back, I remember Dad using his belt. This was before Dr. Spock and enlightened sociologists decreed parents should never hit their kids. Or if they had, their theories hadn't been translated into Yiddish.

I was a lousy student. My elementary school teachers kept me in back of the classroom because I squirmed constantly in my seat. I couldn't spell. The multiplication table was an enigma. As for Hebraic and religious classes, I may as well not have shown up. (My wife, a preschool teacher, once observed that today they put kids like me on Ritalin.)

In my early elementary school years, I'd wait in terror for my parents to return from parent-teacher night because I knew the truth would come out—that I had lied, a lot. I rarely completed homework. I hid bad test results, and they were all bad. On occasion, I forged Mom's signature next to the poor grades. I could tell by the front-door slam that they were enraged. I'd hide under the Formica dining room table or inside the bedroom closet behind heaps of clothes.

Mom would slap and scream that it wasn't about poor grades; it was about lying. Dad didn't speak much. He swung that brown faux-alligator belt instead. Thinking back on it, though, Dad wasn't all that accurate, and the belt seemed to smack the floor a lot more than it did me. Or that's how I want to remember it now.

Still, even if it happened as Alan recalled, what did this specifically have to do with the Holocaust? Many couples argue about money. Who seriously compares their family to TV clichés like *Ozzie and Harriet* or *Leave It to Beaver*?

Alan pointed to our mother. As adults, we always blamed her mercurial mood swings on damage caused by the war. We always felt Mom should have gone for counseling to deal with her demons.

I mentioned this to Eli, the close family friend. "Ah, with your mom, I'm not so sure," he said. "It could have been genetics as much as environment."

Eli had a point. Big personalities and explosive tempers run deep in my mother's side of the family. Her older brother, Fischel, immigrated to the United States in the 1920s. He was known for his jovial personality, playing the ponies, smoking cigarettes from filtered holders—and for mercurial temper tantrums. Mom's younger brother, Ari, the one who fought in the British Army, was everyone's best mate and also loudly temperamental. To what extent were Mom's issues genetic or warped by Holocaust trauma?

My youngest daughter, a social worker, said it wasn't necessarily either/or. A person can be genetically susceptible to a certain disease or disorder. The likelihood of developing that disease/disorder can be increased by environmental factors. For instance, in the case of schizophrenia, someone with a schizophrenic relative may have a certain genetic risk factor. However, the likelihood of developing the disease is increased if there are "environmental stressors" present. Mom certainly had enough environmental stressors to bring out any latent depression.

A recent theory that has leaked into the popular press from some fashionable Jewish journals sounds like a punch line to a Jewish joke: The psychological trauma suffered by our parents mutated their DNA, and this mutation has been passed on to their children, the ultimate Jewish guilt trip. *Happy now, Ma?*

While I embrace the notion of inheriting certain survival instincts, overall I humbly decline this honor. Neither my father's quiet fatalism nor my mother's savage pessimism defines me. Their legacy is so much more than that.

Is Holocaust trauma different from trauma suffered by Tutsi survivors of the Rwandan massacres, or the genocide of Cambodians during Pol Pot's reign of terror? Are not the children of those survivors marked by trauma?

In the new foreword to her book marking its fortieth anniversary, Helen Epstein says she wished her research could have included victims of other manmade terrors.

I agree with her that it requires a delicate balance "to honor the classic Jewish injunction to remember, on the one hand, and to transform one's history and create one's own life on the other. Each member of the second generation has to find his or her own way to do this."

Chapter 8

ETHNIC CLEANSING
TO MASS MURDER

....

"**A**re you sure?"

Maybe I'm not hearing right. Maybe I misunderstood. I ask again, "How could they have survived the war?"

"I saw them myself last week," Jeff Cymbler says.

"But how? I mean, how could they have survived all these years?" Stunned doesn't begin to describe it.

"They're right there in the Katowice archives—must be more than fifty folders of the stuff."

While researching his own family roots, Jeff had stumbled across a trove of files from the "Council of Jewish Elders," known as the *Judenrat*, from my father's hometown of Dabrowa. To this day, the *Judenräte*, pronounced You-den-raht and plural of *Judenrat*, are one of the most controversial institutions spawned by the war. The Nazis wanted as little direct interaction with the Jewish populace as possible, so they set up *Judenräte* throughout Poland as their surrogates to carry out Nazi orders and policies. Where possible, they filled the *Judenräte* with established Jewish leaders who already had the trust of their communities.

It fell to the *Judenräte* to meet the day-to-day needs of the people. They set up soup kitchens and health clinics, managed sanitation, and ran orphanages. They negotiated, cajoled, and bribed local German officials to ease restrictions, obtain more food rations, or free individual Jews snatched off the streets for any number of reasons.

My interest is more specific: the *Judenräte* also were tasked with finding housing for thousands of Jews evicted from their homes and concentrated in larger villages and cities as part of the Nazi ethnic-cleansing program to "Aryanize" the newly annexed parts of Poland.

"Fifty? Did you say fifty folders?" I ask.

"Yeah, maybe more. I thought of you the moment I saw them."

I'd been viewing oral histories and reading about life under the *Judenräte* for months. Most of these accounts were recorded years, often decades, after the war. As any cop or reporter knows, memory can be faulty. Witnesses recall the same events differently. Details get muddied in the retelling. That's why much of the history profession sniffs at oral histories and prefers contemporaneous documents and diaries.

Now here's Jeff telling me that fifty folders of this raw material of history, from my father's hometown no less, are sitting in an archive of a provincial Polish city.

My father's family had been evicted from Pilsudskiego 3, though I did not know when or where they went. Because of its size and opulence, I always suspected some high Nazi official or influential ethnic-German family had seized the house. Given the prominence of the Lajtner family in Dabrowa, it was possible the *Judenräte* files would provide answers.

I had been to Poland less than a year ago. In summing up reasons to justify another trip, the costs and time didn't add up. The *Judenräte* archive had just changed that calculus.

"You're sure?" I ask Jeff again. "And they're accessible?"

"Yes and yes. And I know just the guy who can help you."

....

My father said he had heard the Germans coming well before seeing them. "Shitflies," he would recall. "They sounded like shitflies buzzing around a pile of manure."

The buzzing morphed into a crescendo of roaring motorcycles, armored vehicles, and trucks sweeping into Dabrowa. It was the third day of the war. The Polish army seemed to have disintegrated. Aside from the motorcycle roar, the German arrival itself was unspectacular—no street-to-street fighting, no military parades through downtown Dabrowa.

Dad's older half brother Wolf, a reservist in the Polish cavalry, had been mobilized shortly before hostilities. He had proudly saddled up the big chestnut mare and joined his regiment, leaving behind his wife, Maria, and seven-year-old daughter, Margalita.

Wolf Lajtner, thirty-eight, was never seen or heard from again. Years later, I would find some evidence that Wolf likely was captured, segregated from his fellow Polish POWs, and ended up in Auschwitz.

On the day the German army roared into Dabrowa, the radio announced that Britain and France had formally declared war on Germany.

"Good," my father thought. "Finally, they'll put an end to all this madness."

It was not to be.

A month into the war, Germany effectively annexed the Dabrowa Basin area and incorporated it into East Upper Silesia. Unlike other parts of "liberated" Poland, this "East Strip" had never been part of Germany before World War I. Nor did it have a large ethnic-German population. What it did have were coal and zinc mines, steel mills, foundries, and heavy industry crucial to the German war effort. It also had some one hundred thousand Jewish residents, the majority concentrated in three sister cities—Sosnowiec, Bedzin, and Dabrowa. Maps were redrawn and streets renamed.

The annexation proved momentous in ways none could anticipate. New border checkpoints separated the East Strip from the rest of Poland, now called the General Government. Different rules applied as a nominally civilian bureaucracy governed with its own agendas, policies, and priorities. The change would mean the difference between life and death for those Jews during the first years of the war.

To Hitler, the war with Poland was more than a battle about territorial grievance. It was a struggle between races: the superior German Volk versus the inferior Slavic Pole. Unlike Vichy in France or Quisling in Norway, no collaborationist government was set up; the General Government was run under a harsh military occupation. Unlike the German occupations of France or Norway, the Nazis aimed to eliminate Poland culturally as well as politically. Those aims were shared by the Soviet Union, which seized 52 percent of Polish territory under the secret terms of the Hitler-Stalin pact.

In the opening weeks of the war, German SS *Einsatzgruppen* (Special Action Groups), using lists drawn up with the help of local ethnic-German collaborators, executed sixty-one thousand Polish teachers, priests, academics, officials, landowners, politicians, and journalists—the seeds of any future national leadership.

Still, in the pantheon of German enemies, the Jews figured on top.

"The Germans are beating the Jews without any reason, just for fun," a Polish hospital director recorded in his diary. "Several Jews were brought to the hospital with their buttocks beaten into raw flesh. I was able to administer only first aid, because the hospital has been instructed not to admit any Jews."

Across Poland, synagogues were burned and Jewish-owned shops and businesses looted. Scores of Jews were seized and executed on trumped-up charges of profiteering or partisan activities.

In Bedzin, *Einsatzgruppen ZB V* herded three hundred Jews into the town's largest synagogue, set it and surrounding buildings ablaze, and shot anyone trying to flee. A number of Jews bolted from a side door to the nearby church, where its daring priest threw open its doors and nuns hid the terrified Jews. Today, a plaque telling this story sits near the empty site of the synagogue.

My father's life during this period was a cipher to me. I recalled only one story, which he told with a shrug, like it was no big deal, nothing to worry a young child about.

Everyone knew the routine: You see a German soldier, you step off the sidewalk, lower your eyes, and keep walking.

The soldier with the two stripes thought otherwise.

"*Du verfluchte Jude*," You cursed Jew. "How dare you pass an Aryan without removing your hat and acknowledging your superior." A hard-right sucker-punched *der Jude* Lajtner to the ground. Blood spurted from his nose and mouth.

The next time *der Jude* Lajtner spotted soldiers walking his way, he sprang to attention and pulled off his hat. "*Guten tagen, mein herrin,*" Good day, sirs.

"What?" the soldier said. "You dare to greet an Aryan like an equal?" *Der Jude* Lajtner was again beaten and kicked to the ground. Seeing this, some of his Polish neighbors turned and quickly disappeared. Others lingered and smirked. The Germans laughed.

"You didn't know, you couldn't know, what was permitted and what was verboten," my father had told me. "There were no rules. A German could do anything he wanted for any reason. Just because."

The dreaded knock on the door always came at night.

When it came one night to the Lajtner home, it was a German civilian clerk backed by police. They entered the big Lajtner house and inventoried and tagged linens, silverware, lamps, furniture. The clerk told the family they could continue using the items for now but were barred from selling anything with a tag on it as they no longer owned them.

The edicts kept coming. Jews were ordered to wear white armbands marked with the six-pointed star. Jewish shops and businesses were seized as property of the state and put under the control of ethnic-German trustees, a *Treuhänder*. Bank accounts and access to safe-deposit boxes were frozen. Jews were fired from public-sector jobs and banned from most trades. My father was now an unemployed coal agent. A curfew was imposed. Jews were banned from trains, then trams, then from walking on certain sides of main streets. Food rations were set lower for Jews than their Polish Christian neighbors. Local municipal bureaucrats forced Jews at random to clear war rubble, dig sewers, and collect garbage, all the while subjecting them to public humiliation and beatings. Labor Ministry paramilitary police grabbed Jews off the streets and shipped them to labor camps far from home. Contact with the Polish populace was banned. Any Polish Christian caught helping a Jew risked being shot.

With stunning speed, the Jewish communities found themselves impoverished and isolated. Starvation loomed. Panic, hopelessness, and despair took hold. In this mounting chaos, the Jews had only one place to turn, the Jewish Councils, the *Judenräte*.

....

Blue . . .

Not just any blue, but a luminescent cerulean blue.

The brightly painted entrance to the State Archives in Katowice is all the more jarring against the grimy cement-gray stucco of the buildings themselves. Rusty iron bars and mesh cover the windows facing the street. Cinderblocks and cement seal those on the second floor.

With me is Artur Szyndlar, a Polish archivist and PhD candidate in Jewish studies. Artur is as big as an NFL fullback but with an academic's soft-spoken reserve. I ask Artur how he came to Jewish studies.

"Well, I'm from Oswiecim," he shrugs, like that had preordained his vocation.

The Germans annexed Oswiecim in 1939 and renamed it Auschwitz. The rest, as the cliché goes, is history. Though Artur hasn't really answered my question, his quiet intensity (and large size) doesn't invite much chitchat.

"Ah-hah," I say, nodding.

I follow Artur past the gated security checkpoint. Another surprise: while the outside looks like some Day-Glo entrance to a Soviet-era funhouse, inside is a modern mélange of gray carpeting and ceramic floors, subdued task lighting and padded workstations. Light tables and microfiche readers are spread around the large reading room. The nearly silent whoosh of air-conditioning is the only sound.

Artur fills out the request form and, in a few minutes, the counter is stacked with fifty-six bound and bulging folders. As the reality of the task before us sinks in, so does my heart.

Artur has been here before. "Not so bad. First, we eliminate all folders that say 'budgets.'"

He hands me a thick Sharpie and paper from his backpack. "Write down names—in big—that we wish to find." He tapes the list to the wall of our workstation.

"Now, we look."

Artur selects a folder at random. It is marked No. 23: hundreds of letters, receipts, scrawled notes, and ledger sheets, all double-hole punched and bound to the folder with brown twine.

A letter dated December 1939 from the Geheime Staats Polizei, the Gestapo, announces "der Jude Moniek Merin" as *leiter* (leader) of the newly formed "Central Office of Jewish Councils of Elders in East Upper Silesia," responsible for some forty-five Jewish communities.

History has not been kind to Moniek Merin. He steadfastly believed the only way for Jews to survive was to prove themselves "productive" for the German war effort. He embraced a policy of accommodation with the Nazi occupiers, which meant doing a lot of their dirty work for them.

Survivor accounts pillory Merin as, at best, a naive tool of the Nazis blinded by hubris and, at worst, a collaborationist traitor to his people. Photos show a sallow-faced, slightly built man with dark, intense eyes and slicked back hair. Appearances aside, even Merin's critics concede he was a fiery, persuasive orator and an able administrator with boundless nervous energy. Early on, Merin gained credibility among the Jewish population for negotiating scheduled work arrangements with local municipalities. The *Judenräte* would supply the required laborers based on a set schedule. Jews who signed up received some pay, and the practice of randomly snatching Jews for street work was curtailed.

Merin soon built a sprawling bureaucracy employing seventeen hundred men and women and controlling all aspects of Jewish life in the East Strip. This generated a lot of paperwork, as Artur and I were discovering.

In Folder No. 3, we find a series of oversized, double-wide ledger sheets cataloguing clothing collected in twenty-two cities and towns on December 3 and 4, 1941. In the winter of 1941, with the German army bogged down outside Moscow, Jews were ordered to surrender fur and woolen clothing as a contribution to the war effort.

Twenty-six categories of clothing are listed across the top. The names of twenty-two cities and towns run down the first column. In my father's hometown of Dabrowa, for example, 300 "fur linings," 137 fur collars, and 219 "wool jackets, vests, and pullovers" were collected. On this one ledger sheet inventorying just two days, the twenty-two communities turned over 2,732 fur linings, 3,866 fur collars, and 3,353 woolen coats.

On to Folder No. 39—*Heilwesen*, or medical system: month-by-month breakdowns of medical expenses, receipts for pharmaceuticals, names of available doctors, and lists of patients treated at the *Judenräte* clinic.

Folder No. 47—Food Distribution: rations for Jews were set at seven ounces of bread per person daily and three and a half ounces each of margarine, sugar, and marmalade weekly. Anyone with anything to trade—jewelry, fine linens—bartered them for food with their Polish Christian neighbors. The poor and not-so-poor lined up at free soup kitchens run by Merin's *Judenräte*.

A knot in my gut grows with every missive and memo, requisition and report we peruse. Back in New York, I had only considered this archive for what it might reveal about my family. Sitting here now, on plush task chairs, in this air-conditioned cubicle, I realize these yellowing files are more than source material for a research project.

Folder by folder, page by page, they tell the desperate story of a desperate community racing against time, unaware time was draining beneath them like sand from an hourglass.

....

From the start, German plans called for the Jews of the East Strip to be expelled and replaced by ethnic-German "settlers." A year into the war, even the most ardent ethnic cleanser had to admit the plans were going nowhere. This was largely because Hans Frank, the German in charge of the rest of Poland, refused to allow any more Jews into his territory, arguing he had enough of his own to worry about. Instead, East Upper Silesia itself became a dumping ground for Jews deported from other areas. These included seven thousand Jews expelled from the newly renamed Auschwitz. The Jewish population quickly grew from one hundred thousand to one hundred thirty thousand.

Faced with feeding an impoverished population stripped of any way to feed itself, local German officials demanded that Berlin at least put the Jews to work for their rations.

Seeing an opportunity, Heinrich Himmler appointed SS Brigadier General Albrecht Schmelt as his personal emissary for the "Employment of Foreigners in East Upper Silesia." Answering only to Himmler, the second most powerful man in Germany, meant that Schmelt had complete control of the local Jewish population. He overruled Labor Ministry and local municipal bureaucrats who had come to rely on Jews as cheap labor for pet projects.

Schmelt's goal was to exploit Jewish labor for German war production—and turn a handsome profit for the SS. As an unintended consequence, from this point on, in this one small strip of Poland, economic imperatives trumped Nazi racial ideology in the early years of the war.

Within a year, the Organization Schmelt, as it became universally known, controlled fifty thousand Jewish workers in 177 labor camps and scores of factories. Employers paid Schmelt RM 6 ($2.30) a day for a skilled worker and RM 4.50 ($1.70) for unskilled laborers. Thirty percent of the workers' pay went directly into SS coffers. Schmelt collected another 18 percent from employers in lieu of the social welfare taxes they no longer paid because Jews were "exempt" from benefits.

Vast sums flowed directly to the SS, bypassing the bean counters at the German Finance Ministry. Schmelt kicked back some money to the *Judenräte*, which used it to finance its operations, soup kitchens, and medical clinics.

Compare this to the rest of military-occupied Poland, the so-called General Government. In the city of Lodz, one hundred sixty thousand Jews were sealed in a ghetto and allowed to work only for food, and very little food at that. Mass starvation resulted. This policy was applauded by the deputy Nazi commander in Lodz, Alexander Palfinger. "A rapid dying out of the Jews is for us a matter of total indifference, if not to say desirable."

Knowing of the brutal conditions elsewhere cemented Merin's belief that the only salvation for "his" Jews was cooperation with the Germans. When ordered to provide a detailed census of all Jews in East Upper Silesia, Merin promptly obliged. When this census was then used to draw up lists for forced labor camps, the *Judenräte* sent out the directives under its own letterhead and name.

In the fall of 1940, my father received a written summons from the Dabrowa *Judenräte* for the first *Arbeitseinsatz* (Labor Deployment), ordering him to a camp in Germany. He was told to pack enough food for one day and to bring no more than ten kilos, or twenty-two pounds, of personal possessions. For the next six months, Dad worked on a road gang constructing a leg of the autobahn in Germany. I learned about this not from Dad's stories or the *Judenräte* files, but from a deposition my father gave to the German courts in 1954 when he applied for war reparations. "The camp was separated by barbed wire from the outside world," he had written. "The barbed wire was not electrified." Though Dad did not describe camp conditions in detail, he did say that he was sent back home to Dabrowa in April 1941 after becoming ill.

The Schmelt camps were thrown up quickly and haphazardly, with little thought to adequate food or shelter from the Polish winter. In these early years, Schmelt allowed the Jewish laborers to send and receive mail and packages with food and clothing from home, a calculated kindness meant to reassure families that loved ones were safe. However, many Jewish workers wrote home describing brutal conditions, starvation rations, and violent civilian foremen and guards.

As word spread, able-bodied young Jews ignored the *Judenräte's* summonses. In response, Schmelt threatened to withhold ration cards from the family of anyone who failed to report. Merin sent his Jewish police to round up resistors from their homes. Resentment grew when word got around that those who could pay a tax imposed by the *Judenräte* were exempted from the compulsory labor.

Besides running labor camps, the Organization Schmelt rented out thousands of Jewish men and women to local factories, known as "shops," that had contracts with the German military. More than five thousand Jewish men and women sewed army uniforms. Hundreds more made boots and shoes. Given a choice between labor camps and the shops, Jewish workers did whatever they could to get assigned to shops near home. Pay was minimal and hours were long—ten-hour shifts—but, at the end of the day, workers could return to their families. Though staying close to home made sense at the time, this thinking proved disastrous as events unfolded.

More important than pay, a "Schmelt Jew" qualified for a *Sonderauswiese* (a special pass), simply called a Sonder. It exempted the holder and one or two family members from being snatched off the street and sent to a labor camp, which is how things had often worked before Schmelt. Sonders were color-coded—blue, green, pink, or yellow depending on the importance of the work to the war effort. Blue was the most coveted, given to skilled workers in "essential" military-related industries.

As Merin had hoped, the Jews of East Upper Silesia were becoming vital to the German war effort while greatly enriching the SS.

It was all about to change.

Ethnic cleansing metastasized to mass murder by the end of 1941. More than one million Jews were murdered, most in mass shootings, following the invasion of the Soviet Union and in East European countries. In September, the first "successful" experiments were conducted using Zyklon B gas on Soviet POWs in Auschwitz. In December, the first stationary gas chamber using carbon monoxide was introduced at the Chelmno killing center. The following month, on January 20, 1942, the "Final Solution to the Jewish Problem" was rubber stamped at a conference of mid-level Nazi bureaucrats in Wannsee, Germany.

That winter, a red brick farmhouse in a remote corner of the sprawling Auschwitz Birkenau camp was secretly converted to a gas chamber. Named Bunker I, it was informally known as "the little red house." It could kill eight hundred people at a time. On March 20, 1942, the little red house was tested on a transport of Schmelt Jews from East Upper Silesia who were deemed "unfit for work." The following month, Merin's *Judenräte* posted notices on sidewalk kiosks that transports to new Jewish settlements in the east would begin in May, part of the ongoing campaign to make room for ethnic-German settlers.

The very idea of deportations to the unknown triggered widespread panic in the cities and towns of East Upper Silesia. Until then, only those of working age without a Sonder had been shipped to the camps. This time, it was to be everyone: the old, the infirm, and the very young. Jews who had smuggled themselves to the relative safety of East Upper Silesia from the brutal ghettoes in occupied Poland told of mass executions and starvation that were killing men, women, and children by the thousands.

There's little doubt that Merin knew of this firsthand. The Germans had supplied him with a car and driver for meetings with his counterparts in cities like Lodz and Warsaw, where systematic starvation left the dead on the streets. Despite Merin's determination to cooperate with the Germans, this time *Judenräte* central committee members pushed back. They quoted Maimonides, the great medieval rabbinic scholar, who wrote, "If foreigners come to the Jews and tell them, give us one of yours so we may kill him, lest we kill you all, all must die so that none from Israel shall be sacrificed."

Merin agreed to allow an assembly of local rabbis and religious scholars decide the issue. He argued that by cooperating, he would be able minimize the numbers to be deported and to save "the more valued" members of the community. "I will accept whatever decision you come to," Merin said and left the room. After debate, the rabbis agreed that Merin's plan was the lesser evil.

The Zionist youth organizations, a powerful presence with hundreds of young adult members, argued that Merin's policies only made the Germans' job easier. They passed out flyers urging people to ignore the summonses. When only a fraction of twelve hundred who had been summoned showed up at the assembly point in Sosnowiec, the Gestapo threatened to make up the difference with *Judenräte* members and their families. Merin personally supervised a nighttime raid by his Jewish militia on several apartment buildings. Residents were lined up and turned over to the Germans.

On May 12, 1942, fifteen hundred men, women, and children from Sosnowiec were sent to Auschwitz and gassed in the little red house. By the end of the month, some fifty-two hundred Jews from East Upper Silesia had been murdered there.

....

Six hours and eleven folders later, my eyeballs ache. The bulging disc in my neck throbs. I really, really need a cup of coffee. I glance over at Artur scrutinizing a tattered paper. He hasn't even taken a piss break.

He picks up another folder, No. 52—*Hauptabteilung Finanzen*—III-A, or Department of Finance—III-A. It's a big one, a good four inches thick.

Halfway through, Artur spots Josef Lajtner's name on a green sheet of paper titled "Recruitment of Jewish workers with prior authorization." Josef Lajtner is the second of three "Metal and Carpentry" workers listed. His address is recorded as Meissenweig 3; the Germans had renamed Pilsudskiego after Meissen, the German city famous for its fine porcelain and Gothic cathedral.

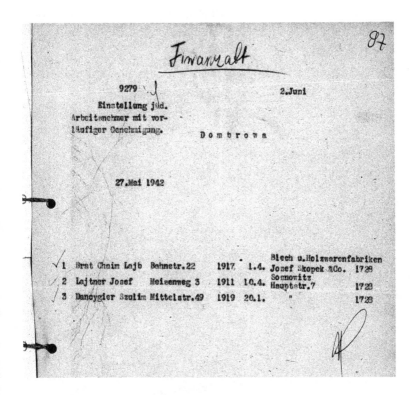

The date jumps out at me: May 27, 1942, during the first mass deportations to Auschwitz Birkenau.

I had just stumbled upon how my father avoided deportation to the little red house. He was working for Josef Skopek & Co., a metal fabricator in Sosnowiec with military contracts. This would have rated a high-level Sonder.

A few pages later, he appears on another list showing him working for Rudolf Irmler, another metal shop in Sosnowiec. That list is dated June 15.

On June 17, two thousand men, women, and children from Sosnowiec were sent to the little red house. On June 20, another two thousand Jews were murdered there. On June 30, a second gas chamber, Bunker II, known as the "little white house" because of its white plastered walls, became operational. Soon trains from France, Holland, and across Western Europe began feeding thousands of victims a day to the gas chambers of Auschwitz.

Dad's luck ran out on July 16, 1942. He's one of twenty-three "arrestees" ordered by the Gestapo Resettlement Division to appear for deportation at the collection point in Bedzin. The document was signed by Nuchim "Israel" Kaufman of the Bedzin *Judenrat*. There were eighty-seven names on that list. Josef Lajtner was number eighty-six.

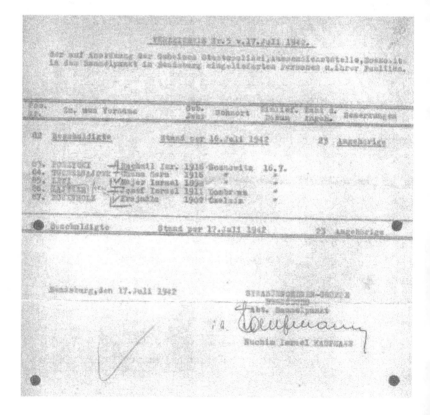

How did my father escape deportation and death in July 1942? Though I could find no paper trail, I had some suspicions.

....

By summer of 1942, Auschwitz in all its horror was common knowledge to the Jews of East Upper Silesia.

In the July heat the mass graves around Bunkers I and II began to putrefy and leak human remains while noxious gases rose from the decomposing bodies. Himmler ordered the graves reopened and the thousands of corpses cremated in open-air pits.

"It stank everywhere, sometimes almost unbearably, of burnt hair," a resident of a town six miles from Auschwitz recalled. "And if the weather was right and you forgot to close the windows, a kind of fatty-slimy soot settled on the furniture, the dishes, and the floor, and got stuck in your hair."

An SS officer wrote in his diary: "The great pyres were spreading such a stench that the whole countryside, many kilometers in width, had been infected. At night, the red sky above Auschwitz was visible for many miles. Railway men used to tell the civilian population how thousands were being brought to Auschwitz every day, and yet the camp was not growing larger at a corresponding rate."

Only after the war did the Big Lie emerge that the crematoria were a carefully kept secret, unknown to the surrounding German population or to the Nazi bureaucrats who rounded up the Jews for deportation.

With the realization that a "productive" job meant the difference between life and death, people scrambled to find work. Oral history testimonials speak of enormous bribes paid to ethnic-German business owners for a job—any job—that provided a Sonder. Yet even this last bastion of security was no longer immune. To make their quotas, the Germans raided "essential" factories and deported hundreds of skilled workers to Auschwitz.

This, in turn, triggered a rush of volunteers to the once-dreaded labor camps.

By now, Merin was not only aware the evacuations meant death, he was also a willing participant in the selections. The Zionist youth organizations branded him a traitor. When Merin learned of a plot to have him assassinated, his militia hunted down the ringleaders and turned in several young men and women to the Gestapo. They were first tortured, then executed.

Not every *Judenrat* leader complied with the Nazis. Ordered to round up hundreds of children for deportation, the head of the Warsaw Ghetto's *Judenrat*, Adam Czerniakow, closed the door to his office and swallowed a cyanide pill. "They demand me to kill children of my nation with my own hands. I have nothing to do but to die," he wrote in a suicide note to his wife. In a second note to fellow *Judenrat* members, he wrote, "I can no longer bear all this. My act will prove to everyone what is the right thing to do."

In July, Merin's *Judenräte* announced that the Gestapo would issue new photo ID cards to the Jews of Strzemieszyce. That's where my father's younger sister, Pola, her husband, and their baby daughter as well as his uncle, aunt, and several cousins had been living for more than a year after being evicted from their homes in a nearby town to make room for new ethnic-German settlers.

Merin personally traveled to Strzemieszyce to reassure the people they had nothing to fear. They were simply to appear on the appointed day in the central square wearing their best Sabbath clothes for the photographers.

No one was buying. When the day came, Jewish *Judenräte* militia and German police clubbed and rifle-butted the terrified population into the square. Photos were taken, documents certified and stamped. Everyone was then sent home . . . just as Merin had promised.

The *Judenräte* next announced a similar photo ID operation for August 12 simultaneously in the province's three larger sister cities—Sosnowiec, Bedzin, and Dabrowa. Merin again traveled from town to town, reassuring the people and urging them to wear their Sabbath best for the photographers, just like in Strzemieszyce.

Thursday, August 12, 1942, dawned hot and oppressively humid. By 7:00 a.m., my father was among several thousand Jews crowded into the square in front of the Dabrowa *Judenrat* headquarters. Tables were set in rows of alphabetical order. At 8:00 a.m., German police and soldiers with machine guns surrounded the square. Snipers looked down from surrounding roofs. The *Judenrat's* Jewish militia prevented anyone from leaving. Hours passed. There were no bathrooms, no water, only the heavy, sultry heat. Children cried. Old people withered under the blistering August sun. Similar scenes unfolded in Bedzin and Sosnowiec, where thousands of men, women, and children were corralled in fenced-in athletic fields.

The *selektion* in Dabrowa began in late morning. Grouped by family, everyone went before Frederich Kuczynski of the Organization Schmelt and Gestapo chief Hans Dreier.

It wasn't until 3:00 p.m. that Kuczynski and Dreier reached Bedzin. Fourteen-year-old Rutka Lasker recalled that everyone had been in a good mood—until soldiers with machine guns were spotted along the perimeter fence. "People were thirsty, and there was not a single drop of water around," she wrote in her diary. "It was terribly hot. Then, all of a sudden, it started pouring. The rain didn't stop."

Pandemonium erupted, with people shoving, everyone shouting, babies crying. "I saw how a soldier tore a baby, who was only a few months old, out of its mother's hands and bashed his head against an electric pylon," Rutka wrote. "The baby's brain splashed on the wood. The mother went crazy."

"I am writing this as if nothing has happened. As if I were in an army experienced in cruelty. But I'm young. I'm fourteen, and I haven't seen much in my life, and I'm already so indifferent."

"The groaning of the old people and the crying of children, of babies in baby carriages, is impossible to describe," another survivor recalled. "The weeping didn't help and, although some people wanted to go together with separated relatives, the guards didn't permit it."

The wife of a senior Nazi official, Alexandra Klausa, witnessed the Bedzin *selektion* from her villa near the sports field. "Today, fifteen thousand Jews here were resettled out of town," Klausa wrote to her mother. "It was so terrible that one would also have liked to leave the place immediately oneself. Russia is as nothing to this"—a not-so-cryptic reference to the infamous Stalin purges of the 1930s.

While Dabrowa had about five thousand eight hundred Jews, Bedzin's Jewish population was twenty-six thousand and in nearby Sosnowiec, about twenty-seven thousand five hundred. With the Germans working only several hours a day, the *selektionen* in the two larger cities took five days.

People were divided into three broad groups: Group 1, those with valid Sonders; Group 2, those who were working or capable of work, but without Sonders; Group 3, those deemed unfit for work, mostly the ill, the aged, and the very young. Group 1 Sonder holders were sent home. Members of Group 2 were mostly sent to labor camps. That left Group 3. In transports of about two thousand people each, some fifteen thousand Jews were sent to the Auschwitz gas chambers.

My father escaped the August *Aktion*. A *Judenrat* worklist dated August 31, 1942, has him again working at Rudolf Irmler's metal factory. He is number 122 of 129 "qualified" workers.

How did Dad land an "essential" job just one month after being ordered to appear for deportation? As a skilled metal worker he could have been hired on merit. But merit alone likely wasn't enough, not given the hysteria and panic and chaos of everyone scrambling for a job to survive.

I'm betting Dad bribed his way to a blue Sonder, or used

6

12

122. Lajtner Josef	Weisenweg 3	1911	1942 31.8.	Rudolf Ingler, Sosn. Sugeten 23 4205
123. Rosenstein Majer	Mittelstr.40	1894	12.8.	Bojsenstein 41b Mittel 40 4275
124. Ingster Hendla	Kreuzstr.58	1908	31.8.	"Ogniwo" Poststr.34 490
	Br.S.B.v.24.9.42.			J.Rudolf, Grodko w-
125. Weltfreind Chil Majer	Schlachthof 6	1912	31.8.	Bendsburg 5074
	Br.P.B.v.2.10.42.			Alois
126. Pasternak Moszek	Kreuzstr.56	1908	29.9.	Busnik 286 Josef Mieczorek, Bendsb.
127. Kajzer Moszek	Mittelstr.54	1874	12.8.	A.Haupt 32 1342
128. Horowicz Henoch	Gr.Heden 28	1927	"	" "
129. Klein Frymeta	Werkstr.14	1922	5.9.	Siegfried Schier Kreuzstr.5 4693

some other influence, as did so many others who lived to tell their stories.

The August 1942 *selektionen* in East Upper Silesia were part of a coordinated operation throughout Poland: Fifty thousand Jews were killed in Lvov; eighteen thousand Jews from the Radom Ghetto were liquidated in the Treblinka death camp. Another one thousand five hundred who resisted deportation were shot on the spot. Some nineteen thousand Jews from the Kielce Ghetto were also killed in Treblinka that month.

A chart compiled by Merin's *Judenrat* headquarters in Sosnowiec put the number of "resettled" Jews at 15,485 plus another 6,516 in labor camps. In all, about one of every three Jews in the six neighboring towns and cities were gone.

On September 24, a group of mid-level German officials, including Gestapo chief Hans Dreier, met in the Bedzin town hall. One can imagine the Nazis toasting themselves with schnapps for a job well done. They agreed the trick of renewing ID cards would never work again. So, how to ensure the next deportation went smoothly?

"In terms of the local preparation for further evacuations," minutes of the meeting said, "the Jews should be brought together as much as possible in one section of town . . . The preparation shall be made in such a way that no disquiet arises among the Jews."

Closed ghettoes had arrived in East Upper Silesia, three years after being imposed in the rest of Poland. Supervised by Merin's *Judenräte*, Jews were evicted from their homes and relocated to two dilapidated neighborhoods that were turned into ghettoes for Dabrowa, Sosnowiec, and Bedzin.

Despite all that had transpired, Merin still insisted cooperation with the Nazis was the only chance at salvation. One account written after the war recounted Merin's defiant speech before an angry crowd in one of the ghettos:

> *I warn you—I am in a cage, confronted by a raging, hungry lion. I stuff flesh down his throat, human flesh, my brothers' and sisters' flesh . . . Why? Because I am trying to keep the lion in his cage, so that he doesn't get out and trample and devour every one of us at once . . . I shall fight all those men who would disrupt my work . . . I shall not let youth distract me from my bloodstained labor . . . I shall fight them with all the means at my disposal, and let history judge me.*

An unexpected reprieve came from a most unlikely source—the German military. The sudden disappearance of Jewish workers from strategic industries caused chaos for German war planners. In a memo to the General Staff dated September 18, 1942, General Kurt Freiherr von Gienanth, a district commander in occupied Poland, wrote, "The evacuation of the Jews without advance notice to most sections of the Wehrmacht has caused great difficulties in the replacement of labor and delay in correct production for military purposes."

Von Gienanth said production in the armaments industry in the affected areas dropped by 25 percent to 100 percent. Repairs of motor vehicles decreased about 25 percent, which translated to about twenty-five hundred fewer vehicles being put back into service each month.

Faced with mounting outcry from the military and the Armaments Ministry, Himmler called a halt to the liquidation of Europe's Jews.

In his reply to the General Staff on October 9, Himmler ordered textile workers, shoemakers, and the like transferred to concentration camp shops, where, he wrote, "we will guarantee the continuous delivery of the items of clothing required." He continued, "Jews in real war industries, i.e., armament workshops, vehicle workshops, etc., are to be withdrawn step by step . . . Our endeavor will be then to replace these Jewish labor forces with Poles . . . But there, too, in accordance with the wish of the Führer, the Jews are some day to disappear."

That month, the German Quartermaster noted that General Kurt Freiherr von Gienanth had retired from the military after a distinguished career.

Chapter 9

LIQUIDATION OF

A SMALL GHETTO

"*Tutaj, widzisz?*" Here, see?

Our guide points to the faded blue plaque as if he had won a scavenger hunt.

"This is where the ghetto was?" I ask.

"*Tak, tak.*" Yes, yes.

The plaque, approximately twelve by twenty-four inches, is bolted to a stucco wall of a hollowed-out building that had once belonged to the Strzemieszyce *Judenrat*.

The Polish inscription reads, "To the memory of the Jews concentrated in the ghetto of Strzemieszyce, formed in April 1942 and liquidated in June 1943." It had been translated into Hebrew with grammatical errors.

I snap a quick photo with my digital camera. *As memorials go*, I think, *this isn't much*.

The first time I had seen the word "Strzemieszyce" was on my father's Auschwitz registration form. It was listed as the place of his "arrest" on June 23, 1943. Now that I had found Dad's house in Dabrowa, I needed to see where he had lived before being deported to a concentration camp.

During the war, Strzemieszyce had been a separate village and important railroad terminus along the Warsaw–Vienna line. It wasn't until 1976 that it became another neighborhood of Dabrowa.

Written in cursive script, Dad's address on the Auschwitz form was listed as "Louge Strasse 40." But our local guide says he knows of no such street, which renders the whole point of coming here moot.

I walk on ahead alone, along quiet streets and pocked roads, past squat, soot-stained houses of red brick with steeply pitched roofs, seeking some landmark that would connect me to the past. It's no good. This is just another hardscrabble neighborhood of Dabrowa, the kind of place that had never seen better days, and never would.

I glance back at the blue smudge of the sign hugging the shell of the *Judenrat* building.

Not much of a memorial, not much of anything.

....

By 1943, successive *Aktionen* had culled the Jewish population of East Upper Silesia from one hundred thirty thousand to seventy thousand.

The remaining Jews of Dabrowa, Bedzin, and Sosnowiec were herded into two closed and heavily guarded ghettoes, an operation managed by Merin's *Judenräte* that took several months.

"The rope around us is getting tighter and tighter," fourteen-year-old Rutka Laskier wrote in her diary on February 5, 1943. "Next month there should already be a ghetto, a real one, surrounded by walls . . . To sit in a gray locked cage, without being able to see fields and flowers . . . I simply can't believe that one day I'll be able to leave the house without the yellow star." The last entry in Rutka's diary is April 24. Soon after, she and her family were relocated to the ghetto in the Kamionca neighborhood of Bedzin.

Instead of either of the two large ghettoes, my father got himself transferred to Strzemieszyce. There he reunited with his younger sister, Pola, and his Uncle Mordka-Hirsch's family.

Even as the village ghetto's population grew with waves of Jews evicted from homes elsewhere, the allotted area remained the same: a single street in the most decrepit neighborhood, with rotted-out houses and no running water or indoor plumbing.

Still, compared to the surrounding larger cities, Strzemieszyce must have seemed charmed. It had escaped the August 12 *Aktion* unscathed. Its ghetto had no walls. Only a wire fence separated it from surrounding neighborhoods. There was easy contact with Polish neighbors. The police were mostly local ethnic-German Silesians and traded openly with the Jews.

Dad landed a job at the Josef Skopek Werke, a branch of the same metal company that had hired him in its Sosnowiec factory the previous May, during that first *selektion* to Auschwitz.

How did he get himself to Strzemieszyce while most of Dabrowa's Jews ended up in much harsher ghettoes? Because he had been previously employed by Skopek? Or was it "arranged" with a bribe? If so, who would he have had to pay off? Someone at Skopek? A member of the *Judenrat*? A German official? All three?

Not much is known about Josef Skopek other than he was an ethnic German from Silesia using cheap Jewish labor to cash in on the war economy. (Oskar Schindler of *Schindler's List* fame had started out the same way.) It was rumored that the Skopek Werke was a place where a Jew could get hired without too many questions or complications.

One survivor, Matlyda Szymiad, recalled that Skopek's managers had helped her and her husband, a chemical engineer, get both a job and housing inside Skopek's Sosnowiec factory. The Strzemieszyce branch opened in 1941 and was run by an ethnic German who was a card-carrying member of the Nazi Party. Despite this, Szymiad said, "We lived well with that director, and in that way people could work there and live."

Soon after arriving in Strzemieszyce, my father was befriended by a sixteen-year-old aspiring artist named Walter Spitzer, who had a heavy crush on Dad's pretty young cousin, Pola Krajcer. Spitzer shamelessly cultivated my father, who was then thirty-two, to get closer to Pola.

"I was very fascinated by Dolek," Spitzer had told me in Paris. "I was a young guy and your father had a lot of, uh, culture. He was big on the matters of women—"

I burst out laughing.

"—Yes, I was very interested in this subject, and he gave me all kind of details, about breasts."

My father? Breasts?

Dad worked ten-hour shifts galvanizing bathtubs, shovels, and buckets destined for the German army.

By mid-1943, Himmler's order that Polish Christian workers replace Jews was becoming a reality at the Skopek factory.

"They started to bring Polish people and we knew it was not good," recalled Sabina Krajcer, Pola Krajcer's older sister. "Whenever a Polish person came, we had to train the Polish people. They took over—worked on the machines. We taught them cutting and welding in different parts of the factory."

With mounting German losses in Stalingrad, North Africa, and elsewhere, logic dictated that the Germans needed all the workers they could get. Heinrich Himmler had other priorities.

Some historians point to the Warsaw Ghetto revolt as feeding Himmler's paranoia. Others say the uprising, which began on April 19, 1943, was the excuse Himmler used to overrule the Armaments Ministry and military planners and do what he had always intended. Either way, on May 21, orders went out that the "evacuation" of all Jews in the Reich was to be completed by the end of June, including those "still in work . . . without any consideration of declining production."

On June 19, Moniek Merin and his top assistants were summoned to a meeting with Gestapo chief Hans Dreier. They were never seen again. Rumors spread that Merin and his circle had been dispatched to Auschwitz and killed.

Two days later, on June 21, the Nazis launched the first in a series of *Aktionen* to liquidate the two large ghettoes.

"All hell has broken out," Alexandra Klausa, the wife of the Nazi official, wrote to her mother. "All Jews are being resettled at the moment, and the whole misery is there to see on the streets . . . Perpetually some Jews are fleeing, there is constant shooting, everywhere dead Jews are lying around, everywhere there is turmoil."

In neighboring Strzemieszyce, Dad, his cousin Sabina Krajcer, and Walter Spitzer were among three hundred Jewish and Christian Polish workers on the overnight shift at Skopek on Wednesday, June 23, 1943. Only sixteen at the time, Sabina worked as a nurse in the factory's infirmary. "It was a very tense evening," she recalled. "We expected they were coming for us, too."

Roaring motorcycles and barking dogs, police whistles and gunfire signaled the start of the *Aktion* just before 6:00 a.m. Screaming *Juden raus!*—Jews out—the Germans stormed the factory and stomped and rifle-butted everyone in their path.

Dad ducked through a side entrance and hid in the high grass of the nearby fields. The Germans sent in bands of *Hitlerjugend*, the Hitler Youth, to scour the fields. "They locked arms in rows and combed through the fields and I was caught," he had told me.

Mark Beck, the survivor I had interviewed in Florida, also remembered the *Hitlerjugend*. "It was a great sport for them. They came with little boys dressed up in Hitler Youth uniforms and would start searching for Jews." Beck was taken from his home with his father, Joseph, and younger brother, Charles.

Walter Spitzer and a few friends also bolted from the Skopek factory to the high grass. "Some girls saw us and began to follow," Walter recalled. "I told them to run low, so the grass would hide them. Then the Germans started shooting machine guns and the girls panicked and began screaming . . . It was hopeless. I raised my arms and surrendered."

The Germans checked identity papers. Polish Christians were sent back to work. Jews were herded outside and ordered to sit on the ground. Names were checked against lists. They were counted and formed into a column three across.

Gunfire and black smoke rose from the ghetto less than a mile away. The Skopek workers began jogging, then running, toward the shooting and their families, outpacing their German guards.

Sabina Krajcer watched it all from a window in the factory's infirmary.

"'What do I do? What do I do?' I had to stay calm, to think."

She saw her friends beaten, counted, and led off at gunpoint.

"I stayed hidden until after the Germans left and then came out, acting all innocent-like. 'Where are the Jews? How come the day shift hasn't shown up?' The Polish workers who were there said, 'Don't you know? There's been an *Aktion* and the ghetto is being emptied out.' I figured I was safe until 2:00 p.m., when the shift changed. Then a Pole would certainly denounce me to the Germans."

Soon after she emerged, however, Sabina was spotted by Jonas, an ethnic-German policeman well known in the ghetto.

Jonas pointed his rifle at her face. "Bend down and cover your eyes."

"If you want to shoot me, shoot me without covering my eyes," she said.

At that moment, an older German, the head of the railroad office, intervened. He told Jonas that he would bring Sabina to the proper authorities. Jonas reluctantly agreed.

Back in the ghetto, Sabina's younger sister, Pola, had spent the night with her mother hiding in an attic just inside the ghetto perimeter. Awakened at dawn by gunfire and screams, Pola Krajcer peeked through a crack and saw a column of SS men coming toward them.

"The first house on their way to the ghetto was the house (where) we hid," Pola Krajcer said. "They put up a ladder directly to the attic and before we knew it, we were downstairs."

Captives in tow, the Germans went house to house. In each house, they would beat and eject people into the street.

At one house, "We heard horrible screams, like a pig was screaming, something I never heard before," Pola recalled, "and all of a sudden we see a man, running in circles and he is being hit and kicked by the Germans and he is screaming, bloody. Those screams—I can hear them even today and they chill my blood. And eventually he fell down a bloody mess, and he was our neighbor, Mr. Zachs."

At one point, Pola's group passed Walter Spitzer and the Skopek workers.

"I suddenly see Pola and Mrs. Krajcer," Walter recalled. "She came forward straight, stiff, noble, with Pola clinging to her arm. They walked like robots, without looking to the left or right. I tried to signal to them. They walked on . . ."

The Jews were marched to an area just outside the ghetto known as the *Umschlagplatz*, the transit point. Pola Krajcer said, "On the way we saw people killed, dead people, screaming, and [guards] yelling continuously, kicking us and beating us and screaming."

In the square, they were reunited with Pola Krajcer's maternal grandparents, Mordka-Hirsch and Bacia Lajtner. With them was my father's younger sister, also named Pola, huddled with her two-year-old daughter, Aviva.

On one side of the square, hundreds of Jews sat on bundles of possessions on the ground. On the other, the Germans ate a leisurely lunch served on portable tables and chairs. "We were lying there and they were eating and laughing, making fun of the broken-down Jews," Pola Krajcer said.

The sky was blue and cloudless, the sun bright and warm. The afternoon dragged on. The Germans were in no rush.

Only after they finished their meal, after the tables and chairs were cleared, did the *selektion* begin. Men were separated from the women—wives from husbands, mothers and fathers from sons and daughters. Mordka-Hirsh was separated from Bacia.

Walter was grouped with other Skopek workers. "We could hear the cries of children—'mommy, daddy,'" he remembered. "Wives tried to reach their husbands, but they are driven away with whips. Hysterics, atrocious cries, overwhelming sadness. Something irreversible has happened."

Two by two, the Jews went before an SS officer who directed them either right or left.

"Most of the young people were sent to the right," Pola Krajcer recalled. "My grandmother, Bacia Lajtner, and older people, children, disabled people, they were all sent to the left. So we knew where they were going."

The family urged Pola Lajtner to hand little Aviva over to her mother-in-law, Bacia. "We all imposed on her, 'You have to give the child away so you can live,'" Pola Krajcer recalled. "We knew that my grandmother was [going to] the death camp. And so, my Aunt Pola gave her the child and is standing with us. And all of a sudden this little girl starts running to her and stretching her arms and calling 'Momma, Momma, Momma.' So my aunt left us and ran to the girl, picked her up, and stood next to my grandmother."

The family again pleaded with Pola to leave the child.

"The baby would quiet down and Pola returned her to Bacia and crossed the square to be with us," Zieute Nier, a cousin, told me. "But then the baby would start crying again. Pola ran back to quiet the child and then again returned to us. She went like this—back and forth, back and forth—maybe five times. In the end, she stayed with the child."

I know my father was there. Did he, too, scream and beg his kid sister to abandon her child? What would I have done? How would I have behaved? Dad never spoke of it, not to me anyway.

Matlyda Szymiad also remembered the *selektion*. "The horrors of that square torture me to this day—the mothers with small children who did not want to be separated from them . . . The grandmothers who took the small children to protect the parents because they knew that they were going [to their deaths] anyway."

Some behaved otherwise.

Another survivor recalled, "A German noticed this girl, a very young girl, and asked who she was with. All of these women, including her mother, denied any connection to her."

Sabina Krajcer may have witnessed this same scene. "One woman went to the line, gave her little girl away [to an older woman]. And the little girl ran to her and the German asked, 'Is this yours?' and she said no. And the little girl looked up at her trying to understand. I don't blame her. You don't know what you would do. You just don't know."

The sorting was complete, the *selektion* made. Working men, working women, and those destined for Auschwitz waited under the sparkling June sunshine.

"We were sitting there, waiting we didn't know for what," Pola Krajcer said. "Suddenly I see a man, a broken-down man, his underwear showing, schlepping boxes and all kinds of things, being pushed by the Germans and I look at him and I see: This is my uncle [Yanik, Pola's husband]! He was such a handsome man, sure of himself. And all of sudden he was a broken man. How could he look any other way when he knew his wife and child are going to a death camp?"

Yanik Lajtner, an engineer by training, was murdered in Strzemieszyce that day.

"Eventually they took all the people from the side that was supposed to go to extermination camp and put them into covered trucks," Pola Krajcer said, "and while they were driving them away, we could hear them singing 'Hatikvah,' the Jewish anthem."

Hatikvah means "The Hope."

With whips and guns and clubs, German soldiers forced the remaining Jews of Strzemieszyce to the nearby rail depot. A sketch by Walter Spitzer, part of a series made in 1945, just months after the war, captures the chaos of the *Aktion*.

Sabina Krajcer was separated from her sister Pola and her mother Regina. They were sent to different labor camps for women.

My father, his Uncle Mordka-Hirsch, Walter Spitzer, and Mark Beck were among some three hundred Skopek workers loaded onto third-class cars of a regular passenger train.

The liquidation of one small ghetto was complete.

....

During the High Holy Days, known as the *Yomtoivim* in Yiddish, our family would attend a small shul, a synagogue, housed in an aged brownstone a few blocks from our home. The main sanctuary could accommodate perhaps sixty families. The wooden floors creaked and the walls smelled of musty books. The congregants were exclusively survivors, like my parents, and their American-born children, like me.

For my parents' generation the atmosphere was comforting and familiar. The rabbi, himself a survivor from Hungary, sported a long white beard and sermonized in Yiddish. Being the High Holy Days, he and many of the men wore long white robes, a *kittel*, which symbolized purity. The women sat behind a high curtain in the back.

There were "Polacks" like Dad, "Magyars"—Hungarians—like Mom, "Litvaks" and "Yeckes" (Lithuanians and Germans, respectively), but no American-born Jews of their generation.

During one of those long days of prayer, Dad leaned in close. "I can understand thanking God," he whispered, "but why do we have to repeat ourselves so many times?"

I was surprised. I was eleven or twelve years old. I asked the obvious, "Do you believe in God?"

He chewed the inside of his cheek for a few moments. Then shook his head. "No God worthy of the name would have allowed what I saw during the war."

Around us, men were loudly chanting the prayer of the moment in unison, focused on their black-covered prayer books. I thought, *Every man here is a survivor like Dad. Obviously, they still believe in God enough to spend long days here in prayer.*

While the setting of Dad's declaration of doubt—in a synagogue, on one of the holiest days of the year—surprised me, he was also confirming suspicions I had felt for a long time.

At home, Mom kept a kosher kitchen, lit candles Friday nights, and enrolled me in Jewish day schools where strict observance was a given. "That's why they call it 'faith'" was how my fifth-grade teacher shut me down when I once questioned something biblical.

Come Saturdays, Mom would loudly chastise my father, "Your son doesn't know what the inside of a synagogue looks like." Dad acquiesced and took me to services more to escape her hectoring than from any sense of religious obligation. A more pleasurable Saturday ritual was going with Dad to the double feature at the Loews movie theater on Broadway and 83rd Street.

As I grew older, I came to understand that it wasn't that my father was an unbeliever, it was that his view of God was nuanced. He'd quote Einstein that something beyond human comprehension must be behind the orderliness of the universe. Like Spinoza, Dad allowed there could be a God, just not the personal kind who listened to, much less answered, prayers.

Yet for the full year after Grandma Felicia died, my father attended daily morning and afternoon services in a synagogue so he could recite the *Kaddish*, the prayer for the dead, within a *minyan*, that religious quorum of ten men.

When I asked him about this contradiction, he just laughed. "I'm hedging my bets."

Of course, there was more to it. There was love, honor, and deep respect for my grandmother and for a revered tradition. That's why I did the same when my parents died.

When the year of official mourning had passed, a member of the congregation telephoned him to help make up the *minyan*. "You've got the wrong customer," he replied.

If Dad's views of God were nuanced, his opinion of the more extreme flavors of organized religion was withering. "Remember," he often intoned in Yiddish, "If they want to speak to God, let them. But if they think God speaks to them, watch out."

He vented his anger at the rabbis in the *shtetls*, the small Jewish hamlets, of prewar Poland. They had vehemently opposed the Zionists who tried to enroll young people to immigrate to Palestine.

As Nazism rose in Germany, anti-Semitism grew apace throughout Europe. Zionist leaders like Zeev Jabotinsky warned of dark days ahead. "Liquidate the diaspora before the diaspora liquidates you," he said in 1938.

The shtetl rabbis viewed the secular Zionists as apostates who threatened their tight-knit communities. They believed that Israel's resurrection must be accompanied by the appearance of the Jewish Messiah. Anything else was blasphemy. Dad dismissed these beliefs out of hand. "They were more interested in keeping control of their little *kehilas* [communities]," Dad would say. "Thousands could have been saved except for their stubborn blindness."

I got to thinking about Dad's views of God while piecing together the story of Strzemieszyce's liquidation. I wonder how much that warm, cloudless, and terrible day forged his views about the God of Abraham, Isaac, and Jacob.

....

In 1967, Yehiel Stern, a survivor of the June 23 *Aktion* then living in Israel, returned to Strzemieszyce to recover the remains of Jews from a mass grave. Stern was aided by Polish officials, a representative of the International Red Cross, and several laborers.

The small group ascended the steep hill overlooking the town. Skeletons revealed themselves under less than a foot of soil. "The bones were slowly withdrawn, even the smallest of them," Stern recalled in his testimonial. "I placed them in plastic bags, and when they were full we put them in a large crate . . . this process was repeated again and again."

Workers found a silver watch among the bones. It was identified by an engraving and later returned to the son of its owner.

They also uncovered a skull with two gold teeth.

"The workers wanted to extract the teeth for their own gain, but I strongly opposed this," Stern wrote. "Thanks to the intervention of the district doctor, the skull was transferred as it was, with the two gold teeth."

The remains were reburied in Israel.

Chapter 10

TIN HAMMER

....

Dolek squinted through windows so grimy the watercolor greens of the countryside passed like an old sepia film in slow motion, punctuated by the *clickety-clack, clickety-clack* soundtrack of iron wheels. *They still need us, they still need us, they still need us,* he chanted in a silent, mindless syncopation.

How absurdly normal we must appear, Dolek thought. *Like ordinary workers going to ordinary jobs on an ordinary passenger train.*

The railcar throbbed with heat and dread. Men sobbed uncontrollably. Others sat in numbed silence.

Where were they taking them? West for sure. Yes, definitely west, into Germany. Dread gnawed at Dolek's intestines.

The train often pulled onto sidings to grant right-of-way to war matériel deemed of a higher priority. At one stop, a German troop transport heading the opposite way—east, toward the Russian front—stood directly across the narrow tracks from Dolek's window. His gaze met the bright blue eyes of a young German soldier, fresh-faced and Aryan. The soldier smiled warmly, then drew his index finger slowly across his throat. The dread heaved up Dolek's esophagus. He swallowed down the rising vomit.

A sudden lurch, and the old coal-fired engine started again and with it Dolek's mantra: *They still need us, they still need us, they still need us.*

It took three hours to arrive at Ehrenforst Station across the old German-Polish frontier, just fifty miles from Strzemieszyce as a bird might fly.

"*Los, Schnell!*" Move! Quick! Screams and blows from clubs and rifle butts. Dolek and his fellow prisoners were hustled into a column five across by regular German Wehrmacht soldiers. The entire area seemed to be one giant staging ground: supply yards, vehicle depots, and encampments.

The column trudged past POW camps with names like BAB21 and E/3. British Tommies in their neat khaki uniforms barely gave the prisoners a second glance. They passed Dorflagers, or village camps, for foreign workers hired for the German war effort. Dolek would also remember the tidy German villages, fresh laundry on lines, and white bedding airing on windowsills.

Two miles later, the column entered a thin forest of beech and elm, fragrant and peaceful, and stopped before a gray concrete guard tower and drop-down barrier and simple swing-out gate. A sign read "Blechhammer," Tin Hammer.

Blechhammer was the Organization Schmelt's largest *Zwangsarbeitslager fur Juden*, Forced Labor Camp for Jews. Like all Schmelt camps, it was independent and distinct from the Concentration Camp Directorate that ran Auschwitz, thirty-five miles to the southeast.

Inside the gate, they passed the red brick houses with neat flowerbeds of the German Security Police, the SD, and high rows of barbed wire strung from an endless march of ten-foot cement pillars. The newcomers were herded along a cinder path flanked on both sides by high barbed-wire fencing.

Hollow-eyed inmates pressed up against this inner fence, which was not electrified, many shouting at the new arrivals. *Anyone know of the family Kalikstein? Did you come across Esther*

*Schwartz from Dabrowa? Hannah Zimmer . . . Mortka Bernstein
. . . Mona Glick . . . Avraham Fein . . . the family Jablowsky . . .*

Some news emerged in this manner, some connections made.

The column stopped in an open area between wooden bunk-houses. The Skopek prisoners knew the drill: stand meekly as possible, arms at sides, avoid even accidental eye contact with any German. They were counted and recounted and then counted again.

A tall, lanky man with a Swastika armband inspected the arrivals. *Lagerführer* (Camp Commander) Eric Walter Hoffmann was a former lawyer who would celebrate his forty-seventh birthday the next day. Dolek would remember Hoffmann's long crooked nose that reminded him of a vulture. Walter Spitzer would recall that the pointed visor of Hoffmann's cap resembled the crest of a rooster's head.

To all prisoners, Hoffmann was derisively known as *Moïsche Houen*, Yiddish for "Moses the Rooster" though colloquially closer to "Blowhard Mike," for Hoffmann didn't just strut and shout commands, he shrieked them.

Military Government
Liaison and Security Office
Det. E 2137 SK Munich
Special Branch

Subject: Trial of Spruchkammer [German
de-Nazification court] VII on 23 July
1947 against Dr. Hoffmann, Erich, Walter,
Fritz, born 24 June 1897

"Respondent was camp commander at camp
Blechhammer [Silesia] where Jews were
interned. He whipped Jews to death, is
responsible for the killing of Jews,
sent Jews to the gas chambers at camp
Auschwitz."

120 WHAT THEY DIDN'T BURN

Witness Mrs. Palluk: . . . I have seen Hoffmann order and supervise what was known as the "cold water procedure" . . . Hoffmann ordered people to be killed by a hosepipe put in their mouths so that they were filled up with water . . .

Witness Schloss: "When my transport arrived at Blechhammer, we were greeted by Hoffmann who told us 'You dogs, you will all die here.' Then he immediately shot two Jews who had just arrived. I have seen him beating people nearly every day. I have also seen him supervising the 'cold water procedure' and had to remove the bodies of the people so killed . . ."

Witness Boatschinki: "I was forced to work as a gravedigger at Blechhammer. I have seen Hoffmann supervising the cold water procedure, as a result of which the victim nearly always died. I have also seen Hoffmann kill several people in a day, by shooting. Altogether, I buried 301 inmates who [had] been killed or died as the result of ill-treatment. I should think about 40 or 50 people were [killed] by the cold water method . . ."

Witness Palluck: "I have seen Hoffman beating people almost every day. He usually hit them on the face . . . I know of one Jewish girl whom Hoffmann raped and when she became pregnant, he ordered her to be sent to Auschwitz to be killed . . ."

Discretely following Hoffmann and the Germans was Karl Demerer, the *Judenälteste*, the "Jewish Elder." Just as the Germans had appointed the *Judenräte* in ghettoes, in Jewish labor camps, they appointed a *Judenälteste* to carry out German orders inside the wire with his own staff. Self-assured and immaculately dressed down to his riding breeches and high black boots, Demerer wasn't particularly tall but had the square features and broad forehead of a 1940s Hollywood character actor and carried himself as one. His voice was deep and raspy from too many cheap cigarettes.

Demerer was from Vienna, had moved to Poland before the war, and occasionally said he was from Berlin. He let it be known that he had been in the Austrian army, which was untrue. He played it all to his advantage. He had been one of hundreds of Jews randomly snatched off the street in the early days of the war and sent to a labor camp. He ended up in Organization Schmelt camps, leaving his wife, son, and daughter in Sosnowiec.

In early 1942, as the Nazis were constructing the gas chambers at Auschwitz, Demerer was among three hundred Jewish workers sent to build Blechhammer, which initially served as a transit camp for those destined to Auschwitz. They cleared trees, dug drainage trenches, and built thirty wooden barracks. When a typhoid epidemic sickened most of the prisoners, the ill were sent to Auschwitz for medical treatment. None returned.

Demerer owed his position to *Hauptsturmführer* Bruno Ludwig, a notorious SS captain who supervised several Schmelt camps, and to his excellent command of German. He had worked for a German branch of an insurance brokerage in Poland before the war and was good at the paperwork and number crunching that *Kommandant* Hoffmann disdained but that the Organization Schmelt craved.

"Ludwig liked me," Demerer recalled. "I don't know why he showed me some sympathy."

Ludwig even agreed to carry a letter from Demerer to Demerer's wife in Sosnowiec. "He took the letter, put it into the sleeve of his coat and went to Sosnowiec, gave the letter to my wife, and gave me my wife's answer," Demerer said. "Later on, I asked him again a favor: to send my wife and my two children to Blechhammer camp."

Ludwig told him, "I shall bring them, but not yet. Your children are still too young." Demerer's son was ten and his daughter eleven and a half. "When the time arrives, I shall help you." That time was at hand: The liquidation of the ghettoes in East Upper Silesia was well under way.

Now, as Demerer stood by deferentially, a German officer addressed the Jews as *Häftlinge*, "inmates," but also "detainees," a very specific legal term.

Dolek, who knew German, considered the irony. German is a very precise language and the term had been carefully chosen. A "convicted prisoner" is "*verurteilte Gefangen*," while a "suspect" of a crime is "*Verdächtiger*." The Jews were neither convicted criminals nor criminal suspects. Until their legal status was determined by the Reich, they were inmates being detained.

"You must give all of your money, watches, jewelry, pocket-knives, and personal documents to the authorities," the German said. "Failure to follow these directions is *streng verboten* [strictly forbidden] and will be severely punished."

With guards watching closely, Jewish *Kapos*—prisoner trustees—passed in front of the newcomers with baskets to receive the booty. Some prisoners dropped more prized possessions on the ground and tried to bury them with their feet.

The Germans had seen it all before. "Is this yours?"

"No . . ."

"But it's under your feet . . ." Punches, blows, and hobnailed kicks. Seeing this, most were too terrified to hold back anything.

The detainees then lined up to have their heads shaved by the special "Hair Kommando." Maybe it was the stress, maybe it was borderline hysteria that triggered the manic laughter by some of the younger arrivals at seeing their friends shaved as smooth as artillery casings.

With his head shaved, Dolek was directed to the showers. "Get undressed, arrange your shoes in pairs, toes out, and

carefully hang up your clothes!" No towels of course, and no complaints; the day was hot and the train ride had been hotter. After the shower, those who had hidden valuables in their clothes were rudely surprised: The prisoners were all given different civilian clothing.

Whose life am I wearing? Dolek would recall thinking. *What happened to the owner of this shirt, these old shoes? Will some-one ask the same about my clothes?*

He and the other *Häftlinge* were marched to the low wooden barracks. Each was about 130 feet long and 24 feet wide and divided into six rooms. Each room was run by a Room Elder, responsible for keeping the room clean, adjudicating disputes, and most important, passing out the dining coupons that would be exchanged for supper, the only real meal of the day. The position was a bit higher in the camp's elaborate pecking order, which meant some extra food or privileges.

Each room had double- or triple-deck bunks for up to forty men. Dolek was assigned to Barrack 17. His mattress was a burlap sack filled with straw. There was a thin gray wool blanket. In the middle of the room, a long table with benches served as a place for socializing. Some barracks had coal-burning stoves while others had central radiators.

The Room Elder ordered his charges to line up for their supper: a slice of black bread, a tin of artificial coffee, and a bowl of thin "camp soup," brown and pathetic, reeking of stale grass and rancid mud.

The camp veterans hung back, allowing the hungry newcomers to rush to the front of the line. Dolek would soon learn this was no courtesy; your chances of getting a bit of turnip in the soup were better when ladled from the bottom of the large cauldron. However, don't wait too long or risk getting a smaller portion as the pot emptied.

Dolek stared at these older veterans with their sunken, wary eyes. Would this be him in a few weeks, would he also look like a ghost?

The old-timers watched closely as the new arrivals tasted their soup. They knew some would give it away in disgust. Some did.

Dolek took in the scene, absorbing his new reality. Certainly his hunger wouldn't abate if he gave away the soup, nor would it taste better tomorrow. Dolek forced himself to drink it all, for he wanted to live.

Then it was lights out for Barrack 17.

Dolek pulled the thin blanket over his head but could not shut out the moans and sighs, the coughs and cries, the keening pleas in Yiddish and half-whispered prayers in Hebrew. He thought of his sister Pola and her baby Aviva. Did all this really happen just today?

Deep exhaustion soon overtook grief and even subdued the dread churning his stomach.

He fell asleep, silently chanting, *They still need us, they still need us, they still need us.*

....

A road sign with a stylized red flame directs the black Chevrolet to turn left off Spacerowa Road to a rutted and muddy track obscured by deep shadows of surrounding evergreen and beech trees.

I get out of the car and count the 250 paces from the turn to the first guard tower, a hulking two-level cement box engraved with graffiti, which, I discover to my horror after climbing inside, is zealously defended by swarms of tiny black spiders.

A sharp right, past ruins of red brick German barracks, and the forest canopy gives way to a large open field. This area had been cleared of buildings after the war and is used for occasional memorial services by visiting groups of survivors.

It had rained overnight. The air is sultry, sweet. Only chirping birds and buzzing flies break the silence.

"I remember the birds," Mark Beck had told me back in Florida. "I was jealous. They were free."

The forest has reclaimed most of the area. Then I see the line of broken guard towers disappear into the dark wood and get a sense of the camp's perimeter. *Where's Barrack 17?* Nothing remains of the thirty wooden barracks.

A lonely memorial stands at the far end of the field, an angled white wall the size of a handball court. The wall is bisected by iron cables thicker than a stout man's arm and twisted to resemble a ribbon of barbed wire. From behind this barbed wire, four hands welded from separate iron cables reach heavenward. It reminds me, a lot, of Picasso's *Guernica*.

At the other end of the field sits a squat gray-cement building with an outsized chimney. Inside a locked gate is what looks like a small gray-and-black locomotive without wheels. This is the crematorium.

....

I follow the line of guard towers around much of the camp's perimeter. They are placed exactly one hundred paces apart. Precisely halfway between and somewhat behind each tower sit squat moss-encrusted concrete mushrooms that resemble hobbit dens. These are reinforced one-man guard bunkers that were used during air raids.

I walk the perimeter again, slowly. I want to absorb the evil of this place. I want to feel my father's presence. I cannot. Despite relics of war and hate around me, I feel neither empathy nor rage but profound frustration, a sense that now, sixty-three years later, this is nothing but a sleepy field in a silent forest in an obscure corner of Poland. It is strewn with archeological artifacts few people will ever see and fewer will ever appreciate. If I cannot grasp this horror, how will anyone else?

Had my brother Alan been with me, we certainly would have paused to recite the *Kaddish*. Here alone, prayer is not in me. I am an apostate standing on hallowed ground. It is this guilt at not feeling more that brings tears to my eyes.

....

Five a.m., reveille, shouts, shuffling. First stop, the shithouse: Inside, rough boards with round holes covered a long pit. The reek was staggering, though the veterans seemed to pay it no mind. Dolek waited his turn to wash at the outdoor spigot. Following the lead of other prisoners, he stripped to the waist—but wait—no one has set down their clothes. Instead, they folded their shirts and jackets and tucked them between their knees while they washed. Even worn clothes, he would learn, were commodities to be traded for food. In Blechhammer, everyone watched out for number one.

Breakfast was a ladle of imitation coffee.

After being counted, the new prisoners were led to an alley between the barracks, where they lined up before a makeshift table of two trestles and a board. Behind sat a German functionary and the Jewish secretary of the camp. Each haftling was handed two white pieces of cloth stenciled with a number. At the next barrack, camp tailors sewed the pieces of cloth to the front and back of the prisoner's civilian jacket. A six-pointed Jewish star was cut from the jacket's back and another along the seam of the trousers. To make the stars visible, the holes were backed by pieces of white cloth.

Thus labeled and marked, the prisoners were marched to their next *selektion*.

A German officer and Demerer, the *Judenälteste*, were waiting. A Jewish secretary hung back, ledger in hand.

"*Achtung!* Attention!"

Kommandant Hoffman arrived with a German civilian who walked with a limp. He was Hausschild, well known in East Upper Silesia as "the lame one." Hausschild was a *Judenhandler* for the Organization Schmelt, a procurer of Jewish workers for private German companies. He pointed his cane at one prisoner, then at another, and another.

....

"Name and profession?"

"Lajtner, Josef. *Elektro-Schweiser.*"

"An electrical welder?" Hausschild asked. "You look soft for a welder. I warn you—lie to me and you'll hang."

"But I am a welder. I worked for Skopek and my family owned metal shops in Dabrowa." Dolek realized he had said too much.

The German paused, leaned on his cane, and contemplated the haftling standing before him for three very long seconds. "So your family owned metal shops? You're one of those bourgeois Jews no doubt?"

The guards snickered. Dolek stared at the ground, barely daring breath. Dread churned his intestines to jelly.

Hausschild said, "So tell us, *herr direktor*, how would you weld aluminum?"

Is this a trick question? "Sir, with respect, before you weld aluminum you have to make sure the oxide coating is removed and you must be careful, for aluminum melts at much lower temperatures than steel—it can puddle with almost no warning. Now, with steel, it is much easier and—"

"He'll do," Hausschild said, pointing his cane at the next prisoner. The Jewish clerk recorded Dolek's name and number with the notation, "*Arbeitskommando* 27, bau 408"—Labor Battalion 27, Construction branch 408.

Dolek walked away as casually as possible, as if the interview was no big deal, nothing at all. Except his heart raced, his knees trembled, and he dripped sweat that had been cooked over brimstone.

As the work assignments continued and his heart calmed, Dolek took in his surroundings. Most of the long, low barracks housed prisoners, about 240 to a building. There was also the tailors' barrack and one for the clothing warehouse. There were barracks for the camp's three kitchens, the laundry, and, separated by a wire fence, the camp infirmary.

Some prisoners wandered about like ghosts, lost and apathetic, their clothes little more than rags. Their arms or legs were wrapped in makeshift paper bandages and, most notably, they draped their heads and bodies with their filthy blankets. Having given up on personal hygiene, they gave off a foul stench. They existed in every concentration camp and were universally known as the *muselmanner*, German camp slang for "Muslims," because their blanket-wrapped heads vaguely recalled Arab headdresses. In the camps, however, a *muselmann* meant a living dead. It was terribly easy to become a *muselmann*. For a prisoner already weak from hunger, any illness, accident, or infection could slow his work. This would result in a beating for malingering, which weakened the prisoner further, which in turn invited more beatings and the inevitable downward spiral. It was accepted wisdom that once a haftling descended to *muselmann*, he would be dead within days.

At one corner of the camp Dolek was surprised to see women in their own barrack separated by a high wire fence. There were between one hundred and two hundred women at Blechhammer. They worked in the camp kitchens and in the laundry room, disinfecting clothing. They were also domestic housekeepers for the guards and their families, though this violated German rules.

Dolek asked the women if any had seen his cousin, Regina Krajcer, or her daughters, Sabina and Pola. The women were sympathetic but none had. As he turned to leave, a woman threw a hunk of dark camp bread through the wire. You'd better learn to organize food if you want to live, she said. He thanked her and devoured the bread. He would not remember her name or face.

....

Soon after his arrival at Blechhammer, Dolek was summoned to a meeting with Karl Demerer.

As befitting his position as *Judenälteste*, Demerer had a private room close to the *Schreibstuben*, the typists' offices, at the front of the camp. The room was clean and spare: a cot, a desk, a couple of wooden chairs, some file cabinets. On one wall hung several bulls' penises from hooks. Weights had been attached to the ends, stretching them toward the floor. Dried and cured, these made for nasty leather truncheons.

Dolek would remember how Demerer offered him an English Players cigarette, obtained from British POWs. *What? Real English tobacco? Here in Blechhammer?* He savored a long, slow drag.

Demerer spoke in a raspy Yiddish. He complimented Dolek for not panicking during the *selektion* with Hausschild. Dolek replied with something vague, wondering what this meeting with the *Judenälteste* was really about.

Demerer noted Dolek was older than most of the *Häftlinge*. How old was he, exactly? Thirty-three this past August, Dolek said.

Demerer lit a fresh Players from the glowing stub between nicotine-stained fingers. With the camp expanding, Demerer said he needed more *Kapos* to help run the place. "*Fershtai?*" he asked in Yiddish, understand?

Dolek nodded.

Demerer came to the point: He wanted to make Dolek a *Kapo*, partly because Dolek was older and would command respect from younger prisoners, partly because he had shown he could keep his head, but also because he spoke German, and they liked that.

Me? A Kapo? Dolek thought.

"Exactly what do I have to do?" he asked.

"Make sure the men work and do what they're told," Demerer said.

"And if they don't?"

Demerer removed a penis truncheon from its hook on the wall. "You use this—but only with permission, fershtai?"

"Thank you, but I don't want to hit anybody or be in charge of anybody. I just want to be treated like everyone else. No better, no worse."

"You don't actually have to hit anyone," Demerer said.

Dolek frowned.

Demerer grimaced. He allowed that occasionally it might be necessary to strike a prisoner to impress the Germans. "Usually," he said, "you just smack the ground. Maybe one in four times you have to actually hit—"

"I don't want to hit even once. Just treat me like anyone else," Dolek repeated, "No better or worse."

Demerer reminded Dolek that as a *Kapo* he would get better privileges.

"I don't want privileges," Dolek said.

Demerer studied the rising smoke of his cigarette. "Look," he said, "you've only just arrived. You don't know what you're facing."

Images of *muselmanner* flashed before Dolek's eyes. "Yes, I believe I do."

Demerer crushed the butt with his polished riding boot.

"Well, if that's the way you feel . . ."

"Yes," my father said. "Absolutely."

....

The workday started with the dawn ablution at the outdoor spigot. This ritual was more than about keeping the lice in check. To wash oneself daily with frigid water, even in winter, was both an assertion of life, of humanity, and an act of passive resistance against a camp system designed to crush the spirit. Stop washing and you became a *muselmann*, and you died.

After their morning coffee, Dolek and three thousand Blechhammer prisoners lined up for the morning head count, the *Appell*, grouped by their assigned *Arbeitskommando*, their work battalions. Prisoners stood at attention—slouching invited a beating—until the tallies of those ready to work, those sick in the infirmary, and the overnight dead were reconciled.

With the *Appell* complete, the *Häftlinge* marched five abreast from the main camp gate. After a mile and half, they arrived at the Blechhammer North Refinery. The complex extended as far as Dolek could see. At the front gate, the camp guards turned their charges over to labor foremen for more than twenty German civilian contractors building the complex.

Inside, a veritable Tower of Babel: forty thousand foreign workers—Czech, French, Italian, Polish, Romanian, German—as well as two thousand British POWs and the three thousand Jews. Each nationality needed a German speaker to translate instructions between the workers and the German engineers, construction managers, and chemists.

Blechhammer North was one of a dozen synthetic oil refineries built with a single goal: make Germany energy independent by turning coal into liquid fuels. Like its ally Japan, Germany was entirely dependent on imported fuel.

IG Farben, the world's largest chemical conglomerate, pioneered the production of synthetic fuels from coal in 1927. One its inventors, Friedrich Bergius, shared the 1931 Nobel Prize in chemistry for it.

Except the high costs of production made no economic sense, especially compared to cheap oil coming onstream in Oklahoma, Texas, and, more recently, the Arabian Peninsula. Farben's American partner in the synthetic petroleum business, John D. Rockefeller's Standard Oil, dropped out of their partnership to drill wells in the desert.

With Hitler's ascension, Farben got the political support it desperately needed. There was just one hitch: Farben had to resolve its "Jewish problem." As the Nazis consolidated power in the 1930s, Farben began building a string of synthetic oil refineries, earning hundreds of millions of Reichsmarks. During this period, Farben rid itself of three Jewish cofounders of the combine and three additional Jewish directors. One was promoted to Farben's American subsidiary. Others resigned or were voted out. By 1938, Farben dismissed anyone else deemed "non-Aryan."

The Nazi government subsidized construction costs, guaranteed government contracts for the synthetic petroleum, imposed high tariffs on imported fuels, and, once the war started, rented out cheap slave labor to Farben and other private industries.

....

While researching the history of the Blechhammer refineries, I come across a rare documents dealer in Germany offering original bond certificates issued by the Oberschlesische Hydrierwerke, the Upper Silesia HydrogenationWorks, the conglomerate created to build the Blechhammer North Refinery.

It is the date of issuance that catches my eye: June 1943, the very month my father was sent to the Blechhammer Forced Labor Camp for Jews. On impulse, I buy a 1,000 Reichmark bond over the internet for about thirty-five dollars, postage included.

I imagine dour, dark-suited financiers hawking the bonds to pensioners, veterans, and widows, promising a 4 percent return on their investment for, in effect, enslaving my father. What would Dad think? Would he be angry? More likely he would smirk at the irony of it all. With its embossed seals and mock-gilded border, this ornate piece of paper is all that remains of Hitler's grandiose dreams of energy independence.

My father survived that nightmare and went on to build a new life.

This thought pleases me.

Chapter 11

AUSCHWITZ IV

··

T he days of the Organization Schmelt were numbered, though
the prisoners were the last to know it.

As far back as October 6, 1942, US and British Army intelligence issued a secret analysis of Germany's growing synthetic
oil industry. It said the Blechhammer North Refinery, still early
in its construction, would occupy 1,150 acres. By comparison,
New York's Central Park is 843 acres. The analysis projected the
refinery's capacity at up to five hundred thousand tons of fuel a
year, more than 3.5 million barrels.

Three months later, the guts of the intelligence report appeared
in *The New York Times* article, "Germany's Synthetic Fuels."
It said Germany was on track to build enough refining capacity
to produce four million tons, or twenty-eight million barrels, of
synthetic fuels annually.

"Another problem—and a growing one—is manpower," the
Times wrote. "The production of four million tons of synthetic
oil yearly . . . requires about thirty million tons of coal and
the full-time labor of fifty thousand miners plus one hundred
thousand workers in the synthetic plants themselves and very

considerable electric power. More synthetic plants mean more labor and more materials to erect them."

The Germans didn't need *The New York Times* to tell them they had a problem. Between June 1942 and June 1943, the Eastern Front alone had chewed up 1.9 million German soldiers. The only way to replace them was to pull German workers off factory lines. The only way to replace the German factory workers was with forced labor.

To increase efficiency, Himmler had agreed to integrate all the Schmelt labor camps into the economic arm of the Concentration Camp Directorate under Oswald Pohl. Pohl was charged with transforming the camps from penal warehouses "into organizations more suitable for the economic tasks."

Lest anyone think Pohl soft, his orders stipulated, "This employment must be, in the true meaning of the word, exhaustive . . . There is no limit to working hours . . . Any circumstances that may result in a shortening of working hours (e.g., meals, roll calls) have therefore to be restricted to the minimum which cannot be condensed any more. It is forbidden to allow long walks to the place of working and noon intervals for eating purposes."

The Nazi Minister of Justice labeled this policy "extermination through work."

Pohl's directorate ran the huge labor camp that was part of Auschwitz near Monowitz. Its ten thousand prisoners worked for IG Farben making *buna*, an artificial rubber. Eli Wiesel and Primo Levi were among its alumni. Farben paid the SS for every worker. The camp was called Buna Monowitz and was officially designated as Auschwitz III. (Auschwitz I was the original camp for political prisoners, Auschwitz II at nearby Birkenau became the notorious killing center.)

Under the planned reorganization, some two hundred Organization Schmelt camps would be consolidated and transferred either to the Auschwitz or the Gross-Rosen camp systems.

Blechhammer would become the second largest labor camp in the Auschwitz system, after Buna Monowitz, and the largest exclusively Jewish labor camp. Some historians and websites refer to it as Auschwitz IV.

In the weeks before the switchover, Schmelt's Security Police weeded out the weak and ill in daily *selektionen*. Karl Demerer walked up and down the rows during morning count warning everyone to stand up tall, keep quiet, and "look healthy." The infirmary was emptied and patients sent to the gas chambers of Birkenau.

....

Inmate 1327 was an old-timer. His low number proved it. He knew all too well that Auschwitz prisoners more likely left the camp through the chimney than the front gate.

So when Prisoner 1327, Kazimierz Smolen, and several fellow inmate-clerks from the camp's administration office were told they had been selected for a special assignment outside the wire, he feared the worse.

For months now, Smolen and a few comrades had been secretly hand-copying the logs of transports arriving at Auschwitz. The lists included arrival dates, number of prisoners, and origination of the transports. When the Germans destroyed Auschwitz's records, these copied logs were invaluable in reconstructing the camp's bloody history.

"I remember the date very well because April 1 is 'Liar's Day' in Poland," Smolen said. "There were five or six of us. We didn't know where we were going and thought they may be taking us out to kill us."

Instead, Smolen's small group was driven to Blechhammer to register 3,052 men and 186 women into the Auschwitz Camp system.

After the war, Smolen helped found the Auschwitz Memorial Museum and served as its first director from 1955 to 1990.

With Les translating, I interview Smolen in the small office he has maintained at Auschwitz since his retirement to learn about the day Blechhammer became part of Auschwitz. Despite his eighty-six years, Smolen stands ramrod straight and studies me with deep-set blue eyes as Les explains our interest.

"We worked for three days and three nights, without a break," Smolen tells me. "There were lots of details, and each one had to be filled out by hand."

I hand Smolen a copy of my father's Auschwitz registration form.

He smiles and nods. "Yes, these are the forms we filled out. This one could be mine. The handwriting is similar, but after so many years"—shoulder shrug—"maybe."

....

The line of prisoners snaked its way into the barrack in rough alphabetical order: Salomon Lierens, thirty-one, a painter from Amsterdam, was just in front of Josef Lajtner, thirty-three, while Marian Landau, twenty-six, an electrician from Bedzin, stood behind him.

Kazimierz Smolen and his fellow clerks filled in the blanks on the registration forms. On the upper right corner, they added a unique number from lists brought with them from Auschwitz. After signing the form, the prisoners moved to the next room where the tattooists waited.

"Make the numbers small," Dolek whispered. He slipped the tattooist several English Players cigarettes. A needle fitted into a wooden squib rapidly punctured the skin on the back of his left arm. Blue ink was smeared over the wound and 177904 appeared in a small, neat line.

"Did it hurt, Dad?" I asked as a child.

"The tattooing? Yes, I guess it did, but it was over fast. What really hurt was the humiliation. I looked at my arm and thought, 'Now I am cattle. I am nothing but a number.'"

The prisoners turned in their civilian clothes for concentration camp blue-and-gray striped pajamas. They were also issued a light jacket and a small cap of the same fabric. Their civilian shoes were exchanged for wooden "Dutch" clogs with cloth uppers. A yellow star with the prisoner's stenciled registration number was sewn to the shirt and jacket.

The 7th Guards Company of the SS Deaths Head Division, which ran the concentration camps, replaced the Organization Schmelt personnel.

Hauptsturmführer Otto Brossmann was named *Lagerführer*. Brossmann, forty-five, a former schoolteacher who had joined the Nazi party in 1938, had a spit-and-polish reputation.

Among their first acts, the SS ordered construction of a sixteen-foot-high cement-and-block wall topped with electrified barbed wire around the Jewish camp, isolating it from nearby British and French POW camps and an adjacent transit camp known as the *Bahnhofslager*.

Until now, the dead had been buried in shallow mass graves outside the wire. The SS changed that too. They ordered a *Taschenofen*, a pocket furnace, from the firm of H. Kori of Berlin. It was easy to transport, quick to set up, and ran on heavy fuel oil. It cost about RM 3,000 and could incinerate two corpses at a time.

Kori's portable human ovens were installed in at least nine other concentration camps. Kori may have been awarded the contract as a consolation prize, having lost the bid to build the industrial-size gas chambers and crematoria at the Auschwitz Birkenau camp. That contract went to another old-line German company, Topf & Sons.

Karl Demerer remained *Judenälteste*. The SS wasn't interested in changing a system that was working. Demerer soon established a working relationship with the new SS regime just as he had with the Organization Schmelt.

"Before it [the camp] was full of vermin, they stopped it," recalled Abraham Schaufeld, who was a Polish Jewish teenager when he was sent to Blechhammer. "Even the food, funny enough, improved slightly under the SS." Other survivor testimonials confirm Schaufeld's account.

Barracks and bunks had to be kept clean. Regular delousing was introduced. Workers with key skills, like electricians and welders, were even inoculated against typhoid fever. "They used the same needle on everyone," Mark Beck had told me.

"They tried to beautify the barracks in some way by painting the bunk beds and oiling the floors," Schaufeld recalled. "But all this was done with stolen material from the factory. Everyone knew it was stolen, but if you brought it back to the camp, you got some sort of reward. It was sort of strange—if you were caught with contraband you were punished. But if you brought some paint or material and it was used to almost beautify the place, no one acknowledged it. It was [a] strange existence."

Concentration camp rules and procedures that had been refined and codified since the 1930s were now applied to Blechhammer.

Foremen for private contractors at the job sites were henceforth verboten from beating their Jewish workers. Complaints had to be filed with Auschwitz III headquarters in Monowitz and punishments would be assessed from there as per established guidelines.

Previously, the Schmelt camp guards had dropped off their prisoners at the front gate of the construction site and patrolled the perimeter. Now, SS guards rode bicycles around the work area. If they spotted something they didn't like—a prisoner trading with a foreign worker, for example—they noted the prisoner's number and punishment would come later. That was the theory anyway. In practice, SS guards did pretty much whatever they pleased.

Chapter 12

PROFILE OF A *KAPO*

···

Bored with the Law and Order rerun, I turn to my computer and, on a whim, type the Polish spelling of my father's name—J-o-s-e-f L-a-j-t-n-e-r—into Google. I had done this once or twice since starting my research a year ago but with no useful results other than learning "Lajtner" was a popular name in the Czech Republic.

This time, a story pops up from the *Jerusalem Post* from April 2006: "Auschwitz Held 'Show Trials' Until Just Before Liberation." The reporter's angle is that the Germans were punishing Jews in labor camps even as the war was being lost. It refers to thirteen "legal documents" on display at the Ghetto Fighters House, a small museum in northern Israel. "Josef Lajtner was given twenty-five lashes for selling a diamond to a non-Jewish worker for 500 marks, money he used to buy food."

In all the months of reading and research, this is the first solid clue about Dad's fate. The museum's curator emails me a high-resolution scan of a two-sided sentencing report.

The front of the form summarizes the crime: On June 7, 1944, fifteen diamonds were transferred to a civilian for 500 Reichmarks that were supposed to be used for food. The charges

Kommandantur
des Konzentrationslagers Auschwitz III   Monowitz, den 13. Juni 1944
                                                        Ort   *Datum*

Az.: K.L. 14 e 3 / Schw.- Mi.   177 904

Grund der Schutzhaft:	
politisch	Jude
politisch rückfällig	
Berufsverbrecher	
Bibelforscher	
Rasseschänder	
homosexuell	
Emigrant	
Ausweisung	
arbeitsscheu	
Fürsorge	

Personalien des Täters:

(Zu- und Vorname): L a j t n e r   Josef

geboren am **11.8.11.** zu **Bendsburg**

Tatbestand: (wann, wo, was, wie?)

hat am **7.6.44.** Uhr

**15 Brillanten an einen Zivilisten für
500.- RM. verschoben.
Das Geld konnte nicht sichergestellt
werden, da L. es restlos für Lebensmittel
verbraucht hat.
Ausserdem wurde bei ihm ein Ausweis mit
Lichtbild von der Reichsbahn Krakau gefunden.**

(Arbeitslager Blechhammer, Kdo. 27 Bau 408.)

Strafverfügung!

Gemäß Strafordnung für die Konzentrationslager und kraft der mir als Lagerkommandant übertragenen Disziplinarstrafgewalt verhänge ich nach reiflicher Prüfung über den Täter folgende Strafe:

Ordnungsstrafen:

____ Verwarnung unter Androhung einer Bestrafung.

____ Stunden Strafarbeit in der Freizeit unter Aufsicht des SS-Unterführers ____

Verbot, Privatbriefe zu schreiben oder zu empfangen, auf die Dauer von ____ Wochen.

Entzug der Mittagskost bei voller Beschäftigung am ____ / ____ / ____

Einweisung in die Strafkompanie ab ____ bis ____ (bis auf weiteres).

Hartes Lager nach der Tagesarbeit in einer Zelle in folgenden Nächten: ____

Arrest:

	Stufe I mittel	Stufe II verschärft	Stufe III streng	Die Stufe III kann als Einzelstrafe oder als weitere Verschärfung der Stufe II tageweise eingeschaltet zur Anwendung kommen.
	bis zu 3 Tagen	bis zu 42 Tagen	bis zu 3 Tagen	Vollzug!
	Holzpritsche		ohne Gelegenh. zum Liegen und Sitzen	Stufe I oder II verbüßt vom ____ mit ____
	helle Zelle		dunkle Zelle	Stufe III (Einzelstrafe) verbüßt vom ____ mit ____
	Verpflegung: Wasser u. Brot; jeden 4. Tag volle Verpfleg.			Stufe III (als Verschärfung von Stufe II) angewendet am ____
Tage				am ____
				am ____

KL 18 4.49 5.000

reference the forged railway identification card. Though it does not explicitly link the diamonds to the forgery, the implication is the Nazis strongly suspected a connection between the diamonds and the ID card.

On the reverse side, a box on the upper left corner is titled "Number of Strokes," with five, ten, fifteen, twenty, and twenty-five running down a column. The box next to twenty-five is initialed.

I had read enough survivor accounts to know how this worked. My father would have been bent over a bench with his hands tied down in front of him. His trousers would be pulled down to his ankles. A thick rod or whip, maybe one of the bull penis truncheons my father had talked about, would strike him twenty-five times on the buttocks. Dad would have likely passed out before the last stroke. His comrades would have dragged him back to the barracks and applied whatever poultice was available.

A dull weight compresses my sternum, making it hard to take in air. I study the Gothic typeface legalisms, the check boxes and fill-in-the-blank spaces, the multiple signatures and rubber-stamped approvals, all the bureaucratic gloss to white-wash utter barbarity. Dad never spoke of this official torture. Yet again, I realize I know more about the camps than the man.

Another detail strikes me: This sentencing form was dated June 13, 1944, but that very first Auschwitz diamond document, the one with tattoo numbers but no names, was dated October 19, *four months later*. This meant my father had been caught a second time, four months after receiving twenty-five lashes.

The surprising story behind this October 19 incident was revealed in yet another unexpected Nazi document sent by the Ghetto Fighters House. In it, the SS charged that Josef Lajtner was the ringleader behind an elaborate scheme to sell a diamond for 480 Reich Marks "and a considerable amount of food" to a civilian worker at the refinery complex.

When the buyer refused to pay up, the SS said, Josef Lajtner "instructed his *Kapo* to pretend to be the owner and to demand

Körperliche Züchtigung:

Anzahl der Schläge*)			Der Täter ist bereits körperlich gezüchtigt worden:	
5			am	Schläge
10				
15				
20				
25	25 St.			

*) Anzahl einsetzen

Vorschriften:

Zuvor Untersuchung durch den Arzt! Schläge mit einer einrutigen Lederpeitsche kurz hintereinander verabfolgen, dabei Schläge zählen; Entkleiden und Entblößung gewisser Körperteile streng untersagt. Der zu Bestrafende darf nicht angeschnallt werden, sondern hat frei auf einer Bank zu liegen. Es darf nur auf das Gesäß und die Oberschenkel geschlagen werden.

Ärztliches Gutachten:

Der umseits bezeichnete H____ag wurde vor dem Vollzug der körperlichen Züchtigung von mir ärztlich untersucht; vom ärztlichen Standpunkt aus erhebe ich keine Bedenken gegen die Anwendung der körperlichen Züchtigung.

~~Gegen die Anwendung der körperlichen Züchtigung erhebe ich als Arzt Bedenken, weil~~

Der Lagerarzt:

SS-Hauptsturmführer

Dienstaufsicht:

Der Vollzug der körperlichen Züchtigung wird im Hinblick auf die Tat und gestützt auf das vorliegende ärztliche Gutachten genehmigt – ~~nicht genehmigt.~~ **SS-Wirtschafts-Verwaltungshauptamt**
Amtsgruppenchef D
Konzentrationslager

i. A.

SS-Standartenführer

Ausführende:

Die Strafe der körperlichen Züchtigung haben folgende SS-Unterführer am 29.6.44. Uhr vollzogen: Hftl. Nr.

eigenhändige Unterschrift { SS- 167598

SS- Braasen Josef

Zeugen und Aufsicht:

Als verantwortliche SS-Führer und Zeugen waren bei der Strafvollzug zugegen:

SS-Hauptsturmführer   Lagerkommandant

eigenhändige Unterschrift   SS-Obersturmführer   Schutzhaftlagerführer

SS-Hauptsturmführer   Lagerarzt

Aktenvermerk:

1. Originalverfügung zu den Schutzhaftakten.
2. Abschrift zum Sammelakt: Strafen.
3. Abschrift an: SS-Obersturmbannführer und Lagerkommandant.

SS-Hauptsturmführer

the stone be returned." *Instructed?* Just how much influence did my father have to be able to instruct his boss to do anything? Clearly, Dad was a key player in the black market, yet another side of his life about which he never spoke.

Turning back to the two-page sentencing report, at the bottom I read that the twenty-five lashes were inflicted on June 29, 1944, by fellow prisoner, Joseph Braasem, tattoo number 167598.

Who was Joseph Braasem? Had he been ordered to whip my father? Or did he volunteer, perhaps for a larger portion of soup that night? What made a man like Braasem tick?

The Auschwitz Museum confirms a Josef Braasem from Amsterdam, Holland, only his tattoo number was 176598 instead of the 167598; the clerk who typed up the report had inverted two digits. With this information, I post queries on several Holocaust-related websites and chat boards asking if anyone knows of a Joseph Braasem from Amsterdam who had been a prisoner at Blechhammer.

Within days, I get a phone call from Max Stodel in Los Angeles. Originally from Holland, Stodel says he had gone to school with "Jopie" Braasem's brother, Abraham.

Stodel tells me Braasem's father had been a fruit and vegetables wholesaler. Braasem's brother, Abraham, was a boxer. Joseph "was a rough, tough guy," Stodel says. "He was a wrestler." Braasem became a *Kapo* and traded food ration coupons with the Germans. "On account of his activities with the Germans, he got a lot of food," Stodel says. He does not, however, confirm that Braasem had beaten prisoners.

I find a Jopie Braasem in an autobiography by a Belgian named Israel Rosengarten. Braasem had bunked with Rosengarten in Barrack 16, Room 15.

"Braasem was one of those with whom the Germans got on relatively well," Rosengarten wrote. "He had been a boxer and had enormous physical strength. Even the SS were stunned by him."

In the fall of 1944, Rosengarten wrote, every night around midnight two SS men would arrive at the barracks. "In the corner of our barracks was placed a pocket torch [flashlight] and an oil lamp. The two SS men sat at a little table opposite two *Kapos*"— and played cards.

One of the *Kapos* was Joseph Braasem.

"To us, these card-playing evenings were extremely ambiguous, mysterious," Rosengarten wrote. "They simply could not be explained."

One of the SS players was the most notorious guard at Blechhammer, known as Tom Mix, after the 1930s American cowboy movie star. Like the Hollywood cowboy, SS Tom Mix sported two pearl-handled pistols slung low on his hips and enjoyed using them.

"These SS-ers were the worst bloodthirsty tyrants imaginable," Rosengarten wrote. "For that same card money, they would easily have sent us to the gas chambers in the morning. Yet they sat there, playing a bit, chatting a bit, as they were the best chums . . . They went on playing until 4 o'clock in the morning, happily drinking together as if they were a small private circle of friends." Rosengarten, however, said nothing about Braasem beating fellow prisoners.

I phone Rosengarten in Brussels. While he remembers Braasem as "a giant of a man," Rosengarten says he has no recollection of Braasem beating fellow prisoners.

A few days later, Lester Burke, another survivor who saw my internet query, calls me from Pompano Beach, Florida.

"He gave me five whips on my behind," Burke says. "He was used like an executioner—he was big, strong, he had a mustache." He then recalls this story: "There was an incident where I brought potatoes [into the barrack]. I stole potatoes, ok? I volunteered to carry the sacks to the kitchen, and I tied my pants on the bottom and dropped in a few potatoes. So I started to cook the potatoes during the night, and the *Stubenälteste* [room orderly] comes over to me. He says, 'I am the Stubenälteste. I want half.' I tell him, 'You want half? Steal your own potatoes.'"

"He took the basin with the cooking potatoes and turned the potatoes into the fire. 'I don't get, you don't cook,' he says. I took my blanket and put it over his head and held on to him and a couple of guys in the barrack beat the hell out of him. He reported me and my friend to the SS."

Burke said the SS summoned Braasem to inflict the punishment.

"It was not of his own will," Burke says. "He was ordered to do that. The guard was standing and watching. It hurts, let me tell you."

During my second trip to Poland in 2007, I visited the Auschwitz Museum archives. I'm shown bound volumes of prisoner documents organized by registration—that is, tattoo—number. There I find seventeen "Penal Reports" in which Josef Braasem had whipped fellow prisoners.

For having been found with 30 Reichmarks, Masier Herchko, 184854, received ten lashes on July 20, 1944. Elizer Papo, 178238, received ten lashes on June 3 for being caught with one diamond. Mendel Jueker, 179381, ten lashes on May 27; Berek Fiszinski, 184824, twenty lashes on July 4; Max Voss, 179226, twenty-five lashes on September 7. . . . By the time I copy these details, I taste blood in my mouth from biting down on my lip.

From Poland, I fly to Israel. On a sunny Mediterranean morning, I drive up the coast to the seaside resort town of Nahariya and the Ghetto Fighter's House museum. There, entombed in an acid-free, clear-plastic wrapper, is the original of my father's punishment report. My hands tremble as I pick up the document turned brown with age.

Tears fill my eyes. I feel proud, and frustrated. Proud, because I had found another tangible link to my father's past, another incontestable piece of Dad's timeline of survival through the war. Frustrated, because I hadn't made the time as an adult to talk to him about so very much.

In the same folder, I find three more forms where Joseph Braasem had whipped prisoners, including Pinkus Potok, who received ten lashes on June 29, 1944—the same day my father was beaten.

Returning home from my trips to Poland and Israel, I proudly show my wife Anat everything I had learned about Joseph Braasem.

"That's amazing," she says. "Did he survive the war?"

Good question.

Before the war, about one hundred forty thousand Jews lived in Holland. All but thirty thousand disappeared, most into the crematoria of Auschwitz Birkenau. Holland is the only country in Europe that has made a national effort to track down each of its Jewish citizens by name. Dutch archivists combed through German, Dutch, and Red Cross records and interviewed every survivor they could find.

An online database, made in cooperation with Hebrew University in Jerusalem, lets you sort and filter information on a number of criteria. Filtering for "place of death = Blechhammer," the database returns two hundred and sixty names. Another two hundred died in Gross-Rosen, and two hundred sixty more in Buchenwald. Joseph Braasem's name is not among any of them.

I email Dutch authorities. An archivist replies that on August 11, 1947, a Joseph Braasem, born on March 5, 1919 in Amsterdam, had been interviewed about his wartime experiences. The Dutch authorities snail-mail me a copy of Braasem's thirteen-page testimonial.

Joseph Braasem had been seized in a mass roundup on September 5, 1942. Two days later, he and twelve hundred fellow Dutch Jews were shipped in sealed cattle cars to Auschwitz.

Braasem's train was stopped at Cosel, a few miles from the Blechhammer refinery complex. Organization Schmelt Security Police pulled some 240 men including Braasem off the train. The remaining men, women, and children continued on to Auschwitz. Most were gassed on arrival.

Braasem couldn't have known it, but he was saved from Auschwitz because of competition between two Nazi bureaucracies for able-bodied workers. During the fall of 1942, Germany was engaged in the battle of Stalingrad, regarded as the deadliest single battle of the war. Some four hundred thousand German troops were killed or taken prisoner. Labor shortages were already acute, and both the Organization Schmelt and the Concentration Camp Directorate needed workers. Braasem's train and others were stopped at Cosel on orders of the Organization Schmelt, with the blessings of the Armaments Ministry.

Auschwitz's *Kommandant*, Rudolf Höss, was outraged by Schmelt's actions.

"These men on their own authority, without informing anyone, and without orders from the Reich's Security Office, stopped the transport trains to Auschwitz," Höss wrote from his prison cell after the war. "They took healthy Jews from the trains and exchanged them for their disabled workers or even dead ones . . . This continued until my complaints moved the higher SS and police leaders to put an end to it." In all, the Organization Schmelt removed ten thousand prisoners bound for Auschwitz before Himmler ordered the practice stopped.

Braasem arrived in Blechhammer some months later via several other Schmelt camps. In each, he had been appointed a column leader or supervisor.

"I had several positions in Blechhammer," Braasem wrote. "At first I declined a couple of times . . . but later I accepted in the interest of the people."

Stunned, I read Braasem's casual description of the nocturnal card games with the SS guards, confirming Rosengarten's account. "At night I sometimes played cards in my room with the SS, for instance, 21," Brassem wrote. "They were mean fellows and I constantly kept an eye on them. As long as they can benefit from you, you can get a lot done from them. After all, we were stuck in that situation and tried to make the best of it."

Among the regulars, Braasem said, was the SS guard who "thought he was Tom Mix. As long as you called him that, everything was okay. The guy was a raving lunatic. He was a terrible man. It was the wisest to stay good friends with him. I sometimes borrowed money from him, not because I needed it, but just to be able to give it back with a pack of cigarettes, to make him feel good. Besides, that way I was always in touch with him."

Nowhere in his thirteen-page, single-spaced testimonial does Braasem talk of beating fellow prisoners. Given the number of punishment reports, I wonder why neither Max Stodel nor Israel Rosengarten would confirm that Braasem beat fellow Jews. It gradually dawns on me that I was experiencing what historians had long known: Certain topics are taboo within the survivor community. Perhaps the biggest involves sexual assault against Jewish women, which is absent in virtually all early Holocaust accounts. Only in recent years, as more women researchers have entered the field, have the many episodes of forced sex and outright rape come to light.

Similarly, survivors have shied away from talking about so-called Jew-on-Jew violence or detailed accounts of theft and fights among Jewish inmates—and there were many. When I asked about this, several survivors told me, in essence, they feared the drama of conflicts among prisoners would ignore the nuanced context of trying to survive in the camps.

I conclude that Jopie Braasem was the worst kind of collaborator, a mean-spirited tough guy turned concentration camp enforcer who played cards with SS killers.

Then I get a phone call from Karl Kaye, a survivor from Poland then living in Mill Basin, Brooklyn, who was also responding to my internet query. "He was the hitter alright," Kaye says. "But he was good."

The Germans had caught Kaye with a bag of onions. When he refused to identify the person who gave them to him, "They told me to eat the onions. And I started eating the onions and my tears went down. So I want to drop the onions but they sat me down and made eat the onions."

The Germans ordered Braasem to beat Kaye. "He told you to yell," Kaye says. "If you'd yell he'd hit to the side. If you didn't yell, he'd hit you so you had to yell. He didn't hit me. He told me to yell and I yelled so much the guard turned away."

Yadja Hammer of Passaic, New Jersey, also contacts me about Braasem. Hammer had been barely fourteen when she was shipped to Blechhammer. She worked in the camp kitchen. She says Braasem kept order when prisoners lined up for food.

"Order?"

"You know, people would get rowdy, especially if they felt they were shortchanged their ration. He kept control and made sure no one pushed ahead."

Before I can ask, she volunteers, "He was used for punishment by the SS. But in his character, he was a good guy. It hurt him very much to hurt prisoners. Sometimes he was crying inside. He told me, 'What can I do with myself?'"

This is getting complicated. I phone several survivors whom I had interviewed in the past. None acknowledge knowing Jopie Braasem and none want to speak about *Kapos* other than to say that, overall, they were better at Blechhammer than in other camps.

I reach out to Motek Kleiman, the survivor in Los Angeles who had known my father. I am depending on Kleiman's solid memory for names, dates, and details.

Kleiman, too, is reluctant to talk about *Kapos* at Blechhammer. Only after I tell him about the punishment reports, he suddenly says, "There was this huge Hollander, Yolie—he was like a bull but a very good man."

Yolie or Jopie, Kleiman says this *Kapo* had "made a club that looked like a baseball bat but made a big noise. If he hit someone on the ass, it made a big noise but not a big pain."

"You mean like a slapstick?" I ask.

"I don't know what you call it, but . . . the guy who gave the lashes was a hero."

Jopie Braasem may not have been the monster I had imagined. But hero? I have a hard time with that. That Braasem never mentioned beating prisoners in his testimonial to Dutch authorities tells me he knew he was on shaky ground, slapstick or not.

Faced with a similar choice, my father had turned down an offer to become a *Kapo* after he was told it would mean beating fellow prisoners, if only occasionally.

"I don't want to hit anybody even once," my father said he had told Karl Demerer.

Perhaps Jopie Braasem did what he thought he must to survive.

My father chose a different path. He never had to hide it.

Chapter 13

BREAD AND OTHER
SURVIVAL STORIES

....

D ad loved making sandwiches and I loved watching him make them. Like a penitent in prayer, he'd sway to and fro assessing each ingredient assembled before him on the red-and-gray Formica table.

"Bread is the most egalitarian of foods," he'd say. "It is both spiritual and secular, a promise of heavenly salvation and a reward for earthly labor."

I'd nod. I'd heard Dad's bread-as-life discourses many times growing up.

"Think about it. Bread is godly, bread is family, bread is penance. We welcome the Sabbath with bread and wine, consecrate our homes with bread and salt, feed prisoners bread and water." He paused. "Of course, not all breads are created equal."

He lifted a braided challah loaf from the wicker basket. "Challah is both spiritual and special. Back in Poland, this was Sabbath bread. It was expensive—made with white flour, many eggs, and sugar. Only rich people ate challah during the week. The *kihila* [community council] would distribute loaves of challah to poor people for Shabbos."

He slid a round, dark pumpernickel from its bag of white waxed paper. "Peasant bread is more like this, but coarser and much larger, maybe five pounds. It is primal and organic, dark and strong, round and full." He brought the loaf to his nose and inhaled deeply. "Ah! We ate a lot of bread like this."

With a serrated bread knife, he cut four thick slices of pumpernickel so perfectly even, the surgery could have been performed by the deli machine down the street. He sliced two of Mom's "special" sautéed hamburgers into mirrored halves. Using a small paring knife, he cut a sour garlic pickle (never a half-sour or dill) into thin, translucent slices. A dollop of Heinz ketchup went on the bottom slice of bread, then came the meat, the pickles, and a final dollop of Heinz on top ("Why should the upper teeth be deprived?"). He pressed the top slice of pumpernickel down hard onto the sandwich, forcing the meat, pickles, and ketchup to bond with the bread.

We sat together in silence at that gray-and-red table, eating these delicious sandwiches of black bread and Mom's burgers. If the mood was right, if Mom and my kid brother were out, my father occasionally talked a little more about the war.

"Now 'camp bread' was democratic and brutal. Democratic, because it was shaped like a brick so it was easy to divide into four equal parts. Brutal, because a loaf weighed a kilo, about two pounds. This meant we each got about eight ounces of bread as our daily ration."

....

Everything in Blechhammer had a price and that price was calculated in rations of bread. The price of a food tin might be set at three bread rations; a spoon might cost a half ration.

"Organizing" more food was easier for those prisoners who could make contact with foreign workers and British POWs at the refinery. There, they could barter for food, beg for food, steal for food.

My father, a welder, said a British POW once asked him to fashion a cage from metal scraps for an injured bird they had found in their camp. "You know how long that bird would have lasted with us? Once a cat found its way into the camp . . . never mind. From the English Players he gave me, I ate well for a week."

Mark Beck and his father Joseph, an engineer, fashioned portable electric stoves from scrap wire and bricks. British POWs used them to heat tins of "bully beef" (corned beef) they received in Red Cross parcels.

"It was before Christmas and I traded a little heating stove for butter and bread with an Englishman," Mark told me. "A German [civilian] saw me. He stopped me and he started writing my number"—Beck pointed to his arm—"and this was my death sentence. So I told him, 'If you write this number and give it to the camp, I'll be hanged.' The German says, 'Yah, Yah. You should be hanged.' So I say, 'But if I am hanged you and your family won't live through this Christmas because a bomb will fall on your house and kill you all.' This is what I said. And he looked at me. He says, 'you *verfluchte Juden! Verschwinden!* ['You cursed Jew! Disappear!'] And so he took my bread and I verschwinden."

Sigmund Walder got himself an indoor job as an electrician in the central operations control of the refinery. Just being indoors and out of the harsh weather was in itself a notable accomplishment and source of envy among his fellow prisoners. Better still, he worked closely with British POWs on a day-to-day basis. This provided endless opportunities for trade.

He put his prewar profession as a jewelry maker to good use. He fashioned signet rings from British two-pence copper coins, engraving them with the initials of his clients. Walter Spitzer remembered them well. "Those signet rings were wonderful," Walter told me. "Polished, they looked like gold."

Sigmund's dealings with the POWs were so extensive, he

never lacked for food and could afford to distribute his daily bread and soup ration to friends at the camp.

Walter parlayed his artistic skills to survive. With a piece of charcoal and paper from cement sacks, he sketched portraits of POWs and German foremen at the building site.

"Walter at the time made a drawing of a British prisoner," Sigmund told me. "He did not have the easy contact I had, so then he handed the drawing to me and I gave it to the Britisher." In return, the POW gave Sigmund bread. "I just turned everything [the bread] over to Walter. I mean, that was not business then; I didn't take a 'finder's fee,' which was how things were done."

Smuggling the bread back into the camp was risky. Guards randomly searched inmates for contraband. "If you had a loaf of camp bread," Sigmund said, "you could split it like the ration with three friends and never get caught. If you had a round loaf of peasant bread it was riskier, but still possible."

Abraham Schaufeld, the teenager from Poland, got extra food by taking on an additional job cleaning the barrack floors and soup barrels. This was after his regular ten-hour workday.

Abraham got the job from a fellow prisoner, a Dutchman, who had volunteered to help defuse unexploded bombs dropped during air raids. The volunteers got more food. "So he stopped washing the floors. I got his job. And this was my salvation. After the food was distributed, we could scrape the bottom [of the vats] and get some food," Abraham recalled. "The tragedy of it was, they were winching one of those bombs up and it slipped and a lot of them got killed."

Marcel Klein from Holland had been in five labor camps before arriving in Blechhammer in May 1944. Using the only tool he had—a spoon—he fashioned figurines out of chamotte, a clay used to insulate the huge hot water pipes at the refinery. He traded the figurines to foreign workers for food.

One day Marcel was told the notorious SS guard Tom Mix was looking for him.

"I thought I was a dead man," Marcel said. "I sat on the toilet for hours, avoiding the inevitable. I could delay no longer and went to see him."

Tom Mix asked if it was true that Marcel made figurines out of chamotte stone? Yes, Marcel confessed, though he knew that was enough to have him executed.

"Can you make a dog because my girlfriend wants to have a dog?" Tom Mix asked.

"So I made one for him and I got something for it," Marcel said, "I think some bread."

Josef Braasem recalled, "At night in the camp there was a full market exchange going on between the barracks. Anything was for sale, and everybody was trying to sell stuff . . . Part of this went to the SS . . . and they pretended not to see anything."

....

Someone was stealing bread from prisoners at night as they slept, right from under their pillows where they'd squirrel away part of the ration for the next day.

As *Judenälteste*, Karl Demerer was allowed to run things much as he saw fit—as long as there were no problems. This was a problem, a serious one. Stealing a shirt to sell to Polish workers was one thing. But bread? Prisoners were killed for stealing bread.

Every day, between four and six inmates complained to Demerer their bread was missing. "In tears they came to tell me that their piece of bread had been stolen," Demerer recalled. "Once, twice, three times I gave them from the bread available. It couldn't go on like this, however. The situation had to be brought to an end."

The daily bread ration was distributed in the evening with the camp soup, after inmates returned from their ten-hour workdays. The barrack's *Kapo* divided the rectangular loaf into four sections. Fights broke out if a prisoner felt he was being shortchanged. Some *Kapos* used crude scales to weigh each piece to avoid violence.

Demerer ordered the barrack's *Kapo* to quietly assign a prisoner to an all-night watch. The watchman would be excused from work the next day.

That night, the watchman saw a man creep from his bed to another's, remove the pillow of folded clothes, and take the bread.

The thief turned out to be a teenage boy. Caught and crying, he was taken to Demerer's office.

"You know what you have done?" Demerer asked. "You have stolen bread from your brother, who had exactly the same bread. He might have starved."

Demerer summoned a *Kapo* nicknamed Jumbo to inflict the punishment.

"Give him ten solid strokes on his back," Demerer ordered.

The boy accepted the punishment without a sob or tear as red welts rose on his back. He then turned to Demerer. "May I get another ten strokes but, please, let me have a little piece of bread."

Demerer gave him the bread without the strokes and assigned the boy to kitchen duty for four weeks, where he could eat well. After the four weeks, the boy begged Demerer to be allowed to remain awhile longer.

"No, my dear friend," Demerer said. "We are no boarding house for thieves or a sanatorium. For four weeks we gave you to eat as much as you liked. Now you are in good health; but take care never again to take anything."

With that, the boy was returned to the construction site.

....

As part of the expansion of the SS Concentration Camp Directorate, smaller Organization Schmelt camps in the area were shut down and their prisoners sent to Blechhammer.

One transferee was Robert Widerman from Paris. Though only sixteen, Widerman had been a modestly successful cabaret singer and dancer when his family was swept up by the war. At war's end, Robert Widerman changed his name to Robert Clary and became an actor best known for his role as Frenchie (formally, Corporal Louis LeBeau) in *Hogan's Heroes*, a TV sitcom about Allied inmates in a German POW camp that aired from 1965 to 1971. From here on out, I'll refer to him as Clary.

French police collaborators working with the Gestapo arrested Clary, his mother, sister, and other family on September 23, 1942. They were put on a sealed freight train two days later that became Transport 37 bound for Auschwitz.

"The moaning and crying never stopped," Clary recalled. "More than anything I remember the unbearable stench. The [waste] buckets had no lids. They filled up very quickly and there was no way to get rid of the defecation."

At his mother's urging, Clary wrote a note to his older brother, Jacques, who was being hidden by friends in Paris. "We are a hundred in sealed cattle cars, and frightening things are happening in them, that I hope you will never see."

Clary put the note in an addressed envelope and slipped it through the cattle car slats. An unknown passerby found the letter and posted it.

Like Joseph Braasem's transport from Holland, Clary's train was stopped at the station in Cosel, where Schmelt's Security Police ordered all men between the ages of sixteen and fifty off the cattle cars. The Germans weeded out those who looked too young, too old, or too ill for work. Though Clary was sixteen and a half, he looked twelve. A German took one glance and ordered him back on the train.

Clary stood by the open door of the train car helping distribute cans of water. Another guard passed and asked him how old he was. Clary spoke no German, but the old man next to him said Clary was sixteen. This German ordered him down on the ground. Clary was sent to the Organization Schmelt labor camp at Ottmuth, where he worked in the shoe factory.

Researchers have chronicled the French Jewish deportations in detail. Of the 1,004 people on Clary's Transport 37, 175 were pulled off at Cosel by Schmelt guards. Upon arrival at Auschwitz, another 131 were selected for work. The rest—698 men, women, and children—went directly to the gas chambers. Of the 306 people selected for work both at Cosel and at Auschwitz, Clary was one of only fifteen known to have survived the war. None of the women did, not Clary's mother, not his sister.

At Ottmuth, Clary was overheard singing and became a camp favorite, regularly entertaining the *Judenälteste* and senior *Kapos* there on Sundays. When the notorious Judenhandler, Hausschild, made his weekly visits to select workers for other Schmelt camps, the *Kapos* kept Clary out of sight. "In the nineteen months I remained at Ottmuth, I saw that same agent at least once a week, when he came to make selections," Clary said.

On April 2, 1944, Ottmuth was closed down as part of the consolidation of Organization Schmelt camps and Clary was sent to Blechhammer, tattooed, and became Prisoner A-5714. Word soon reached Demerer of this new French prisoner with a marvelous singing voice. Clary began entertaining the Jewish leadership at Blechhammer on Sundays, along with several other talented musicians and singers.

Clary and Demerer both said that an SS officer gave permission to stage musical reviews for the prisoners, as well as for the SS guards and their families. "We had lights, sets, costumes and wigs for the female parts played by men," Clary wrote in his autobiography.

"I remember going to two performances of theater sketches by the prisoners," Abraham Schaufeld recalled. "Even the SS came and sat in the front row. And the SS, sometimes on Sundays, used to come and put chairs near the front gate, with their families, and they would ask for some performance. And the performers were on this side of the front gate, and they [the SS] used to sit on the other side enjoying themselves, watching the dancing or the singing."

Demerer said he used the performances to reunite, however briefly, wives and mothers separated by the wire from their husbands and sons. "They always wanted to meet each other, but with rare chances," he said. "Of course I first chose women whose husbands or sons were in the camp, to give them a chance to meet, to talk together. The performances were, indeed, nice and beautiful."

There apparently was more fraternization between men and women prisoners at Blechhammer than Demerer lets on.

Frederika Kohensius, who tutored Demerer's children at Blechhammer, said Demerer performed nuptials between male and female prisoners.

She dropped this tidbit as I was wrapping up an interview at her home in Nahariya, Israel. I had mentioned that several couples that had met in Blechhammer had gotten married after the war.

Nodding, she said, "Yes, there were some stories like that, in the end happy stories. Demerer also helped things along. He conducted 'camp marriages' in his capacity of *Judenälteste*. Of course, no one knew if we would live to see the end of the war."

Kohensius would say no more. An austere woman with thick white hair, she had received her doctorate in philosophy and philology from Jagiellonian University in Krakow before the war. She was not a woman who could be pressed into gossiping, even sixty-five years later.

Yadja Hammer, whom I had interviewed about Joseph Braasem, also hinted at romances between women and men at the camp. Like Kohensius, Hammer turned mum when pressed for details.

None of the men I interviewed and none of the recorded testimonials I had viewed discussed possible romantic liaisons at the camp, sexual or otherwise.

My father certainly never did.

Another prisoner to arrive in Blechhammer from Ottmuth was Motek Kleiman, who had gone to school with my father's younger sister, Pola.

"The first time I hear the word 'concentration camp' was at Blechhammer," Motek says. He was tattooed and became Prisoner A-5691.

"When I got to Blechhammer, first thing I saw—all my friends," Motek tells me. He was reunited with his cousin Mark Beck and his uncle Joseph. They got him assigned to the same barrack (Block 17) and same work battalion (number 27) as my father. "They called me an electrician, but I knew nothing," he says. "I went up a pole and I was scared to go down. Basically, I did nothing."

"We had a group in Blechhammer," Motek says. "We were a very, very tight group, and we made Dolek our *Unterkapo* [assistant *Kapo*]. When we went to sleep, he was watching. Dolek was a great guy, a terrific guy. He was watching over us."

This could not be. Dad specifically told me he had refused to become a *Kapo*.

Motek can tell I am distressed. "Look, it was no big deal—it was nothing, a little more than me. He'd give a report to the SS. After all, somebody must take care of the twenty guys. Someone must be responsible for the group."

Motek suggests I get in touch with Martin Izsak, who had been head *Kapo* of the electricians and welders. "We called him Red Martin because of his hair," Motek says. "He knew your dad."

Martin Izsak . . . I know I know that name, but from where? It takes some digging but I find him in my notes. This is the same Martin Izsak whose number was on that first diamond document, the one dated October 19, the one with only numbers and no names that said they were guilty of a criminal offense—the possession of diamonds.

This meant Martin Izsak was the *Kapo* who, the SS said, my father had "instructed" to retrieve the diamond from the civilian buyer who welched on the deal.

I am furious—at myself. I had spoken to Motek Kleiman several times over the past year. He had never suggested that there might be other survivors who knew my father and, like an idiot, I had never thought to ask.

Through Motek's friends in Los Angeles, I reach Martin Izsak's son on his cell phone. He is with his father, but it's too late: Red Martin is in the grip of late-stage Alzheimer's. "He doesn't know where he is anymore," Martin's son says.

Hoping against hope, I suggest that maybe hearing a name from the past might jar loose some memories. The son agrees to give it a try. He puts the receiver to his father's ear.

"Do you remember Dolek Lajtner?" I shout into the phone. "From Blechhammer? He was a welder . . ."

No response.

The son comes back on the line. "Sorry, a year ago he could have helped. Now . . ."

I am too late. Again.

Martin's son tells me his father had recorded a video testimonial with the Shoah Foundation, the organization founded by Steven Spielberg that has videotaped thousands of Holocaust survivors. It's in French, and thinks he might have a copy in the garage.

I thank him and tell him not to worry about it. I know how to get ahold of testimonials from the Shoah Foundation.

I next call Sigmund Walder and Mark Beck in Longboat Key and Walter Spitzer in Paris.

"Your father definitely was not a *Kapo*," Spitzer tells me. "He was older than most of us, in his thirties, so he probably got more responsibilities—but Dolek wasn't a *Kapo*."

Mark Beck, who was in the same work battalion as my father, said he would have known if Dolek Lajtner was a *Kapo*. "Maybe a *Stubenälteste* [room orderly], if that."

Sigmund Walder agrees. "As he was older, he would have been seen as a natural leader, someone the younger boys would look to for guidance. That's probably why Demerer wanted to make him a *Kapo* in the first place. Sounds to me like he may have been put in charge of a room within the barrack."

Unterkapo or not, Motek says he and my father tried to bolster the spirits of their fellow prisoners. "Your father and I would sing songs and tell stories to raise our morale as we marched to the refinery. We would sing in Yiddish, the kind of songs from the burlesque shows. If a guard said no singing, we would whistle."

Mark Beck remembers this well. "Motek used to lead us in singing bawdy songs, the kind that would not be appropriate for ladies' ears. The Germans were very amused by this: 'These stupid Jews are marching to work and they sing songs.' It helped keep our spirits up."

Mark also said they would gather around a fellow prisoner who had worked in a candy factory. "We would congregate around him and ask him, 'How you make the candy? How you make the sugar?'" They did this so often, Mark said, "after the war, I [could] go and make candy . . . Instead of food we talked about food."

As for Motek, Blechhammer was his seventh labor camp. He knew all about organizing. "I got some cocoa from a French worker. I gave it to a Czech worker. He brought back five rolls. I gave three back to the French and kept two for myself. That's how it worked.

"We all made business with Germans, with the French, with the Englishmen, a lot of Czech, a lot of Polish. Your father—he had a lot of connections."

....

When it came to black market trade, however, few prisoners would likely match the written record of Avram Halerie for sheer audacity, inventiveness, or scope.

French police seized Halerie, a 38-year-old tailor, and his wife, Marguerite, from their Paris apartment on Sunday, September 27,

1942, and shipped them to the Drancy internment camp. Luckily their daughter, Fernande, eluded capture.

The next day, the Haleries and nine hundred men, women, and children were loaded onto cattle cars that became Transport 38 to Auschwitz Birkenau, three days after Transport 37 carrying Robert Clary and his family.

Like Clary, Halerie scribbled a note, addressed it to a friend, and shoved it through the slats of his cattle car. Like Clary, a passerby found the note and posted it.

"Dear friends, my wife and I are in a cattle car without air or light, destined for Poland. I hope everything is going well at your home with regard to Fernande. Do all that's possible to care for her and keep her at Monique's home or at Mme. Germaine's home. Be brave and we will see you upon our return."

Also, like Clary's Transport 37, Organization Schmelt security police stopped Transport 38 at Cosel and removed Halerie and about a hundred men from the cattle cars. Marguerite continued on to Auschwitz, where she and most of the remaining eight hundred passengers were gassed upon arrival.

Within months, Fernande Halerie began receiving letters and postcards from her father, who apparently sent them via several French civilian workers at the refinery complex. Halerie signed the letters and postcards variously as Adolf (Halerie's common name), Marcel, Georges, Paul, Bernard, or André. Some correspondence was postmarked from Dortmund, Germany, about 560 miles west of Blechhammer.

In all, Fernande kept some seventy postcards and letters from February 1942 through July 1944.

But there's more.

In return, Fernande and the friends mailed Halerie a steady stream of packages with food, clothing, and small luxuries hard to obtain in wartime Germany that the Blechhammer prisoner then resold, used as bribes, or traded for favors.

So many letters and packages were sent, Fernande numbered

them so that father and daughter could keep track of the shipments. Taken together, they provide a unique, contemporaneous record attesting to the depth and breadth of the black-market trade inside Blechhammer.

June 6, 1943: "I have received your package #6. That was a good idea you had to send me the rum. It's been a long time since I have seen its color and tasted it." By March 25, 1944: "I received your letter #28 as well as packages #50 and #52, and the little one with mending needles. All was intact."

How all the goods were smuggled into the heavily guarded forced labor camp remains a mystery, though it was common knowledge that for a price guards would look the other way.

One recurring request early on was for four meters of flowered cloth "in silk or rayon or a light and solid cotton, very pretty for a woman of about twenty-five years of age," white shoes size thirty-seven with medium heels, and a powder compact engraved with the letters "HR." Halerie explained the items were for the wife of his boss at the camp infirmary, to whom he owed his good job.

In many letters, Halerie instructed Fernande collect money from acquaintances, neighbors, and possibly relatives of fellow prisoners who were indebted to him.

Besides the detailed shopping lists, Halerie expressed affection for his daughter—"I kiss you very sweetly with tears in my eyes"—and encouraged Fernande to stay positive. Occasionally, he included poems to her as well.

But after receiving a letter from a friend critical of Fernande's behavior, Halerie admonished his daughter to stop gossiping and straighten up, lest she alienate her protectors. "You must turn your tongue seven times in your mouth before saying a word. This word could be hurtful. Do not pronounce it. I insist that you do this well."

Missing from the letters are specific details about day-to-day life in Blechhammer. Was Halerie being cautious, avoiding anything that might lead German investigators back to Blech-hammer? Or did he not want to upset his daughter, who was already under enough stress.

In one undated note, Halerie alluded to his dark situation. "Courage is necessary in order to bear our miseries. We would very much like to return before winter because here it is hard to endure. It is cold and one cannot fall ill, for there is not much here to heal oneself."

....

Society in Blechhammer was turned on its head. Shoemakers who could make custom boots were royalty, protected by the German guards and never suffering a shortage of bread. Skilled laborers—electricians, welders, machinists—were the nobility and received more bread than unskilled workers. Professionals—teachers, accountants, lawyers—were expendable serfs assigned the hardest work with the highest mortality rates.

If you survived in Blechhammer for more than a few months, you were an old-timer, a veteran. You had mastered how to raise your shovel just enough to simulate work, but never to needlessly expend energy. You had learned to never draw the attention of the guards for any reason. You could tell which of your fellow prisoners would live, and for how long.

Newcomers always asked the old-timers, What type of camp is Blechhammer? Is there real work here? How are the *Kapos*? Only those new to the camp system would ask silly questions like, Is there torture here?

Torture? You'll get beaten, of course, but you probably already have, so that's a given.

More important: How will you handle the hunger? Real hunger, not like that headache behind your eyes after the Yom Kippur fast. No, this Day of Atonement does not end at sunset. This hunger gnaws. It saps your strength, your will to survive. Will you learn to hoard your bread to make it last? Will you learn to organize? Because for food, your comrade is also your competitor. How will you cope? For how long?

The only reality in Blechhammer is hunger.

Well . . . not true.

The lice are real. They breed in the seams of your clothes. No avoiding them—no getting rid of them. No matter how hard you scrub the barrack. Will you scratch yourself raw? How will you sleep? How will you cope?

The cold is real. You get sick. Your nose runs. It drips. Constantly. No handkerchief. Nothing to clean your nose, nothing to stop the dripping. Will you cope? For how long?

Sooner than later you'll get diarrhea. No toilet paper—or any other paper. Some grass, maybe. How will that affect you? How will you deal with it? How many days, how many weeks, how many months?

Torture? There is no need for torture at Blechhammer. The system is torture perfected.

....

Karl Demerer learned of plans to deport 102 women to Auschwitz. They had apparently been given duplicate tattoo numbers as other women prisoners at the main Auschwitz I Camp. The solution was quintessential SS: liquidate them.

"I needed money, I needed gold, I needed diamonds, I needed valuables to corrupt the *Lagerführer*, who was, thank God, corruptible," Demerer recalled. He gathered between $4,000 and $5,000 in jewelry and cash from prisoners with the help of his *Kapos*, who knew which prisoners had valuables.

The next morning Demerer and the Camp commander were on their regular inspection rounds when the German turned to him. "Tell me, Demerer, not as '*Lagerführer*' talking to the 'Lageralteste,' but tell me, What do you think? Who will win the war?"

"I am a German Jew, Herr *Lagerführer*. Of course we—"

"What do you mean by that?"

"Of course, we Germans, Herr *Lagerführer*."

"As if today," Demerer recalled, "I remember the *Lager-führer* offering a cigarette to me, giving me fire, and how we two were smoking."

Demerer brings up the matter of the women. "Herr *Lager-führer*, I want to ask you a favor; please, help me. Leave the women in the camp. They are more important than a hundred workers. They keep the laundry and kitchens going."

Demerer paused to gauge *Lagerführer's* reaction, then plunged ahead. "I found some valuables, which I would have had to deliver to you anyhow; they were hidden in the *Kleiderkammer* [clothing warehouse]. There is gold, there are diamonds, there are dollars. I don't know—I haven't counted how many there are. You know, they are of no value for me. Take the parcel. Perhaps you can use the dollars, and perhaps you can do something for the women."

The *Lagerführer* turned to look at Demerer. "Where is the parcel?"

Demerer took him to the clothing warehouse and handed over the bundle wrapped in cloth and tied with twine. The German unwrapped it, examined the contents, and slipped the package into his pocket.

"Does anyone else know about this?" he asked.

"No, Herr *Lagerführer*. No soul on Earth. I am the only one to know."

"And you will keep silence?"

"I shall keep silence, Herr *Lagerführer*. As an ancient Austrian officer, I promise you an oath."

"The women may stay!" the German said and with that, departed.

That following night, two tattoo "specialists" arrived from the Auschwitz main camp and gave the 102 women new numbers. The cover story was that 102 women had died and these were their replacements.

This episode is included in Demerer's testimonial, buried in two five-inch thick folders of Israeli police documents on Blechhammer in the archives of Israel's Yad Vashem Holocaust museum. Like many survivor stories, it was rich in color but poor on context. Demerer never said when the exchange took place. Neither did he identify the *Lagerführer*, the camp leader. There were two after Blechhammer became part of Auschwitz, Otto Brossmann and Kurt Klipp, who assumed command that September. Had Demerer even placed the story within a season, I could have deduced which.

When I get back to the States, I phone Yadja Hammer, the Blechhammer survivor I had interviewed earlier. I start telling her about Karl Demerer and 102 women who supposedly got a second tattoo—

"I have two tattoos on my arm," she says. "The first is 79102 and the second, 34437." She pauses and, almost as an after-thought, says, "We were on trucks to be taken to Auschwitz and the crematoriums." An hour later "they changed their minds" and the transport was cancelled. She was told a large transport of new prisoners was arriving at Blechhammer and "they needed us girls to work in the kitchen."

I read her the part about Demerer bribing the *Lagerführer*.

"I had no idea about this. Never knew a word of it," she says.

I also phone Rosa Plawner, who worked in the camp office. She, too, confirms that she had received a second tattoo number. "The first one I can't even read it, because they crossed it out. It was 79016. I will forever remember this."

Though she ate lunch with Demerer almost every day and remained in touch with him after the war, she, too, had no knowledge of the story behind the second tattoo. Or how it saved her life.

Chapter 14

DIVERSION BY DOCUMENT

··

I t was a copy of a copy and a poor one at that. It was a *Rent-abilitatsberechnung*, a profitability calculation, of how much profit the SS expected to realize from the average forced laborer.

I had received the document from Sigmund Walder, the survivor I had interviewed in Florida. He said he had gotten it from the widow of a rabbi who had it in his files. "It's shocking, unless you were there and saw it."

It listed "income" of RM 6 a day, the price the SS charged private companies for a skilled laborer. Subtracting 70 pfennigs for food and overhead left a gross profit of RM 5.30 per day.

This was multiplied by 270 days—nine months—the average life expectancy of a forced laborer.

This yielded RM 1,431.

Add another RM 200 from "Proceeds per rational value of corpses"—gold teeth, clothing, items of value, and money. After deducting RM 2 for cremation but adding back the proceeds from "bone and ash recycling," the projected net profit per slave laborer came to RM 1,631, about $652 in 1942 dollars or, adjusted for inflation, $10,568 in 2019 dollars.

Rentabilitätsberechnung
der SS über Ausnützung der Häftlinge
in den Konzentrationslagern

Täglicher Verleihlohn durchschnittlich RM 6.--
abzüglich Ernährung   RM -,60
abzüglich Bekl. Amort.   RM -,10
durchschnittl. Lebensdauer   9 Mt.
       9 Mt. = 270 x RM 5,30   RM 1

Erlös aus rationeller Verwertung der Leiche :
     1. Zahngold 3. Wertsachen
     2. Kleidung 4. Geld
abzüglich Verbrennungskosten RM 2.-
durchschnittlicher Nettogewinn   RM   200,-

Gesamtgewinn nach 9 Monaten   RM 1 631,-
                                                  ============
zuzüglich Erlös aus Knochen und Aschenverwertung.

This was as cold-blooded an indictment of German slave labor policies as I had seen. Here, on this single piece of paper, was a revelation truly worthy of the Nazis: the value of human life reduced to a cold calculation of profit and cost. What made it compelling was that it pulled together many numbers from known facts.

The SS did rent out laborers to German industry for between RM 4–6 a day. They spent mere pennies—"pfennigs"—on food. The Germans set daily food rations in labor camps at 1,300 calories for unskilled prisoners and 1,700 for skilled workers like my father. A man doing physical labor requires about 2,500 calories a day. The body makes up for a caloric deficit by eating itself to stay alive. This policy of starvation was deliberate and carefully planned. When it was applied to Soviet prisoners of war, one German general called it the "annihilation of super-fluous eaters."

The Germans did have a conscious policy of working labor camp prisoners until they dropped dead. The Nazi justice minister infamously called it annihilation through labor.

Bodies were stripped of gold teeth and valuables before incineration, though some scholars discount reports that bones were used for fertilizer.

There were problems with this document: no letterhead, no date, and no signature, not even a rubber-stamped one. This lack of provenance bothered me. I never came across this blatant a calculation in any book or paper about the Nazi forced labor program. That made me wary. Deniers have long charged the Holocaust was fake news and have leveraged historical inaccuracies to deny the genocide altogether. The thought of inadvertently undermining this horrible history with a suspect document left me queasy.

Sigmund was insistent when I told him I needed some corroboration. "It is 100 percent genuine," he said. "This is exactly how the Nazis carried out their policies."

Searching the internet for variations of "SS *Rentabilitats-berechnung*," "SS Profitability Calculation," or "SS prisoners 270 days," I was surprised to see it come up many times in many languages. Interestingly, no matter the language—English, German, Russian, Hebrew, or Polish—every reference faithfully reproduced the same numbers and math.

Yet every citation, and everyone I contacted, had quoted what turned out to be a secondary source. Often the search followed a trail of footnotes citing other books but never the document itself. The brave new world of internet copy-and-paste had spread it around even more.

In 1997, an economics instructor at Clark College in Vancouver, Washington, used it in his Economics 101 class as a cautionary lesson about the dangers of striving for ultimate efficiency. When I reached the instructor by phone, he was at a different college and specializing in Native American studies. He said he had gotten the document "right from the Auschwitz archives." My contacts at the Auschwitz Museum said they had never seen it.

In 2002, a German graduate student reproduced it as an annex to a paper on worker compensation. One writer said it came from the Buchenwald Concentration Camp, while another placed it in the Ravensbruck camp and a third sourced it from Dachau. I downloaded a translation of the calculation in a Slavic language from the US Holocaust Memorial Museum's website. Its source? The Museum of Yugoslavia. Two rabbis who had quoted it in their sermons told me they had found the profitability calculation on the internet . . . and on and on.

In 2019, it was referenced in the audio guide of the acclaimed exhibit, *Auschwitz, Not Long Ago, Not Far Away* at The Museum of Jewish Heritage—A Living Memorial to the Holocaust, in New York City.

At the end of Audio Stop 54, under the "Life in the Camps" section, the narrator intones, "During World War II, the SS calculated that, after costs such as cremation, but not including the value of bones used in fertilizer, the profit made from each prisoner was roughly $745."

This reference was dramatic enough to have been picked up and paraphrased by *The New York Times* in its May 8, 2019, review of the exhibit.

The earliest reference to the profitability calculation I found was by Eugon Kogon, a respected Catholic journalist and an outspoken anti-Nazi who was imprisoned in the Buchenwald Concentration Camp for six years. Indeed, a curator for the Auschwitz exhibit cited Kogon as their source for the audio guide reference.

Kogon is also cited by the Jewish Virtual Library, a popular online resource about the war, under its "Prison Labor" subsection on the concentration camps.

The profitability table appears in Kogon's 1946 book, *The SS State*. Today, an English translation of the more popular 1950 rewrite, *The Theory and Practice of Hell*, can be downloaded for free. It has been published in a number of languages over the years.

"Let it not be thought that this calculation is my own handiwork," Kogon writes. "It comes from SS sources, and [concentration camp director Oswald] Pohl jealously guarded against 'outside interference.'"

Kogon provides no further details or context about the calculation—who wrote it or when, where it came from, or how it had come into his possession—nothing. The curator of the Buchenwald Memorial museum, Dr. Harry Stein, had previously reviewed Kogon's archive and confirmed to me that he has never been able to find the original source.

None of this surprised Robert Jan van Pelt, the preeminent Auschwitz expert and lead curator of the Auschwitz exhibit, which was produced by Musealia, a private Spanish exhibition company, in cooperation with the Auschwitz-Birkenau Museum in Poland.

"I've never seen anything but a transcript [of the profitability calculation]," van Pelt told me. "Never seen it anywhere, in any archive, or original, or carbon copy, or photocopy of a carbon copy."

How, then, did it find its way into the audio guide of a prominent New York museum exhibit in 2019?

"It fell through the cracks," van Pelt said. Production of a new audio guide for the New York exhibit was running late. In the last minute, hurly-burly deadline of getting the exhibit opened on time, van Pelt said the reference to the dramatic SS profitability calculation was left in.

Soon after I raised questions about the document's provenance, the exhibit's curators quietly deleted the reference from the audio guide.

Still, Van Pelt cautioned against dismissing Kogon entirely based on the questionable background of the profitability document.

Within days of Kogon's liberation in 1945, the US military's Psychological Warfare Division asked him to assemble an in-depth report on conditions in Buchenwald. Kogon's work is still considered a benchmark study of the concentration camp system. The single-spaced, four-hundred-page report was also the basis of Kogon's later books. These reportedly sold more than half a million copies in Germany alone.

"I can't believe he really made it up," van Pelt said of Kogon and the calculation, "because he just doesn't seem to be the man [to do so]."

Still, the *Rentabilitatsberechnung* doesn't pass van Pelt's sniff test for legitimacy. His standards were molded in 2000 when British historian David Irving sued American scholar Deborah Lipstadt and her publisher for libel after she accused Irving of systematic Holocaust denial.

Van Pelt, an architectural historian, was the defense expert witness on the Auschwitz gas chambers.

"I needed to show [the court] due diligence in everything I quoted," van Pelt said. This meant not only presenting German records, but proving those documents were bona fide and not forgeries. "Especially where it relates to the Holocaust, you feel the problem of denial is sitting there. I am more cautious than I would have been twenty years ago, before I had experience with Holocaust denials." (Irving lost the case.)

If Kogon did not invent the profitability table, who then were the "SS sources" he obliquely referred to?

One may have been Major Erwin Ding-Schuler, the SS doctor who ran deadly medical experiments on hundreds of prisoners. Kogon wrote that he worked as an inmate-clerk for the SS major and gradually cultivated him. After a few months, "There was no political or military event about which he failed to consult me . . . On many nights he sat in his room until eleven or twelve o'clock, talking with me, accepting my counsel." When Ding-Schuler learned that Kogon was on a list of prisoners to be executed by the SS, he smuggled Kogon out of Buchenwald in a crate and hid the prisoner in his home in Weimar.

One can imagine the late-night intellectual discussions between the coldly clinical Waffen-SS surgeon and the devoutly Christian Kogon, debating the value of a human life in the context of war and the concentration camp system. Some hard numbers were surely known—the daily fees the SS charged for renting out prisoners, the sums spent on food and shelter. Was the profitability calculation the result of an intellectual exercise, albeit one based on facts? Ding-Shuler committed suicide after the war.

Interestingly, Kogon never used the word "document" or the German term "*Rentabilitatsberechnung*." That term first appeared when the calculation was included in *Power Without Morality*, a 1957 volume largely of SS documents, edited by Reimund Schnabel. The 582-page tome has become something of a go-to reference about the operations and structure of the

SS, and the profitability calculation attained greater legitimacy, and became more widely quoted, after it was included in Schnabel's work.

Most of the book is made up of photocopies of actual Nazi documents. The SS *Rentabilitatsberechnung*, however, is set in plain text type. Next to it is the notation, "Z 32." Under the book's Key to Abbreviations, "Z = *Zitat*" or "Quotations," while "D = *Dokumente*" or Documents.

This meant Schnabel was not reproducing a document but reprinting a quotation.

In explaining the *Zitat* entries, Schnabel wrote, "In each case, the quotations indicate their accurate source." Except there is no "source," only a description: "Profitability calculation of the SS exploitation of the prisoners in the concentration camps."

While Schnabel does not specifically cite Kogon as the source for his *Zitat*, Kogon is listed in the book's bibliography.

None of this has stopped websites, historians, and museums over the last sixty years from misrepresenting "Z 32" as a document number or quoting the calculation as historical fact.

Googling variations of "Nazi Document Z 32" turned up a story from August 5, 1960, in *The Detroit Jewish News*. It reported that Catholic delegates to a Eucharistic Congress in Munich visited an exhibition in the nearby Dachau Concentration Camp and were handed brochures that included "SS Document Z-32," the profitability calculation.

Alex Pearman, an archivist at the Dachau Memorial museum, emailed me that he was unable to locate the source of the document mentioned in the 1960 article. Pearman, however, attached a poster image of the calculation—in English—from a 1964 exhibit at Dachau. It, too, had "Z 32" printed at the bottom, which meant it was taken from Schnabel.

From the Yad Vashem archives, I found a photo of a similar poster, in German, displaying the calculation at an unidentified exhibit; "Z 32" also appeared at the bottom. Surprisingly, no one at Yad Vashem could tell me the source of the photo, much less the location of the exhibit.

Often a historian's use of the SS profitability calculation is obscured by a cookie crumb trail of footnotes.

In 2004, Stuart Eizenstat described the SS calculation as, "one of the most chilling documents I have ever seen," in his book, *Imperfect Justice*. He quotes the document and its arithmetic in detail.

Eizenstat is no intellectual lightweight or dilettante. He's a former ambassador to the European Union, served as a deputy treasury secretary, and was a senior domestic policy advisor to President Jimmy Carter.

His source for the SS document? A footnote cited in a German book about Nazi slave labor. That book, in turn, footnoted yet another German book about Nazi treatment of its enemies. This book's source? Schnabel's *Power Without Morality*.

All this meant that while the *Rentabilitatsberechnung* might be spectacular and based on some hard numbers, without confirmed provenance, it proved to be a lengthy diversion by document—and cautionary lesson in Reporting 101.

Chapter 15

OF AIR RAIDS

AND EXECUTIONS

....

June 7, 1944. News of D-Day tore through the Blechhammer refinery complex like spontaneous combustion.

Dolek first heard about it from his British POW friends, who had learned of it on their hidden radios tuned to the BBC. Word spread to the thousands of foreign contract workers speaking all of Europe's languages. It could be seen in the frightened eyes of German civilian foremen, and in the gun-barrel scowls of the SS guards.

"The Germans had blood in their eyes that day," my father had told me. "You didn't dare look a German in the face. It was a death sentence if they saw you smiling or looking happy. I stayed out of their way as much as I could."

Three weeks later, on June 27, the US 15th Air Force launched its first attack against the Blechhammer refineries. The target was Blechhammer South, which had been tasked with the production of aviation fuel, making it a priority for the Americans. However, the bombers missed their primary targets because of poor weather.

The Nazi Armaments Minister, Albert Speer, grasped the implication of the bombing campaign against the synthetic petroleum refineries. He warned Hitler that failure to protect the facilities would lead to "inevitable tragic consequences."

The Germans had been fortifying Blechhammer for months before it officially came on line on May 27, 1944. High cement curtains surrounded the sensitive refinery installations and effectively protected them from everything but a direct hit. Cavernous aboveground shelters that looked like elongated igloos were built of reinforced concrete seven feet thick. Hundreds of antiaircraft guns ringed the area and scores of Messerschmitt fighters rose to challenge the Americans.

The first successful raid came on July 7, when 350 B-17 and B-24 bombers targeted both Blechhammer South and North.

"Oh, the joy we felt with each explosion," Dad said. "D-Day and Normandy, the Germans were saying they were repulsing those attacks. Seeing hundreds of American bombers overhead, the Germans couldn't hide that. We really believed the war would end in a few weeks."

Prisoners scattered everywhere. Some crawled into sections of huge pipes lying about the construction site. Others hid in the subbasements and tunnels under the refinery. My father told me he ran into an air-raid shelter and found it was full of women office workers. An SS man pulled out his pistol and ordered the Jews to get out. "He said the shelter is not for *Untermenschen* [subhumans]," Dad said. "We had no choice but to leave right in middle of the raid. Everyone was running around, looking for places to hide."

Scattered throughout the refinery complex were mini shelters that looked like large cement bells with slits for the guard to look out. "But when the bombing started the guards ran away to the real shelters," Dad had said. While they protected against shrapnel, the mini shelters were useless against anything close to a direct hit. Still, for the prisoners, it was better than nothing.

Sigmund Walder, Mark Beck, and other survivor testimonials say the Americans always came at noon. "It was predictable," Sigmund said.

As soon as the all-clear sounded, thousands of workers set about cleaning up the rubble and repairing the damage. American post-bombing intelligence assessments were surprised at how quickly the Germans recovered from the raids.

Into the fall and winter, the Americans returned whenever the Germans rebuilt. While there is no official breakdown, researchers estimate that at least 150 B-17 and B-24 bombers were lost during the five-month campaign against Blechhammer North and South and the nearby Odertal refineries.

With the bombings came the first prisoner hangings in the camp.

"It was the SS telling us not to become too happy, that they were still in charge," Sigmund Walder had told me in Longboat Key. "Every time they bombed, the SS would hang someone, and sometimes in between" bombings as well.

One particularly gruesome account comes up in multiple survivor testimonials: a triple hanging on Yom Kippur, the Jewish Day of Atonement, which fell on September 27, 1944. I first learned of it in Sigmund's Yale video, and he elaborated on it when I interviewed him in Florida.

A Dutch prisoner, no more than a teenager, came across some yellow powder lying by the side of a road and, thinking it was laundry detergent from a broken crate, scooped up a handful. The powder was explosives from a bomb that had cracked open but not exploded. A German guard saw him and, accusing him of sabotage, noted his tattoo number. A fellow prisoner intervened, telling the guard the Dutch boy was just a confused kid and had no idea what he was doing. The German noted that prisoner's number too. Then the group's *Kapo* tried reasoning with the German. The *Kapo's* tattoo number was also taken down.

Following concentration camp protocol, the guard sent his report to Auschwitz Monowitz, the giant Auschwitz subcamp that was in charge of all of the forced labor camps in the area.

On September 27, the columns of prisoners returning from work were marched to a makeshift scaffold, where three nooses were tied to a beam, a table set underneath with stools on the table. The camp *Kommandant* called out the numbers of the three prisoners who had been reported by the guard and ordered them to step forward. Reading aloud an official judgment, he declared the three guilty of sabotage and sentenced to immediate death.

The three were forced onto stools. Nooses were placed around their necks. SS guards then kicked the stools away.

"The drop was not steep enough to break your neck," Sigmund told me. "So what happened was, the noose was tightened and the guys were killed by suffocation. The younger guy, the Dutch fellow, he struggled so much his shoes came off and his pants came off. And it took maybe twenty minutes until he died from suffocation."

Sigmund paused, lost in reflection. "After this particular hanging, they didn't cut the guys down for three days and every time we left the camp and came back into the camp we had to go by the gallows where the guys were." Sigmund had told this same story, with the same details, in his Yale testimonial twenty years earlier.

Walter Spitzer also described the triple hanging in his autobiography. Only in his telling, "The dry scrape of the stool followed by the cracks of the necks of these unfortunate men resonated in the absolute silence and crushed us all. It was all so sudden. The muffled, barely audible murmur of a *Kaddish* spread throughout our ranks in response to this despicable act."

Spitzer and at least seven other accounts say the young Dutch prisoner had picked up a piece of wire, not powder. Depending on the account, the wire was used to fasten his wooden clogs or to secure his metal food tin, which all prisoners carried with them. In this telling, the SS guard accused the Dutchman of cutting telephone cables.

Which was it? Did the Dutchman pick up a piece of wire or did he scoop up powder? Did the three die of strangulation or were their necks broken? Both versions couldn't be right. In the scheme of things, this seemed minor. Yet the differences rankled.

Insight came from Dr. Oliver Sacks, the renowned British neurologist and author whose book *Awakenings* was the basis of the Oscar-nominated film of the same name.

Sacks recalled German air raids during World War II when he was a child in England. In one attack, a German incendiary bomb exploded in the garden of his home. "My father had a stirrup [pedal] pump, and my brothers carried pails of water to him, but water seemed useless against this infernal fire—indeed, made it burn even more furiously. There was a vicious hissing and sputtering when the water hit the white-hot metal, and meanwhile the bomb was melting its own casing and throwing blobs and jets of molten metal in all directions." It was an incredibly vivid recounting of what must have been a petrifying event.

Months after the autobiography was published, Sacks was talking about the bombing incident with his older brother, Michael.

"You never saw it," Michael said. "You weren't there."

Sacks was staggered. He could see the whole episode in his mind's eye: his dad furiously manning the pump, the hiss and sputter of the molten metal, every horrific detail.

Michael reminded him that at the time of the bombing, they had both been evacuated to the English countryside. The brothers had received a very vivid, dramatic letter from home describing the attack in detail. "You were enthralled by it," Michael told him.

Sacks realized he had reconstructed the scene in his mind "and then appropriated it, and taken it for a memory of my own . . . It is startling to realize that some of our most cherished memories may never have happened—or may have happened to someone else."

I thought of Sacks while trying to reconcile the accounts of the triple hanging. While every reporter has wrestled with details and versions that change with the retelling, now, thanks to Sacks, I could also better appreciate how incidents only overheard can become memories entrenched though never actually experienced.

Nevertheless, the basic facts triangulated in all survivor accounts: a young Dutch prisoner was accused of sabotage. Two fellow prisoners who tried to intervene were then also charged. All three were by hanged on Yom Kippur, the holiest day in the Jewish calendar. In all accounts, Blechhammer prisoners were marched past the dangling bodies for three days when leaving and returning to the camp.

....

Between July and December 1944, the 15th Air Force launched nineteen raids against the Blechhammer North and South refineries, each carried out by between two hundred to four hundred heavy bombers. Besides the twin Blechhammer refineries, the Silesian campaign also targeted two other refineries.

The route to Blechhammer took the bombers virtually over the gas chambers and crematoria of the Auschwitz Birkenau camp. By then, the genocide had already been widely reported in the world press. Nevertheless, the War Department rejected pleas by Jewish organizations to bomb the rail tracks leading to the death camp, if not the gas chambers and crematoria themselves. The War Department cited a number of reasons: Bombing the rail lines would have limited effect as they could quickly be repaired, and diverting resources would hamper the strategic oil campaign and prolong the entire war.

It's estimated that more than one hundred thousand Jews were murdered in Auschwitz from June 27, the date of the first Blechhammer raid, to November 25, when Himmler ordered the gas chambers decommissioned and dismantled.

Chapter 16

DEATH MARCH TO BIG ROSES

....

At 10:00 a.m. on Jan. 12, 1945, the Red Army launched its winter offensive with the goal of ending the war in forty-five days. Some four hundred thousand German soldiers faced two million fifty thousand Russians across a 558-mile-wide front. The Germans, dug in close to the front lines, were within easy range of the seven thousand Russian artillery pieces. They were pulverized and then sent reeling.

On the Western Front, Hitler's last-gasp Ardennes Offensive, known to Americans as the Battle of the Bulge, was near collapse. The Germans suffered some one hundred thousand casualties and lost eight hundred tanks.

Four days later, Hitler moved into his underground bunker at the Reich Chancellery.

The previous summer, Himmler had issued orders that in the event of a major pullback, concentration camp prisoners and POWs were to be evacuated toward the west, deeper into Germany. Only no one followed through with the detailed logistic planning required. When the Soviet offensive hit, the SS was left scrambling, improvising as developments unfolded.

Himmler's order said no prisoners were to fall into the hands of the advancing Russian army. When senior concentration camp commanders inquired exactly what this meant, they received conflicting answers. Interpretation was essentially left to the SS guards in the field who would accompany the prisoners. They weren't called the Death's Head Division for nothing. . . .

As the Russians took Warsaw five days later, on January 17, Berlin ordered the gas chambers at Auschwitz blown up, all documents of its activities destroyed, and all prisoners immediately evacuated toward the west.

That morning, the last roll call was recorded for Auschwitz and its subcamps: 66,020 prisoners in twenty-two camps, including 3,959 Jewish inmates at Blechhammer.

In Blechhammer, rumors of German intentions seemed to outnumber the prisoners spreading them.

Eddie Gastfriend, a Polish Jewish teenager, recalled one persistent grisly rumor: the SS had already wired dynamite under the barracks and would blow up all the prisoners before the Russians arrived. "Terror took hold of the inmates. I was trembling with fear." He and his cousin considered hiding inside the shit holes in the toilet barracks.

Motek Kleiman heard the exact opposite: The Germans had already packed up and were planning to abandon Blechhammer and leave the prisoners behind.

Red Martin, the head *Kapo* for the electricians, understood from a German civilian foreman at the refinery complex that railcars were being readied to evacuate the prisoners to camps farther west. *After all*, the reasoning went, *they still need us.*

The problem was, with the front collapsing, where would the Germans get the railroad cars necessary for a mass evacuation? The possibility of a forced march was generally discounted, given that it was winter, cold, and snowing. To march any distance in that weather would have been insane.

Sigmund Walder knew otherwise. His POW friends told

him that their officers had passed along orders to prepare for just such a forced march. Extra clothing and food were being distributed. Sigmund "organized" several pairs of brand-new army boots from his Canadian POW contacts. He gave one pair to Walter Spitzer.

Dolek knew about this because Walter had shown him the boots. Walter spattered them with paint from the construction site to make them look old and worn. Dolek was wearing standard concentration camp footwear—"Dutch shoes"—tattered cloth uppers tacked to unyielding wooden soles.

Four days later, on January 21, word that twenty-five hundred prisoners from other labor camps had arrived overnight—on foot—blew through Blechhammer like the storm howling in from the east, from the Russian front. Exhausted, hungry, and cold, the new arrivals told of a three-day forced march through heavy snow and subfreezing temperatures. Guards shot those who couldn't keep up.

At the morning roll call, instead of being counted and marched to work, everyone was kept in line by the *Kapos*. One hour elapsed, then a second, and a third.

At 10:30 a.m., the camp's loudspeakers barked the orders of the day. Blechhammer was being evacuated to a safer area to the west. It promised better working conditions and food. Prisoners would receive double food rations for the trip. They were to bring their food tins and spoons and, if they wished, their blanket and personal possessions. All able-bodied detainees were to evacuate. Only those too ill to walk could stay behind.

No one believed this. It was a given the SS would kill anyone remaining in the camp.

Pandemonium erupted. Some prisoners broke into the food stores, grabbing whatever they could until the *Kapos* arrived and beat everyone back. The Germans remained outside the wire.

Dolek made for the clothing warehouse. Inside the dimly lit barrack, prisoners fought over any bit of extra clothing they could grab. Amid the shouting and shoving, he wrestled two men for a pair of ankle-high leather shoes. Dolek emerged hugging the shoes to his chest like a mother suckling her baby. The warehouse was unheated, the shoes were frozen stiff. He worked them with his hands, back and forth, back and forth, careful not to crack the brittle leather.

Before the war, Dolek had many shoes, like the shiny black ones with buckles on the side that he had taken dancing with Mania Faske. Before the war, he had knee-high riding boots that he polished like burnished mahogany. Before the war, he had climbed hills in steel-toed hiking boots laced high and tight and secure. But now on this frigid January day, any thoughts of Before the war were an abstraction and a distraction. All that mattered were the worn, cracked, and beautiful shoes thawing in his hands.

Dolek kicked off his wooden clogs and unwound the rags about his feet. A bit of adhesive tape from the infirmary secured his last diamond between the large and middle toes of his right foot. All in place, he rewrapped the rags and coaxed his feet into the shoes. He would remember one still had a lace in it.

On the food line two beefy German *Kapos* distributed the promised double ration: half a loaf of black camp bread, a double portion of artificial honey, a dab of margarine, and a slice of horsemeat sausage. Dolek devoured part of the bread and all of the honey on the spot.

Snow fell thick and white. Dolek wrapped his blanket like a prayer shawl over his thin blue-striped jacket. Beneath his shirt he wore a "camp undershirt" fashioned from the paper sacks used for cement. The bags were constructed of several layers of brown industrial paper. The innermost layer, the one most impregnated with cement dust, was stripped out and discarded. Holes were cut for the arms and head. They worked fairly well, considering the alternative was nothing. Many prisoners wore these paper undershirts, though the guards considered them contraband. Any prisoner caught wearing one was stripped, beaten, and left in the snow to freeze.

Dolek joined his comrades from Arbeitskommando 27, lining up as usual in rows five across. The distant thump of Soviet artillery made the German guards anxious. No slow and meticulous count today. Beneath ashen skies, they spurred the prisoners on with clubs and dogs. "*Macht Schnell! Schneller!*" Move quickly! Quicker!

Still, it takes time to move out some sixty-five hundred men.

Red Martin's Arbeitskommando 27 was among the last to be called. By now, the path out of the camp was a gray slushy rut. After 577 days, Dolek was being hustled out of Blechhammer by guards more anxious to leave than he.

Outside the concrete walls, the prisoners joined the deluge of German civilians and soldiers, trucks and horse carts, tanks and armored cars all retreating west, away from the Russian guns. Prisoners were kept on one side of the road while German civilians, many with carts piled with household possessions, were on the other. The center was reserved for military vehicles.

For nearly two years, these same German *burghers* had smugly sneered at Dolek and his fellow prisoners being marched to and from the refinery complex. Seeing them now, frightened, fleeing in panic, gave Dolek a sense of serenity. *Soon*, he remembered thinking, *soon the Russians will be here and we'll be liberated and they'll know how to handle you.*

Two rough hands yanked Dolek from the edge of the road— and from the path of a careening truck being towed by another vehicle with stout ropes. The truck swung wildly from one side of the road to the other, scattering both Jewish prisoners and German civilians. Prisoners struck by the truck were left by the roadside, either dead or injured, which amounted to the same thing.

Stunned, Dolek turned to his rescuer.

"Oy, Motek . . ."

"Oy, Dolek."

There was nothing more to say. Exchanging nods, they rejoined the column that stretched like a long gray worm slithering through the white countryside.

Wind cut like razor wire. Snow stuck to the soles of the wooden clogs. To move forward, the prisoners had to lift their legs high like quarter horses, stopping every few steps to knock the accumulating snow off the wooden soles. But on whom could you lean for support? After a while, the fabric uppers would tear from the tacks holding them to the wood soles. Prisoners then walked with only rags around their feet. Caking snow weighed down the blankets the prisoners had wrapped around their heads and shoulders. Many prisoners discarded them, too.

After a half-day's march, Arbeitskommando 27 arrived at a bridge at the same time as a long column of British POWs. They were among the two thousand POWs from a half-dozen subcamps assigned to the Blechhammer refineries.

The POWs wore layers of woolen winter khakis, heavy coats, hats, and leather boots. Before starting out, they had each received a four-day ration of tinned meat, bread, margarine, sugar, and cigarettes from Canadian Red Cross packages.

Eddie Hyde-Clark, a POW from Suffolk, England, was just settling down to eat when he looked up and "coming towards us I see what can only be described as a shuffling collection of living skeletons. Never have I witnessed such utter despair on the faces of human beings with such hollow faces and protruding bones, all dressed in filthy uniforms that looked like gray-striped pajamas." One prisoner staggered toward Hyde-Clark, reaching out for the turnip the POW was eating, "but was driven back when the ugly-looking bully in charge of them cracked a whip about his shoulders."

Most of the Blechhammer column already crossed the bridge before the POWs arrived. Now that the Brits were there, though, they had priority over the Jews. Some four hundred inmates, including Red Martin's Arbeitskommando 27, waited for the POWs to cross the bridge.

When the four hundred Blechhammer inmates finally did cross, their SS guards turned the column to the right, whereas the main column had gone left.

"We lost the rest of the column," Red Martin recalled.

The SS officer in charge requisitioned an abandoned factory on the outskirts of a small town and settled in. The prisoners slept on clean straw mattresses marked "Red Cross." There were some potatoes and bread. They could even shower.

As for the main column, after crossing the bridge, the Germans shunted the prisoners onto side roads to reduce congestion on the main roads jammed with fleeing German civilians and military vehicles.

The flat, echoing crack of a gunshot ruptured the silence every few minutes.

"The great terror was knowing that, despite your exhaustion, you had to stay on your feet and keep walking," Robert Clary recalled. "If you sat down to rest or were too weak to go on, you were shot. On the march, we heard constant rifle and pistol shots."

Karl Demerer was walking with his son when an SS major passed in an open horse-drawn carriage filled with straw. "He called me to come near and told me, 'Demerer, here in the straw at my side, there is a revolver with [bullets]. Take them, run away with your son to save yourselves.'"

Demerer said he declined. "I did not want to abandon all these thousands of Jews who had been living with me. What happens to them shall happen to me, too."

Any pretensions of order soon dissolved. Like an amorphous mass, the column surged and ebbed onto itself. Prisoners drifted from the front to the middle to the rear and back to the front. Those at the head of the column had to forge a path through the fresh snow. Those in the back risked being shot by the German rear guard for falling behind. Those with the presence of mind tried to stay in the middle.

At night, the guards crammed prisoners into abandoned barns or warehouses. Food was haphazardly distributed, the rations from Blechhammer long gone.

"The Jewish column stretched right back to the horizon behind us," said George Trundle, a POW from New Zealand. "They carried nothing—each person had nothing to carry." Trundle and his mates each had a rucksack with food and extra clothing. "As night fell, we lost contact with them and never saw them again."

Peter Black, a POW from Scotland, said, "The Jewish columns were ahead of us. Most were in a pitiful state and if they didn't keep up, they were shot and their bodies left by the road."

POWs weren't the only witnesses to the carnage.

Rudolf Höss, who had been promoted from Auschwitz *Kommandant* to a headquarters job, was dispatched to the Eastern Front for a firsthand look after communications were cut off by the Soviet advance.

"I now found columns of prisoners who were suffering terribly as they tried to make their way through the deep snow," he recalled. "There was no food. In most cases, the [German officers] who were leading this parade of walking dead had no idea which direction they were supposed to go."

Writing from his prison cell awaiting execution for crimes against humanity, Höss said, "It was easy to follow the route of this ordeal of suffering because every few hundred meters lay bodies of prisoners who had collapsed or been shot."

Investigation

```
Testimony of SS Pvt. Heinrich Schaefer,
German Prisoner of War,
Taken at 1130 hours on 18 August 1945, at
Romilly, France

Q: How long did you stay in Blechhammer?
A: Until the 21st day of January 1945
Q: When did you first observe the killing
of someone in Blechhammer?
A: I never saw anyone killed.
Q: . . .You cannot really claim,
honestly, that during your whole time you
were on guard duty in concentration camps
you never saw killing.
A: I cannot remember. I did not see
anything.
```

....

On the fourth day of the march, Abraham Schaufeld awoke with a sore foot and limped from the barn where he had spent the night.

A German guard spotted him. "*Du canst nicht aufen?*" You can't walk?

"*Ja natürlich, Mir geht es gut.*" Yes, of course, I'm fine.

The guard ordered him to a nearby horse and cart. There were three in all, the last with SS men and machine guns.

"This was not good," Schaufeld recalled. "There was no one in good shape [on the carts], and this wasn't the International Red Cross."

At dusk, the small horse-drawn convoy pulled up to a freshly dug ditch against a low brick wall of a village cemetery.

"They said, 'remove your clothing,'" Schaufeld recalled. "People started shouting and screaming because they could see the ditch and people against the wall, people crying in all sorts of languages . . ." Amid the pushing, shouting, and tumult, "I went over the wall, into the cemetery. I lie down near a gravestone, near the wall. By now it's dark. I could hear the shooting. The screams and the shooting, the full massacre. And then it was quiet."

An SS man entered the cemetery to relieve himself. Schaufeld could see the eagle insignia of his SS uniform belt in the moonlight. "There were two possibilities: He didn't see me or he didn't want to see me."

Schaufeld lay as silent as the tombstones. "I gave it some time. This was winter. Sodden fields. I walked through these fields. In this mud, in this field, I lost my wood shoes. I walked barefoot. No overcoat. Nothing."

Schaufeld made for the lights of a village. Behind a house he found an open barn, fell into the hay, and passed out.

Suddenly awakened by a barking dog and the dancing light of a lantern, Schaufeld saw a German farmer standing over him with a pitchfork and the farmer's wife shouting. "They were dancing around but nobody hit me."

The local village policeman arrived and, together with the farmer and his wife, took Schaufeld to the police station. Some women from the village also showed up. They asked if he was from the transport that had passed. "I told them my father was an officer in the Polish army. They gave me something to eat, some coffee.

"Soon a policeman came with handcuffs and said, I must take you to the SS. In middle of night and we're marching. He started telling me that he was sorry, that the SS would probably shoot me."

The SS guards, who were spending the night in a farmhouse being entertained by women, "immediately start smacking me around, kicking me. Luckily some women came around and said, 'Why are you hitting that boy' and they stopped. They said, 'take him to the barn, we will deal with him later.'"

Schaufeld avoided the SS by mingling with hundreds of prisoners leaving the barn and rejoined the column.

For Arbeitskommando 27 and the four hundred other prisoners, their sojourn in the abandoned factory was about to end. As Red Martin remembered it, the mother of the town mayor confronted the SS, telling them they had to leave and take their Jews with them.

"On the second day after leaving the factory, we began seeing corpses in ditches, against trees, or just lying by the side of the roads," Red Martin said. One of Martin's men pulled up the sleeve of a dead prisoner. The tattoo number was from of the original series assigned to Blechhammer.

By the time they caught up with the main column, hundreds had been killed. "We realized how lucky we were that we stayed at that plant for a few days," Red Martin said.

Just then, a young prisoner, barefoot except for rags wrapped around his feet, ran by. "Don't let them put you into a cart," he shouted. "You must keep walking at all costs."

Days merged into a nightmare of hunger and exhaustion and gunshots. Unable to walk, more and more prisoners fell to the side of the road.

"Not being able to go on, they resigned themselves to certain death," Walter Spitzer said. "I saw people look straight into the eyes of their executioner as they waited for death."

"We were seldom shouted at or beaten," Israel Rosengarten recalled. "Should a confrontation arise with the SS, the chances were now greater of being killed on the spot by a bullet through the head."

Investigation

Testimony of Private Franz Ludwig, German
prisoner of war,
13 August 1945

A: . . . We marched 14 days. The whole
march was very poorly organized and
conditions were simply terrible. Many
people froze to death, others died from
hunger and others were killed.
Q: Who killed them?
A: I do not know anything about the
killing. I just heard rumors about it.

Of the roughly sixty-five hundred prisoners who left Blech-hammer on January 21, an estimated eight hundred were shot or otherwise died during the march. Assuming prisoners had been forced to walk twelve hours a day, that meant an average of more than four prisoners were shot every hour, every day, for those thirteen days.

Chapter 17

BIG ROSES

·····································

"So where did they take you after you left Blechhammer?"
Dad and I were in our favorite spot, sharing the overstuffed
tasseled green armchair. I snuggled against the soft bulge of his
belly, my head resting on his shoulder.

"To a place called Gross-Rosen," he said. "We walked.
Through snow. As high as your knees, boy. For more than ten days,
we walked. And it was cold, a real Polish winter."

"Gross-Rosen?" I asked.

"It means 'Big Roses.'"

"That sounds nice."

My father did not reply. I felt his breathing become short. I
looked up. His eyes were unfocused, or perhaps focused on the
past. I hugged him a bit tighter, listening to him breathe. His
silence magnified other sounds—the hum of our Amana refriger-
ator in the kitchen, the ticktock of the faux cuckoo clock on the
dining room wall, the cars passing below our window on 83rd
Street. Though I was only eight or nine years old, I understood
this was something Dad could not talk about.

I buried my face in his neck. He sighed deeply. I did not press
him, and soon we were on to different subjects. We never spoke
of Gross-Rosen again.

....

On the second leg of my Poland trip, I ask Les to retrace as closely as possible the 180-mile route of the death march from Blechhammer to the Gross-Rosen Concentration Camp. The highway would have gotten us there in about three hours. Driving back roads through the countryside, it took nearly double that. My father trudged this same route through snow and slush for twelve or thirteen frozen days.

Today, Gross-Rosen is a Polish national museum. Not as large as the Auschwitz Museum, it's every bit as solemn, with stained glass windows depicting inmates in striped pajamas and a number of memorials and monuments to the various nationalities of prisoners. There's also a preserved crematorium manufactured by H. Kori, similar to the one at Blechhammer.

Before coming to Poland I had been told that the government tended to play down the Jewish aspect of the war, preferring to lump it together within the overall Polish experience. That certainly was not the case at Auschwitz. Nor was it at Gross-Rosen. The multi-language video presentation at the museum's visitors center presented the full story of the death march and the horrific treatment of the Jews in Gross-Rosen, at least in the English version.

The story began during the war, when Gross-Rosen grew to include some one hundred subcamps and thousands of prisoners, many of them inherited from the Organization Schmelt. Three months before the Soviet offensive, the *Kommandant* of Gross-Rosen received instructions from Berlin advising that his camp would be the destination for thousands of prisoners should there be a general evacuation of camps from the east. Little, however, was done to prepare. When the Soviets launched their attack in January, the camp was not nearly ready for the arrivals from Blechhammer and elsewhere. Gross-Rosen quickly swelled to more than ninety-seven thousand prisoners.

Many guards and *Kapos* at Gross-Rosen were Ukrainian nationals working for the SS. "They were totally dehumanized, filled with hate and anger," recalled Edward Gastfriend. "As we passed them, they exploded with fury and violence . . . and beat our heads with whips and sticks. There was no way to escape the gauntlet. We pushed forward and in our panic trampled over other unfortunates who did not have the strength to run."

Walter Spitzer remembered the corpses, stacks of them. "This incredible sight that has haunted me for many years since: a constant line of prisoners, pulling corpses, or skeletons more precisely, holding them by the tendons and the skin . . . The white of the bodies stands out against the gray and dark brown of the muddy earth. In the total silence, the only thing we can hear is the dull sound of the skulls and the open mouths scraping on the ground," he said.

"It's a terrifying spectacle to see the dead carried by the half dead."

Robert Clary was also haunted by his memories. "Oh I have tasted hell on Earth and I know what it is," Clary recalled. "They did not know what to do with us. They shoved us into unfinished barracks, no windows, no doors, no bunks, no straw on the floor, just cold cement and its freezing and muddy outside."

The roll calls were held in a newly plowed field on a plateau above the main camp, exposed to the winter winds. The prisoners stood in slush for hours, many dropping into the mud and dying there.

"I think back and it was really quite unbelievable—I can't even believe that we stood there hour after hour in that wind," Sigmund Walder told me.

After three days in this frozen hell, thousands of prisoners were loaded into open coal railcars and shipped three hundred miles west to Weimar and the Buchenwald Concentration Camp.

Chapter 18

FROM A NUMBER TO A NAME

Three transport lists have survived the war with the names of 6,439 prisoners shipped from Gross-Rosen to Buchenwald in February 1945.

The lists themselves are a marvel of Nazi bureaucratic efficiency at a time of retreat, chaos, and collapse of the German military. Each typed, single-spaced list was assembled from handwritten logs. Each list is first divided by nationality—French, Polish, Dutch, Hungarian, Greek, Czech, Russian, and so on. Each nationality is then subdivided into "politicals" and "political Jews" with occasional insertions for "mixed race." Within each of these subcategories, names are in alphabetical order.

Each line is numbered and records, in order, the prisoner's new Buchenwald registration number, last name, first name, date of birth, place of birth, work assignment, and the abbreviation and registration number of his previous camp.

Thanks to the efficiency of the SS, it takes me only five minutes to find my father's name on line 1,945, page thirty-three of the fifty-six-page List II.

1944.	125964	Lajtner	Herss	14. 5.14	Sosnowitz	Klemp. GR 24985
1945.	127575	Lajtner	Jozef	11. 8.11	Bendsburg	B.Schwß.Lol77904
1946.	128211	Laks	Abram	12.12.23	Slawkow	Zimmern.GR24929
1947	130517	Taks	Dawid	2. 3.19	Kielce	Tischl. B 597

I also find the name of Joseph Braasem, the *Kapo* who beat my father. He is under *"Politische Hollander/Juden,"* line 2,210, page thirty-eight of the forty-three-page List I. His profession is listed as "worker."

Every survivor quoted in this book who claimed to have been on the death march is on one of the lists.

List III is the shortest of the three. Its twelve pages account for 833 prisoners. A note on the bottom of the last page matter-of-factly reports the fate of 192 inmates: "642–833 Unknown. The detainees died before admission, and therefore will not get any Buchenwald prisoner numbers."

I had used these lists to reconstruct who had been standing in front of and behind my father when the Blechhammer prisoners received their Auschwitz tattoos. Sifting through the Jewish subcategory of every nationality on each list, I copied all the last names starting with "L"—264 of them—into a spreadsheet. I then sorted the list by their tattoo numbers.

130282	Lajtenberg	Ksyl	2.12.25	Bendsburg	Schloss.	177902	Polish
124828	Lierens	Salomon	29.1.13	Amsterdam	Maler	177903	Holland
127575	**Lajtner**	**Jozef**	**11.8.11**	**Bendsburg**	**E. Schwss**	**177904**	**Polish**
125175	Landau	Marian	28.1.18	Bendzin	Elektr.	177905	Polish
126508	Lask	Samuel	23.2.28	Dabrowa	Elektr.	177908	Polish

A year before I came upon the lists, Marian Landau's son had responded to my query about Blechhammer prisoners on a survivor website. When I learned that Landau's number was one higher than my father's, I thought it a fantastic coincidence, not realizing the bureaucratic thinking behind it.

The lists proved themselves a valuable research tool in an unexpected way.

....

If you search the internet for images of Blechhammer, you'll find pictures of the camp's crematorium, its hulking concrete guard towers, and the white wall monument.

There are very few of prisoners.

One of the most prominent is of a man identified only as a Jewish prisoner from Blechhammer working at an electrical workshop.

The man has a pleasant face, open and clean shaven with a broad forehead and close-cropped hair. He stands at the work-bench strewn with hammers, pliers and clamps, eyes focused on the screwdriver in hand gingerly working some mechanical box. He does not at all appear malnourished or abused.

His fingers and nails are blackened with grime as is his boldly striped concentration camp jacket. If you zoom on the patch sewn to the jacket you can make out a six-pointed Jewish star and a number—177242.

I had stumbled upon the photo soon after beginning my research, and downloaded it from the Yad Vashem archives because of its vague connection to my father. Yad Veshem had no information about the photo's provenance, other than it belonged to its very early collections. "Many of those early photographs do not have additional information due to lack of proper cataloging, the various sources they come from, and the general chaos that characterized this period," said Emanuel Saunders, a spokesman for the photo archive.

Though Saunders discounts it, the photo seemed too care-fully framed, too composed, to have been completely random or candid, as if the photographer was told to get a picture of a concentration camp inmate engaged in "productive" work.

Either way, the photograph of unknown Prisoner 177242 had resided on my hard drives for years.

During my first trip to Poland, I met Edward Haduch, who belongs to a group of local history buffs, the "Blechhammer 1944 Association," dedicated to maintaining the memory of the region during the war, with major emphasis on the American air raids against the Blechhammer refineries.

Members of the group have helped track down remains of missing American airmen shot down over the area. In 2019, they completed a years-long conversion of a derelict air raid shelter into a museum with artifacts from the air campaign and the many POW and labor camps that dotted the area.

Edward also began to seriously research the Jewish Forced Labor Camp motivated by, he said, a "deep conviction that the inmates of the camp need to be honored and remembered, and the knowledge that my town is not widely recognized as a significant place on the map of the Holocaust." We had been exchanging tips and leads for years.

With some funding from the local community council, he organized an exhibit about the Blechhammer camp at the town's library. As part of the exhibit, he enlarged the photograph of Prisoner 177242 to poster size. The Auschwitz Museum loaned the exhibit a replica of the blue-gray striped concentration camp uniform. For added realism, it put the number from the poster on the pajama jacket, just like in the photo.

So when Edward Haduch asked me to help identify Prisoner 177242, I turned to the death march lists.

Searching line by line, I found him under "French Political/Jews," line 2,044, page thirty-five of List I: Jean Grynberg, born February 9, 1904 in Brest. His job is listed as electrician, just as the Yad Vashem photo had identified him.

I had put a name to a number.

Other archival databases filled in Grynberg's backstory. Trained as an engineer, Grynberg had moved to Paris before the war with his wife, the former Yocheved Bergerman, originally from Bialystok. The couple had one son, Claude, born in 1931.

Vichy French police collaborators seized the Grynbergs from their Paris apartment at Boulevard Jourdan 32. Today, a pizza and pasta restaurant occupies the ground floor of the six-story neoclassical limestone building.

The Grynbergs were sent to the Pithiviers Transit Camp, about fifty-five miles south of Paris. Jean was kept in Barack 16, separated from Yocheved and Claude, in Barrack 10. On September 21, 1942, they were among 1,051 men, women, and children sealed in cattle cars that became Transport 35 to Auschwitz Birkenau.

Just like Robert Clary's Transport 37 and Avram Halerie's Transport 38, Jean Grynberg's Transport 35 stopped at Cosel. Organization Schmelt Security Police pulled him and some 150 other men from the train. Yochevet and Claude continued on to Auschwitz. They were gassed on arrival. Of the 1,051 Jews that made up Transport 35, only twenty-nine are known to have survived the war.

Grynberg ended up in Blechhammer. Because prisoners were tattooed and given striped camp uniforms only after Blechhammer became part of Auschwitz, Grynberg's photograph must have been taken sometime after April 1944. This meant he had already survived nearly two years of forced labor. Even a cursory examination of the photo confirms some universal truths about what it took to survive in the labor camps.

A key goal was to be classified an "essential" worker. An engineer like Grynberg, or a welder like my father, would have made the cut. This qualified them for more food, about 1,700 calories a day, compared to 1,300 calories for "unskilled" laborers.

A second goal was getting assigned to indoor work, out of the harsh winters that sapped a man's strength and diminished any chance of survival.

Prisoner 177242 checked both boxes: an electrician working indoors.

However 1,700 calories was still far below the 2,500 required by an average man doing physical labor. Grynberg's relatively good physical appearance in the photograph suggests he had also learned how to "organize" additional food. As an electrician, he likely would have worked, like Sigmund Walder, near British POWs and foreign contract workers, presenting many opportunities for black market trade.

Then came the Russian offensive, the death march to Gross-Rosen, and the perilous train transport to the Buchenwald Concentration Camp near Weimar, Germany.

Chapter 19

BEECH FOREST

....

D olek Lajtner huddled in the open coal car for three days, snow his only sustenance, the bodies of his fellow prisoners his only source of warmth. Coal soot blackened his filthy striped pajamas.

Sirens screamed an approaching air raid as the train entered Weimar. The alarm adrenalized the listless, half-frozen prisoners. Those strong enough jumped off the train and made for nearby fields. Others cowered beneath the railcars as the Americans bombed and strafed the train. By all survivor accounts, scores of prisoners were killed.

The remaining prisoners were formed into columns and marched six miles to Buchenwald.

The words above the gate—*Jedem das Seine* (To Each His Own)—were prophetic. The loose brotherhood of Blechhammer prisoners disintegrated as each man had to make his own way in this new camp. *Kapos* ordered everyone to strip out of their filthy clothes. Dolek also surrendered the ankle-high leather shoes from the Blechhammer warehouse. With SS guards closely watching, the *Kapos* searched mouths, under tongues, and in anuses for contraband.

Israel Rosengarten had taped some Reichsmark notes to the sole of his foot. When his turn came, the *Kapo* neglected to look at the bottoms of his soles and Rosengarten passed through with his secret stash intact.

Dolek was not so lucky. Walking naked through a gauntlet of *Kapos* and guards, an SS man spotted the tape around his toes.

"*Vas is Das?*" What's that? He ordered Dolek to raise his leg back like a horse being shoed and removed the diamond. Glancing about quickly, the German slipped the stone into the vest pocket of his jacket.

"*Raus, schnell!*" Out, quick!

Naked, the prisoners huddled together against the cold for hours before being brought to the disinfection block. Two *Kapos* baptized Dolek in a large wooden barrel of brown disinfectant that smelled like tar, dunking his head several times. After cold showers to wash off the oily liquid, he was issued standard striped concentration camp clothing.

Only then was he fed and formally registered into Buchenwald on February 10, 1945, the same day as Jean Grynberg.

....

Nearly a year and a half had passed since I found my father's Auschwitz registration form and, in search of more information, had written to the International Tracing Service at Bad Arolsen, Germany. With all the documents, interviews, and data I had gathered in Poland, Israel, Washington, and Germany, my query had become little more than an afterthought until I spotted an article about Bad Arolsen by an old journalism buddy, Art Max, then a correspondent for the Associated Press.

I reached out to Art, who contacted the public affairs office of Bad Arolsen on my behalf. Within two weeks, an envelope arrived with copies of nine documents from Buchenwald. These included a registration form similar to one from Auschwitz, with my father's signature at the bottom and his new Buchenwald number—127575—in the upper corner. These numbers, however, were not tattooed; only Auschwitz used tattoos to catalog its prisoners.

When I think back on it, I was lucky Bad Arolsen had not responded early on. If it had, I might have stopped looking then and there, satisfied that those were all the documents that existed.

....

In February 1945, Buchenwald held one hundred twelve thousand prisoners mostly divided into two sections, the "Big Camp" and the "Little Camp."

The Big Camp warehoused political prisoners, common criminals, and German soldiers convicted of various crimes. Early in the war, the Communists had fought criminal gangs for internal control of the camp. They imposed discipline, curbed gang activity, smuggled in guns, and built a resistance movement. By February 1945, they pretty much ran things inside the wire.

The Little Camp was down a hill from the larger camp and used as a quarantine area, separated from the rest of Buchenwald by a double row of barbed wire. Seventeen barracks had been built in anticipation of the influx of new prisoners from Gross-Rosen. They proved woefully inadequate. In January, there were six thousand prisoners in the Little Camp. By April, there were seventeen thousand. Barracks designed to hold four hundred to six hundred prisoners were packed with as many two thousand. Prisoners were stacked like logs on shelves five levels high.

Jopie Braasem, the Dutch *Kapo*, shared a blanket with four prisoners in the same box. "To possess a blanket was a tremendous thing, and you had to be careful that the blanket wasn't stolen after the lights went off." Indeed, someone yanked off the blanket one night, despite attempts by a much-weakened Brassem and his bunkmates to hang on. "Quick as lightning we dived out of our box. In the dark we started throwing punches. It turned out that I had the wrong person, because I was beating up [my bunkmate] Broeks while the thief had rushed out with our blanket."

Typhoid and dysentery swept through the Little Camp. Mass starvation was a given.

My father spoke of pushing two-wheeled carts stacked with bodies. He dumped them in shallow ditches. Between January and April, fifty-two hundred prisoners died.

Among them was No. 177242, Jean Grynberg, the prisoner from the Yad Vashem photo. Grynberg's Buchenwald personnel card says he died of *lungenentzündung*—pneumonia—on March 3, 1945, about three weeks after his arrival.

Mark Beck's father, Joseph, No. 177593, died of dysentery eleven days before Buchenwald was liberated by the 6th Armored Division of Gen. George Patton's American 3rd Army.

Avram Halerie, No. 177396, the master black market smuggler, also didn't make it. An acquaintance told Halerie's daughter after the war that Halerie had been shot just before liberation.

By early March, the Germans began shipping Jews out of Buchenwald. Prisoners hid in ditches and toilets or bribed *Kapos* and guards to avoid being put on the new transport lists. My father told me it was not just the terror of another death march, but real fear of American warplanes, which were bombing anything that moved on rails.

Walter Spitzer smuggled himself to the Big Camp, where his artistic skills saved him yet again. He bartered quick portraits of prisoners for food. His skill impressed the Communist barracks leader, who took Walter under his protection in return for Walter's pledge to use his art to show the world the truth about the camps.

Robert Clary was saved by the foreman in charge of delousing, a German named Karl. Karl had been a Buchenwald prisoner since 1938. "Looking back and remembering how good he was to me and to a few other young men, I wonder if perhaps he was a homosexual," Clary recalled. "In my innocence then, and because he never made a pass of any kind, such an idea never occurred to me." Three weeks after Clary arrived in Buchenwald, Karl arranged for him to be transferred to the Big Camp under the protection of a French Communist cadre.

My father's last diamond was gone. "I had nothing left to bribe. A friend offered to pay the bribe for me. He said, 'Dolek, stay. The Americans will be here soon.' But I turned him down. I felt my destiny was to leave. He said I was crazy . . ."

Dad said he learned after the war that a few days before the Americans arrived, his friend was among three hundred prisoners taken out to the forest and shot.

So you see son, in the end it didn't matter if you had money or not, were smart or dumb. Life was worth nothing—absolutely nothing. You needed luck.

Dad never told me where the Germans had sent him. The records from Bad Arolsen did. One card written in block letters was stamped Natzweiler March 9, 1945.

My father's name was also on another Bad Arolsen document, a partial transport list titled "Wurst I" (Desert 1). So was Joseph Braasem's. In his testimonial, Braasem said he had been shipped to the Bisingen Concentration Camp, about 110 miles from the French border. Bisingen was a subcamp of Natzweiler, and Wurst I was a facility tasked with turning oil shale into fuel.

Conditions at Bisingen were murderous. In the year before my father's arrival in March 1945, more than 1,500 of the camp's 4,150 prisoners had died.

The shale oil operation itself was a sham. Hundreds of prisoners chipped out shale from nearby quarries and crushed it with hand rollers or hammers into small pieces. The shale was then shoveled into long shallow trenches. Once ignited with a minimum of air, the theory was the warmed shale would release its oil. The oil would be gathered by a series of pipes and processing tanks that my father and his fellow welders constructed. It never worked. Only drops of oil dripped into the waiting pans.

Fearing transfer to the Eastern Front, the German camp *Kommandant* surreptitiously added oil to the shale slags to keep the project going. It didn't help. The *Kommandant* was relieved of his command by Oswald Pohl, head of the Concentration Camp Directorate.

With French Allied forces closing in, Bisingen was evacuated between April 14 and April 16, 1945. The prisoners were sent on yet another forced march toward Bavaria. Fearing attack by Allied warplanes, the columns moved through the German countryside only at night.

Chapter 20

ESCAPE AND FREEDOM

D olek knew he was fading. This night's march had been long, too long. *It's not fair*, he thought, *not fair to have come so far and to have survived so much to end like this, to die like a dog by the side of a road.*

The black night grudgingly surrendered to the predawn gray. A rising breeze smelled of spring and pine needles. Ahead, a giant willow tree loomed over a wide bend in the road.

Most of the German guards were aging pensioners drafted into the Home Guard. The old-timer in front of Dolek's row sported a World War I great coat that reached his knees and a rifle of the same vintage. He seemed more focused on lighting his big-bowled pipe then on his prisoners, vainly striking match after match in the stiffening breeze.

No time to think, to weigh, to consider. Just act. As he passed beneath the willow's branches, Dolek dropped into a ditch at the bend of the road. His fellow prisoners closed ranks. The old guard never stopped sucking at his pipe.

Dolek buried his face in the dead leaves, his body enshrouded by the willow's drooping branches. He inhaled the sour smell of rotting vegetation and damp soil, willing his body still, absolutely still. Above, the hollow clack-clack of wooden clogs shuffling past. *Maybe they think I'm already dead.*

Minutes passed. The scraping feet began to fade. The SS Rear Kommando would soon arrive with their dogs and machine guns. He jiggled off his wooden clogs.

A bird chirped. Dawn.

Now!

Dolek sprang from the ditch into the thick forest beyond, seeing little of what lay ahead, certain only of death behind.

"*Halt! Juden Halt!*"

The crack of rifle fire echoed through the forest.

With only rags on his feet, Dolek ran, stumbled, and ran again until confronted by a wall of weathered stone. His hands exploded in pain as he reached over the top: shards of glass imbedded in the mortar slashed his palms. Dolek wrapped his hands with strips of cloth ripped from his camp jacket and clambered over the wall using adrenalin his body had no right to own. Shivering, near collapse, he paused long enough to hear the barking of dogs.

Through the emerging dawn, he found himself at a farm. He made for the barn, climbed the wooden ladder to the loft, and fell exhausted into the straw.

The sun was high when he awoke to voices from below. Peering over the edge of the loft, he saw an old German farmer roll in a small wooden cart, the two-wheeled kind that always creaks. It was covered by a sheet of canvas.

The farmer left. Dolek climbed down from the loft. Lifting the canvas, he saw the cart was filled with food—round loaves of black peasant bread, hard salami, and a large crock of schmaltz (goose fat). It took a couple of trips to get it all up the ladder. He filled a bucket with water from a trough in the barn. No good: It was too heavy and he was too weak to wrestle it up the ladder. He drank his fill and climbed to the loft, exhausted and afraid.

For the next two days, Dolek did not leave that barn. He used the far side of the horseshoe-shaped loft as a toilet. Mostly, he slept, ate, and slept some more.

On the second night, the countryside erupted with artillery that lit up the sky like a spring lightning storm. The barn reverberated with the rumble of passing armor and trucks.

The third morning dawned peaceful and still, sunny and warm. Dolek climbed from the loft and, armed with a piece of wood, confronted the farmer in the yard.

The Allies came through here last night, the old man said. "*Für Sie ist der Krieg vorbei.*" For you, the war is over.

Dolek stared at the old man. No cry of joy, no sob of relief—certainly not in front of this German stranger. He was wary even as the farmer's wife brought out a thick country soup and black bread smeared with goose fat. He never let on he was the thief who had stolen their food. If they suspected, they never mentioned it.

"*Du riechst wie ein Scheißloch,*" the farmer said. You smell like a shithole. He dragged a shallow zinc tub into the yard, much like the ones Dolek had galvanized at the Josef Skopek Werke back in Strzemieszyce, back a few lifetimes ago. The farmer began shuttling buckets of warm water from the farmhouse.

Dolek stripped off the striped pajamas and stepped into the low tub.

Seeing Dolek's naked body, the farmer dropped the bucket. "*Jesus Maria! Schauen Sie, was diese Bastarde haben fertig!*" he shouted. Jesus Mary! Look at what these bastards have done!

Dolek's skeleton nearly pushed through his skin. His legs and arms were stalks of bruised skin and bone.

With rough hands and a gentle touch, the old farmer helped wash away the impacted dirt, all the time muttering, "*Ach, Gott im Himmel, Gott im Himmel.*"

The farmer's wife wrapped the worst of the sores with clean bandages and salve. Clucking to herself quietly, she rinsed out Dolek's striped pajamas at his request and hung them to dry in the morning sun. They were his only form of identity and Dolek feared being mistaken for a German by some trigger-happy Allied soldier.

That afternoon, fed, bathed, and rested, he thanked the farmer and his wife and walked up the road toward the village where the farmer had told him French forces were encamped. At a roadblock, soldiers scrutinized the identification cards of German civilians. Any male of military age was pulled to the side.

"Who are you?" a soldier asked in broken German.

"I am a Polish Jew and escaped from the Germans," Dolek said, exposing the blue line of numbers on his left arm.

The soldier turned out to be a Polish national fighting with the Free French Army.

Right away, they were talking in Polish like long-lost cousins. He told Dolek they had been finding Jews wandering the countryside and were putting them up at the village school.

Another soldier with stripes on his sleeve wrote out a pass and pointed Dolek toward the school. "What else do you need?" he asked.

"Well, some clothes . . ."

The Polish soldier pointed his M1 Garand rifle at a middle-aged German waiting at the checkpoint. "Strip," he said. The German immediately dropped his trousers and took off his shirt and jacket.

Dolek took the clothes without a second thought.

"This'll do for now, thanks."

"Well, you are free now. And safe."

The date was April 21, 1945, forty years to the day before I would eulogize my father at the Riverside Memorial Chapel, on Amsterdam Avenue, in New York City.

Chapter 21

AFTERLIFE

....

The French military evacuated Josef Dolek Lajtner to Paris in May 1945.

Dolek's four half brothers—Wolf, Kysl, Solomon, and Benjamin, and their families—were never heard from again. There is evidence, however, that Wolf, who was in the Polish army, had been captured by the Germans. Jewish POWs were separated from their Polish Christian comrades and summarily executed or sent to concentration camps. A Wolf Lajtner born on February 15, 1899, the same date as my father's half brother, is listed on an Auschwitz "registry of dead inmates" as prisoner 134312, having died between December 1943 and January 1944.

My father's half sister, Natka, was luckier. She had been on a skiing vacation with her husband in Eastern Poland when the war broke out. They were in the part of Poland annexed by Russia under the Hitler-Stalin Pact. The Soviets sent them and thousands of other refugees from Hitler to a labor camp in Siberia, where Natka's husband became a truck driver.

In Paris, Dolek was put up at a mansion owned by the Rothschild banking family, who had lent it to the American Jewish Joint Distribution Committee for use as a DP, or displaced persons, camp. There he met Henci Gross, a twenty-one-year-old survivor from Hungary. She had been separated from her father on the infamous ramp at Auschwitz Birkenau on May 27, 1944.

For eight weeks Henci had been in Women's Section C, Block 16, a short walk from the Birkenau gas chambers and crematoria. She shared a sleeping shelf with four other women. They became a close-knit group, watching over and encouraging one another. They called themselves the *finiv schvesters*, the five sisters. I learned of this not from my mother—she never spoke of the war—but in a group interview with three of the five surviving "sisters" in Jerusalem more than fifteen years after my mother's death.

Starting on July 25, 1944, the five were transferred to a series of concentration camps and rented out to companies like Siemens Electric, where Henci inserted filaments in light bulbs. Because the work required dexterity and care, food rations were adequate and abuse by guards minimized. She was liberated at Salzwedel satellite camp by the US Army's 84th Division on April 14, 1945.

Henci had an older brother who had immigrated to the United States in the 1920s and lived somewhere in New York, though she had no idea where, much less how to contact him. Dolek wrote of Henci's dilemma to his sister, Dorothy, living in Brooklyn. Yiddish newspapers in New York at the time were running pages of classified ads from families seeking information about missing loved ones. Dorothy's ad was spotted by Henci's older brother, Fischel, who was living in Brooklyn's Coney Island neighborhood, and contact was made.

Dolek and Henci were married before a rabbi in Paris in 1945.

Despite both having siblings, and in Dolek's case, a mother, living in the United States, US Consular officials did not approve their visa application until late 1948. Washington had slowed immigration approvals to a trickle for fear that Communist agents might infiltrate America along with the refugees.

By the time their visas were approved, Henci was very pregnant with me. A consular officer gently suggested she wait until after the birth before travel. "I told him I would not have my baby born on European soil drenched with Jewish blood," she had told me. Though entering her ninth month of pregnancy, travel was approved. Flying into the old Idlewild Airport, my parents arrived in New York City about three weeks before I did.

They Americanized the spelling of Lajtner to Laytner.

Dad joined the Amalgamated Clothing Workers Union on March 3, 1949, and began pressing suits at Ripley Clothing. They lived briefly in Brooklyn before, Mom liked to say, she "escaped" to Manhattan and a fifth-floor walk-up on the Upper West Side. A more likely reason was that Grandma Felicia and Aunt Dorothy lived four blocks away. Within a couple of years, we moved to the West 83rd Street apartment with its functioning elevator.

In August 1954, my parents took me to the old Polo Grounds baseball stadium, then home of the New York Giants and Willy Mays. To a child of six it seemed all fifty-six thousand seats were filled with immigrants like my parents who, on command, stood and solemnly swore "to support and defend the Constitution and laws of the United States of America."

Under "visible distinctive marks," Joseph Laytner's Certificate of Naturalization notes, "mole on left cheek, concentration camp number on arm."

That same month, Dad formally applied for reparations from Germany.

While his Auschwitz tattoo was pretty compelling evidence that he had, in fact, been a concentration camp inmate, the Germans required affidavits from friends affirming his identity. The German calculations were largely based on the number of days my father was a prisoner of the German camp system—fifty-three months and eighteen days. For this, he received a one-time payment of about $1,400 ($14,010 in 2021 dollars), and a monthly stipend. Later, he also received a smaller payment covering the time between the German invasion of Poland, September 1, 1939, and when he was first sent to a labor camp in October

1940. Over the years, the monthly stipend was recalculated for inflation. When my father died in 1985, he was collecting $84 a month. Mom had also applied for reparations but never received them, she said, because she couldn't prove her timeline to the satisfaction of the German courts.

In 1961, Dolek became Joe, the candy store man. By 1970, New York City was a dark, dangerous place. Crime was soaring, pegged to a rising heroin epidemic. Prostitutes in hot shorts and long fur coats strutted Broadway and the Upper West Side, the tricked-out Cadillacs of their pimps always idling nearby. I started carrying a small can of pepper spray—and used it once to ward off a determined mugger with a knife in 1972 near Columbia University.

Burglars broke into the candy store with increasing frequency. They'd use a car jack to bend up the scissor gate a couple feet, smash the lower glass transom of the door, and crawl into the store. They stole mostly cartons of cigarettes. Dad moved the cigarette inventory to our apartment around the corner. After the next break-in, he started bringing home the boxes of cigars.

The burglaries were part of a much bigger problem. In 1960, New York had 482 murders. In 1970, that rose to 1,117. In 1960, guns were blamed for 19 percent of the murders; by 1970, that figure had jumped to 48 percent.

Fewer and fewer people ventured out at night. Helen and Joe started closing the store by 8 o'clock on the longer days of spring and summer and by 7 o'clock on the short days of winter. Though their hours were less brutal, the worsening business rekindled the fiery arguments over money that had tapered off in the previous few years.

....

On March 28, 1970, I drove Dad to a wedding in Schenectady, in upstate New York. The bride was the daughter of my father's cousin Sabina, whose testimonial I would use more than thirty-seven years later in reconstructing the liquidation of the Strzemieszyce ghetto. We planned to spend the night after the wedding with Pola, Sabina's sister, whose testimonial I also used for the Strzemieszyce story. We would return to New York the next day, which fell on Easter Sunday.

Mom never got on with Dad's side of the family, and keeping the candy store open with the help of her cousin was a convenient excuse to remain behind. Business promised to be slow on Easter weekend.

Back then, I wasn't much into extended family and forgot how Sabina and Pola were related to us within five minutes of Dad's explanation. I was looking forward to having quality time alone with my father, without Mom dominating the conversation or him splitting his attention with my kid brother, who was an annoying thirteen-year-old at the time. Thankfully, Alan was even less interested in coming than I was in having him tag along.

The road trip was incentive enough. I was twenty-two and infatuated with my first car, a well-used, dark blue Volvo 144. It boasted a six-speed stick shift and features that came to US-made cars only years later: front-wheel drive, radial tires, four-wheel disc brakes, three-point seat belts, and reclining bucket seats. True, the four-cylinder engine burned a quart of oil per thousand miles. True, the car spent too much time in the shop for things I had never heard of, like timing gears. Still, I hit 110 mph on the Napeague Run between Amagansett and Montauk before adrenalin started to make my hands shake.

The wedding was beautiful. The bride was my second cousin Shula, whom I had never met. She was breathtakingly lovely, with thick black hair and a stunning smile. There were quite a few relatives among the hundreds of guests, yet I knew no one well enough to schmooze for more than ninety seconds. Instead, I drank quietly at the singles table and listened to Shula's girl-friends talk trash about her in a most mean-girls sort of way.

Back at Pola's house, my father slept in the guest bedroom and I on a pullout sofa in the living room.

Dad woke me about 3:00 a.m. He couldn't pass urine. At fifty-nine, he had been suffering from an enlarged prostate for some time, but a total blockage had never happened before. I rushed him to the emergency room, where a doctor drained the bladder with a catheter. We were back at Pola's in an hour.

At 6:00 a.m., Dad woke me again, and again we hurried to the emergency room. That same doctor again drained the urine and suggested we get back to New York City and the care of his regular physician. This time, the doctor left the catheter in place, attached a flexible tube to the end, and folded it closed with a rubber band. Should Dad need to urinate, the rubber band could be loosened. The doctor also gave him drugs to help him relax.

I phoned Mom that we were driving home. She would notify the doctor and arrange the hospital. Dad soon fell asleep in the reclined bucket seat. Turning onto the New York State Thruway, I pushed the Volvo hard and drove the first ninety miles in one hour.

It began to snow. Light swirls at first, then heavy flakes. Just south of New Paltz, Exit 17, Dad woke moaning and complaining of pressure. I pulled the car over and helped him undo the rubber band and drain the bladder into the bottle we had brought along for that purpose.

It took just ten minutes, but when I got ready to drive again, the snow was piled thick against the windshield.

The Volvo wouldn't start. Dad, passing in and out of consciousness, was now moaning in Yiddish, "Oh my God, Oh my God."

I pulled two road flares from the trunk. Of course we had no matches. I used the Volvo's cigarette lighter to ignite one flare and then used it to light the other. I placed the flares about fifty feet behind the car.

I begged the Volvo to start up. The motor turned over on the first try. I got back out and buried the flares in slushy dirt at the side of the highway. Wind-driven snow cut like glass. My socks were soggy and my fingers numb.

The snow was blinding, what radio announcers call near whiteout conditions. Keeping the Volvo mostly in second gear, the entire highway appeared littered with cars upended in ditches or sitting dark and dead like roadkill along the shoulders. Dad alternated between sleep and moans.

The snow tapered some closer to the city, but it was afternoon before I pulled up to our apartment building on West 81st Street and buzzed upstairs. My mother and brother rushed down. Mom was whiter than the snow. This was before cell phones, and we hadn't been in contact since that early morning phone call. We drove to the Medical Arts Center Hospital across town.

The storm had surprised forecasters. Newspapers called it the Easter Sunday Blizzard. It dumped more than nine inches along the Thruway and four in New York City, which cancelled the Easter Day Parade.

That week, as my father lay recuperating from surgery in the hospital, the candy store was burglarized again.

It never reopened.

With business declining, my parents had been talking to their friend Sam Kliger about opening a linen store in the candy store space. Sam's wife, Anne, and my mother were alumni of the Bedford Hills tuberculosis ward. Sam had been selling "domestics" out of the trunk of his Oldsmobile, going door-to-door in Italian neighborhoods of Brooklyn. It helped that Sam spoke fluent Italian.

Even if the candy store had been thriving, working twelve-hour days, six-and-a-half days a week, was now out of the question. So, nearly sixty, an age when many men begin contemplating retirement, Dad reinvented himself again, starting a business with his wife about which they knew absolutely nothing.

As for me, I was entering graduate school where I would tell Helen Epstein that my parents' Holocaust trauma had nothing to do with me.

The soda fountain, cooler, and ice-cream freezer were ripped out. The old mahogany-stained shelves were painted white and repurposed for sheets and towels. The front glass counter that once boasted boxes of cigars now displayed lacy ladies' handkerchiefs and boudoir pillow shams. Dad installed a stout brass door chain to screen customers and control entry. At night, a heavy opaque roll-down gate covered the entire storefront. A bright orange sign overhead read, "Laytner's Linen Shop."

Citibank declined my parents' application for a loan or line of credit even though they had been customers for nine years. This made building inventory tough. Dad subwayed to Soho and the Lower East Side to fill individual customer orders from local "jobbers"—small wholesalers who accepted only cash payment. Schlepping multiple shopping bags in each hand, he'd return by subway in time to open the store at 10 o'clock in the morning.

Sam Kliger also introduced my parents to his cousin, Sidney Pitter, a big, loud-talking, cigar-chomping jobber who operated out of a basement warehouse in Soho in the decades before gentrification. One day, Sidney visited the linen shop, looked around, and declared that if my parents sold every sheet, towel, and pillow in the place, they still wouldn't generate enough cash to pay the rent.

"But we can't afford merchandise," Dad said.

"Don't worry about it," Sidney said. "Pay me in ninety days."

Mom's cousin Dave drove Dad and me down to Soho in his faded blue Valiant and packed the car—trunk, seats, roof—so full of merchandise that Dad and I had to take the subway back uptown. This was repeated several times. The inventory was a godsend. It helped stabilize the store, and business gradually improved.

About two years later, the elderly proprietor of the portrait studio next door died unexpectedly. My parents bought out the lease from the widow, who had left behind some photo equipment. Alan, still in high school, brought the old Beseler enlarger, chemicals, and photo paper up to the apartment. He turned the bathroom into a darkroom and taught himself how to develop black-and-white prints.

Combining both stores into one was too expensive. Instead, a local carpenter cut a doorway in the plaster and lath wall and built shelves from two-by-four pieces of lumber. The new space became the bath and tabletop departments. From the street, it looked like two separate stores. An orange sign over the new space read, "Under One Roof/Bath & Table Decor."

Instead of a chocolate-stained apron, Dad now wore a suit and tie. Instead of "Joe," customers now called him "Mr. Laytner." My brother and I came to understand that, at heart, Dad was an Old World European gentleman, and these seemingly small things mattered to his sense of self. He seemed more relaxed and smiled more. It was clear that he cared more about the linen shop than he ever had the candy store. This time, the lease was in his name as well as my mother's.

By 1980, Dad was turning sixty-nine and it was time to either pack it in or pass the business on. By then, I had been working for United Press International in New York City for eight years, and was about to be posted to London. Joining the family business didn't even come up for discussion.

Alan stepped up. He had been helping in the store through-out high school and college and even while pursuing an MFA in theater at Columbia University.

"I felt we were going to be forced out of the Upper West Side right when it was starting to get better," he said. "I didn't want us to be gentrified out of the neighborhood." Alan also readily admit-ted to another motive: He wanted to be respectable enough, with a steady enough income, to marry Rachelle, the girl he was dating.

Alan negotiated a new ten-year lease, hired an architect and contractor, and renovated the store to a modern space appro-priate for the improving neighborhood. Since crime was still rampant, Alan installed a new roll-down gate and a buzzer on the door like in apartment buildings to screen customers before allowing entry. He married Rachelle four years later.

Over the following years, Alan oversaw several expansions that grew the store from its original three hundred square feet to about one thousand three hundred square feet. By the mid-1980s, Laytner's Linen had become a neighborhood fixture. Though Dad could now well afford taxis, he still took the subway downtown occasionally to fill customer orders, schlepping the shopping bags back by subway to the store.

It was the day after one such subway jaunt that he suffered his fatal heart attack.

Chapter 22

POLAND REDUX

In October 2015, the Auschwitz Museum honored Walter Spitzer, then eighty-eight, with a one-man show. He was to be wined, dined, and feted for three days. He left after thirty-six hours.

At the show's opening, I meet Walter in Block 12 of the main Auschwitz I Camp, where several rooms have been converted to a temporary gallery space. Walter stands no more than five feet four, and appears alarmed as boisterous millennial Poles surge around him like groupies at a rock concert.

The Auschwitz Museum owns several of Spitzer's works. Others were shipped in from Paris. Copies of early drawings came from the Ghetto Fighters Museum in Israel, the same museum that houses my father's sentencing report in an acid-free plastic wrapper.

Museum officials navigate us—Walter, his son Benjamin, and me—past dozens of oil paintings, watercolors, and prints depicting scenes of daily camp life, emaciated *Muselmanner*, and the death march. From there, Walter is guest of honor at a symposium about art in the concentration camps. The auditorium is packed but the discussion is in Polish. I peel off and head to the archives to double-check the number of punishment reports with Joseph Braasem's name on them.

That evening, I catch up with Walter and Benjamin in the restaurant of the five-star hotel at which they're staying on Krakow's gloriously medieval Market Square. When I arrive, they are debating the merits of a bottle of red wine with the waiter, who happens to be an Israeli national working in Poland.

After learning of the museum's plans nearly a year before, I had rescheduled my third trip to Poland to coincide with this exhibit. In the nine years since I was last here, I had come to realize I had missed the significance of some places I had seen and missed seeing some significant places. The delay would be worth it: Walter had agreed to accompany me to the sites of the Strzemieszyce ghetto and the Blechhammer camp.

Now Walter is apologetic but firm. "Too hard, too many memories, too much pain. The people at the museum have treated me correctly—very correctly—I have no complaints. The young people especially are very interested. But I am not comfortable being here. I need to go home, to Paris."

Protest is pointless. It's hard to argue with a determined eighty-eight-year-old survivor. Walter will return to Paris the following afternoon, after showing Benjamin his family home in Cieszyn, about an hour's drive from Auschwitz. Walter was just thirteen when he and his mother were evicted from that home in 1940 as part of the Nazi ethnic-cleansing program. They ended up in that small ghetto in Strzemieszyce.

....

The next day I visit Strzemieszyce without Walter Spitzer to help navigate my way. I had last been here on a sweltering June day nine years ago to find the house where my father had lived before he was deported to Blechhammer.

I had gotten the address—Lauge Strasse 40—off his Auschwitz registration form. But our local guide at the time said he had never heard of a Lauge Street, which made the entire visit pretty pointless, with no sense of place, nor closure.

Some years later, I had discovered a small error in translation that made me want to kick myself: A survivor's testimonial identified the one-street ghetto as being on Ul Dluga, Polish for Long Street, which translates to Lange Strasse in German.

In retrospect the mistake was obvious: The translator I had hired had misread the cursive script on the Auschwitz form as a "U" instead of "N."

My guide this time is Jakub Czuprynski, a professional genealogist. Jakub had arranged for the local historian, Jan Kimoitek, to show us around Strzemieszyce. An active and gregarious eighty-two-year-old, Jan has a PhD in chemistry and had retired as a director of a factory that made chemicals for the soap and detergent industries.

Jan and his wife welcome us to their modest home with coffee and cake. An upright piano sits against one wall of the low-beamed living room, a coal-burning heating stove at another.

Before we can remove our coats, Jan says, "Yes, I'll remember that day all my life—the wagons stacked with bodies, blood dripping from the bottom."

I grab my digital recorder and ask Jan repeat what he just said, with Jakub again translating, slowly. Here was another witness to the destruction of the ghetto that tore my father's family apart more than seventy years before—and from a very different perspective.

Jan was ten years old at the time. During the ghetto's liquidation, Strzemieszyce's Polish Christian population kept to their homes. After the gunfire had tapered off, Jan and some friends, as kids do, edged closer to the ghetto to see what they could see.

One boy spotted a line of horse-drawn carts. The boys rushed to the street in time to see four or five carts pass on their way to the hills above the village.

The carts, Jan says, were stacked with bodies "of men too old to walk, women and children . . . it is difficult for a child of ten to absorb this, and it affected me greatly."

The coffee in my cup is cold, the cake on the plate uneaten. Neither Jakub nor Jan had finished theirs, either.

From Jan's home we drive to the site of the ghetto, the same neighborhood I had walked nine years earlier, the one that had never seen better days nor, I was sure, ever would.

I was wrong. The street is in the midst of gentrification.

Ul Dluga, or Lange Strasse, has been renamed Gruszczynskiego, which has way too many connected consonants for me to pronounce. Nine years ago, the street was potholed and cracked, and all the red brick buildings dilapidated. Now most of the houses are modern, single-family homes in pleasant pastel greens, tans, and browns. There are fenced-in driveways, neat flower beds, and expansive backyards. Some of these newer houses stand next to derelict, heavy red brick buildings with peeling tarpaper roofs and crumbling facades.

The hollowed-out *Judenrat* building with its sad blue sign is gone, its footprint now an open grassy field. A modern red brick and gray granite monument sits close to the corner. A large bronze plaque is engraved with a simple drawing of a Jewish Menorah. The Polish inscription reads, "To the Memory of Jews from the ghetto in Strzemieszyce. It was established in April 1942 and it was liquidated in June 1943."

The plaque is dated July 2006. This means the *Judenrat* building had been torn down and replaced by this monument just a month after I had visited the village.

Jan provides a running commentary that Jakub translates into my digital recorder: This was where the wire fence ran, no, not barbed wire, just a wire fence . . . This is where the Jews were gathered for the *selektion* . . . That grocery store used to be a Jewish tailor's shop; Jan's parents were friends with the owners . . . A local *volksdeutsch* (ethnic-German) policeman had his uniforms custom-made there, and Jan had acted as translator.

"What was the policeman's name?" I ask.

Jan thinks a moment. "Yohen."

A chill marches up my spine. *Is "Yohen" the "Jonas" who nearly shot my father's cousin, Sabina? The same Sabina whose daughter's wedding we had attended the weekend of the Easter Sunday Blizzard?*

We get out of the car in front of number 40. It is a two-story mid-century modern in light ochre and contrasting brown stucco. *So much for finding Dad's house.* Jan offers that many houses are not really "new" but have been given facelifts of fresh stucco and paint, new windows and roofs. "So," I wonder out loud, "how do we know if this was No. 40 Lange Strasse in fresh paint or a completely new structure?"

"We ask," Jan says, as he turns and knocks on the front door.

The woman who answers smiles as Jan explains our mission. She confirms that while the facade is new, the house itself dates back to the war—and invites us inside for a look. The woman digs through old family photo albums and comes up with a snapshot of the prerenovated house: dark red brick, a sharply peaked roofline, and heavily mullioned windows.

It is strange walking through these pleasantly furnished rooms, wondering in which one Dad had lived, whether the heating stove had always been in that corner . . . I try to imagine several families jammed into this small house.

The woman says the house had belonged to distant relatives before the war and that the Nazis had evicted all the Polish residents to make room for the ghetto. Her parents had told her that after the ghetto's liquidation, "many, but not all" of the Poles who moved into the now-empty houses had ripped up floors and walls looking for hidden Jewish gold.

"Even then they thought the Jews had secret treasure," she says, shaking her head.

Whatever closure I had hoped to find, I wouldn't find it here. Time had moved on. A former slum was becoming hip and fashionable, much like Krakow's old Jewish quarter of Kazimierz. Still, there's a respectful monument dominating a quiet street corner recalling the terrible events of June 23, 1943.

We drive a half mile to the former Josef Skopek Werke. It is still an industrial site, a sprawling, dusty cement and coal yard, with rows of small buildings that Jan says had been part of the old Skopek factory. In truth, they could have been any worn factory workshops in any rust-belt town across America. Again, any sense of closure eludes me.

Then, beyond the low buildings and high piles of coal, across a knee-high wire fence, I see expansive fields of hip-high grass dotted with hundreds and hundreds of yellow flowers. Jan and Jakub stop chatting and stare as I walk to the edge of the fields and snap photo after photo of the tall grass gently rippling in the breeze. In my mind's eye, it is no longer a blustery October afternoon but a warm, cloudless June morning. Dolek Lajtner, frightened and panting, crouches in the tall grass and yellow flowers, "*. . . But they sent in bands of Hilterjugend. They locked arms in rows and combed through the fields and I was caught.*"

The next morning, we arrive at my father's house in Dabrowa at what is now Augustynika 3. I had learned that a small foundation funded by a survivor from the region has, with the cooperation of Dabrowa City Hall, placed signs on a number of buildings with the names and professions of their prewar Jewish owners.

Sure enough, there's the sign prominently posted on the front of the house: "W. Lajtner/Coal Sales/Wholesale and Retail/ Pilsudskiego 3." The "W" was for Wolf, my father's half brother.

Time had moved on here, too. When I had seen the house last, the hallways reeked of urine and graffiti covered the walls. Now, they are freshly painted and clean. Workmen are installing a new roof, metal flashing, and gutters. Many windows have been replaced with modern double-glazed glass.

The next day, we drive to Blechhammer, where we meet Edward Haduch, the Polish researcher who had organized the exhibit about the forced labor camp at his community library.

With Edward leading me through dense brush, I get a better sense of the camp's layout than I had in my previous two visits. I confirm details that only matter to a writer: Was the entrance to the camp a pull-down or swing-out gate? (Hinges indicate it was a swing gate, though some old photos also show a drop-down barrier.) Was the sixteen-foot wall that had surrounded the camp made of cement slabs, as some survivor accounts suggested? (No, the remaining sections show it was constructed of large reddish-and-gray blocks.) Was it really topped with electrified barbed wire? (Yes, and I have a piece of a ceramic insulator to prove it.)

Blechhammer is as I remembered: the white memorial wall with the stylized barbed wire at one end of the open field, the squat crematorium at the other. Both had recently been repainted, bright white and glossy black, respectively.

There is one surprising new addition: a large colorful sign near the crematorium building. In four languages, it directs visitors to tune their CityWalk smartphone app to Stop 501 to learn about the Blechhammer Forced Labor Camp for Jews and the crematorium. It's sponsored by the Blechhammer-1944 Association and funded by a European Union grant. It is one stop along fifteen miles of bicycle and hiking paths with forty-three sites. These include the remains of underground hospitals, air-raid bunkers, antiaircraft emplacements, and the Blechhammer camp.

The recorded lesson may be only a minute or two, but it is an eon beyond what I would have dreamed possible nine years earlier when I believed in my heart that Blechhammer was doomed to be forgotten.

I try making sense of it all: Walter Spitzer honored by the Auschwitz Museum . . . the Lajtner name commemorated on the wall of Grandpa's house . . . a new memorial to the liquidated ghetto in Strzemieszyce . . . the history of Blechhammer a click away on a smartphone app.

To the dwindling ranks of survivors like Walter Spitzer, none of these matter. Their lives, like my parents' lives, were ripped apart and indelibly scarred by Hitler-and-the-Nazis. Would Dad feel any different than Walter? Would he have even wanted to see the Lajtner name on the wall of his childhood home?

For many of my "Second Generation" peers, nothing Poland can do will atone for its dark anti-Semitic history. As I write these words, anti-Semitic incidents have flared across Europe and in the United States. Yet neither Augustynika 3 nor Strzemieszyce are anyone's idea of tourist destinations, and the inscriptions on both memorials are *only* in Polish.

For whom, then, are they meant?

....

On a cold, rainy November morning soon after returning home, I drive alone to the cemetery in suburban New Jersey where my parents are buried. I feel guilty because I don't come out here often enough, not even the customary once-a-year pilgrimage during the High Holy Days. Now, after Poland, I am drawn here though I cannot fully articulate why any more than I could fully explain to friends why I had journeyed into the heart of my father's darkness.

The cemetery entrance is easy to miss—a sharp left from an underpass beneath Interstate I-80. I bear right before the cemetery offices and slowly drive up Abraham Avenue, past Naomi Walk and Maimonides Circle, past row after row of gray granite markers that fade like forgotten memories into the rainy mist.

When it came time to unveil Dad's headstone a year after his passing, Mom, Alan, and I discussed the inscription at length, wanting to keep it simple but get it right, knowing in our hearts the words would never be adequate. We settled on "Beloved Husband/Father/Grandfather" even though Dad had missed the last part by four months.

I scrounge pebbles and small stones from the ground and, following custom, place them on the headstones. Thinking back, Dad never dwelled on the past, never bemoaned his lost life of privilege and wealth, never complained about the hard years in America . . . In fact, he never complained about anything. He also never talked much of his childhood or his vanished family, only those vague vignettes about the war, and even those had been largely scrubbed of blood.

I take off my gloves and caress the cold gray granite. Everything I remember about my father has been colored by what I've learned since about his life before me. I had always thought him cerebral and contemplative, or was he just depressed and defeated? Did he read incessantly because he was intellectually curious or because he was avoiding the reality of dead-end jobs and money woes? At some point during the years of research I realized that my father had suffered from depression through most of my childhood. Though hardly a revelation now, at that moment it was startling and sad and explained so very much.

The father I knew never listened to music; that he had led fellow prisoners in song while marching to slave labor was unthinkable. The father I knew never wanted to exercise and was never in shape, and yet he had been tough enough to survive a thirteen-day death march through a frozen Polish winter. The father I knew was never any kind of wheeler-dealer, much less a black marketeer of schnapps and diamonds to POWs and Poles. I never had a clue how much the war had changed him.

In his later years, he became visibly happier, more content. I simply assumed it was the success of the linen shop and working with Alan that was behind the change. Looking back now, perhaps it was time itself more than material success that was the great healer. Or maybe material success could have come only with the passage of time.

Elie Wiesel said he waited ten years before writing about the war. Jorge Semprun, a Spaniard who became Minister of Culture in Spain, said it took him nearly forty years before he could fully write about his experiences in Buchenwald. Both Robert Clary and Sigmund Walder said it took decades before they could confront their own traumatic histories. Dad never wrote a memoir. Unlike his cousins Sabina and Pola or his friend Motek Kleiman, he never videotaped his stories. That's on me: I should have, and could have, recorded them myself. I'll forever regret that I didn't.

Growing up, I had always preferred the macho gregariousness of Uncle Ari, Mom's younger brother, to my father's quiet circumspection. Where Dad was self-effacing, Ari instantly became the center of attention whenever he walked into a room. Ari was tall and handsome. He flirted easily with women. Dad was short and round and, well, Dad. Ari had smuggled himself from Hungary to Palestine, fought in the British army, then fought in Israel's battles. Ari seemed infinitely more exciting than my father and became my role model in many ways.

Standing before my parents' perpetually cared for graves, in this manicured suburban cemetery on a rainy November morning, I understand that whatever Uncle Ari did as a warrior pales in comparison to what Dad did to survive.

Josef Dolek Lajtner was indeed a most Beloved Husband, Father, and Grandfather. He was also, as Walter Spitzer had said so long ago, one smart, tough bastard—and I found the Nazi documents that prove it.

EPILOGUE

·····························

Walter Spitzer was liberated in Buchenwald by the US Army on April 11, 1945. He soon was drawing portraits of American GIs and was adopted as their unit's mascot. Quickly picking up English, he served as a translator for the 3526 Signal Service Company of the US Signal Corps. The GIs literally passed a hat and raised money to send him to art school in Paris. I have a letter from a former American Army lieutenant confirming this.

On a whim, Walter joined a friend in July 1945 on a weekend trip to Moissac, in the South of France, and was surprised to see his old friend Dolek. Each had assumed the other dead. The two friends embraced and kissed like the family they no longer had.

Walter stayed on in France to become a successful artist. He has illustrated books by Jean Paul Sartre and André Malraux. In 1994, his melancholy sculpture of men, women, and children awaiting deportation to Auschwitz was dedicated by French President Francois Mitterrand in a quiet Paris park about a ten-minute walk from the Eiffel Tower.

He was named a knight of the Legion of Honor, an officer of the National Order of Merit, and a knight of Arts and Letters.

Walter Spitzer died of complications from Covid-19 on April 13, 2021. He was 93.

....

Karl Demerer, the *Judenälteste* credited with savings dozens of lives at Blechhammer, and his son were liberated by American troops from a death march on the road to the Dachau Concentration Camp. Demerer was later reunited with his wife and daughter, both of whom survived the war in a women's labor camp.

Much like Oskar Schindler of *Schindler's List* movie fame, Demerer was never able to match his wartime achievements in civilian life. After failing at several business ventures in Germany, Demerer immigrated to Israel in the early 1960s, where he was welcomed as a hero by Blechhammer survivors. At a birthday party in his honor, Demerer was presented with a huge "birthday card"—a large placard signed by more than 150 Blechhammer alumni. Each added their Auschwitz tattoo number beneath their signature.

Financial success eluded him in Israel too. He suffered several heart attacks and relied on old friends for support. I have a copy of a letter Demerer wrote to friends in New Jersey thanking them for sending $20 while he was recuperating from one heart attack.

Demerer died in Israel in 1973.

On April 11, 2018, Karl Demerer was awarded the Jewish Rescuers Citation in Jerusalem. The award, sponsored by the B'nai B'rith organization, was accepted by his granddaughter, Minia Joneck. While Israel's Yad Vashem Memorial Museum has long honored gentiles who saved Jews as "Righteous of the Nations," there was no such recognition for Jews who saved fellow Jews prior to the B'nai B'rith award.

....

I stopped my search for **Joseph Braasem**, the *Kapo* who beat my father and many others, with the discovery of his 1947 testimonial to Dutch authorities. I had found some clues that might have led to Braasem's family. I had intended to confront them about their father's checkered past. Then I thought, to what end? After weighing possible outcomes, I decided to just let it go. I think my father would have done the same.

....

After their father died in Buchenwald, **Mark Jarzombek** and his brother Charles avoided the final transports from Buchenwald and were liberated by the US Army. Both brothers moved to the United States. While Charles kept his last name Jarzombek, Mark changed it to Beck and became an accountant in Gary, Indiana, before retiring to Longboat Key, Florida.

....

Beck's cousin, **Motek Kleiman**, immigrated to the United States in 1954 and, after multiple stints as a chef in Florida, moved to California and opened a small chain of women's clothing stores. With his powerful memory for faces and details, he frequently helped Holocaust researchers identify photographs of Jews from family albums found in the camp and ghetto remains.

Motek Kleiman died on December 20, 2013, at the age of ninety-six.

....

Sigmund Wachholder immigrated to the United States, changed his name to Walder, and became a successful wholesale commercial jeweler in Connecticut for forty-five years before retiring to Longboat Key, Florida, where I had interviewed him. I've concluded that Ziggy, as he preferred to be called, never really knew my father. I've come to believe he had noted Dolek Lajtner's name in Walter Spitzer's autobiography and "appropriated" it into his memory, much as described by Oliver Sacks. Either way, it was Ziggy who started me on this multiyear quest, and for that I will always be grateful.

Sigmund Walder died at age ninety-three on January 12, 2015.

....

Kazimierz Smolen, the Polish Auschwitz prisoner who likely filled out my father's registration form, cofounded and served as first director of the Auschwitz Memorial Museum from 1955 to 1990. Asked why he felt obliged to return to Auschwitz, Smolen said, "Sometimes when I think about it, I feel it may be some kind of sacrifice, some kind of obligation I have for having survived."

Kazimierz Smolen died on January 27, 2012, on the sixty-seventh anniversary of the camp's liberation. He was ninety-one.

....

By his own account, Robert Widerman distanced himself from the Holocaust for thirty-six years. After liberation he changed his name to **Robert Clary** and concentrated on his show business career, first in France and then the United States, most notably as Frenchie on the television show *Hogan's Heroes*. It wasn't until 1980, outraged by the revisionist historians "who were writing articles denying the Holocaust, calling it a myth," that Clary arranged to appear on the Merv Griffin television show to speak publicly for the first time about his experiences.

Clary published his autobiography, *From the Holocaust to Hogan's Heroes*, in 2001.

....

Over the years, I would return to my search for **Bill Ball,** the POW who sent the postcard to my father's family in Brooklyn, New York, and who was the initial catalyst of this book.

I posted queries on British POW websites and read everything I could find by veterans of Stalag VIIIB, the camp that fed thousands of laborers to German industries and farms during the war, including two thousand to the Blechhammer refineries. No luck.

After Sigmund Walder told me "Bill" was a Canadian who

had escaped, I tracked down lists of Canadian POWs who had been in Stalag VIIIB but could find no name even close.

On one POW site, however, I found a German punishment report—typed in English—about POW Robert Bell, who was sentenced to ten days of "severe detention because he purposely left the camp, deceiving the guards and being in possession of civil clothing and German currency."

The report was from BAB21, one of the subcamps that sent POWs to the Blechhammer North Refinery. It's dated September 20, 1944. That meant Bell's attempted escape occurred within the time frame described by Sigmund Walder, the fall of 1944.

Given everything I had learned of the fragility of memory, Robert or Bob could well have been Bill, and Bell could have become Ball in my father's recollection.

Then I came across a Pvt. William "Bill" Leonard Ball of the 1st Battalion, The Queen's Royal Regiment, West Surrey. This Bill Ball died in the crash of a British plane ferrying former POWs back home to England on May 9, 1945. He was thirty-one years old.

The Lancaster III bomber transporting Bill Ball was part of "Operation Exodus" and went down with twenty-four POWs and a crew of six. A poor-quality photo of Bill Ball was included with the obituary posted online. No other information was available, except that Pvt. Bill Ball had also been a prisoner in Stalag VIIIB.

When I began my search, I thought how cool it would be to find Bill Ball and thank him or, if he were no longer alive, thank his family, for the kindness he had shown my father. I've since reconciled myself that I'll probably never know whether this Bill Ball was that Bill Ball.

....

The **Organization Schmelt** disintegrated soon after most of its camps were incorporated into the Auschwitz and Gross-Rosen camp systems. Its commander, Brig. Gen. Albrecht Schmelt, retired in late 1944. Accounts about his fate vary. Some say an SS audit found Schmelt had diverted RM 100,000 to his personal accounts and that he was tried by an SS court and executed. Other accounts say he committed suicide soon after the war ended in May 1945.

....

The fate of Gestapo Kommissar **Hans Dreier**, who organized the liquidations of the East Upper Silesia ghettoes, is in some dispute. An entry in the Yad Vashem website says that he reportedly was killed in action fighting the Russians in January 1945. However, in 1948–49, the Central Committee for Liberated Jews claimed he was alive in Hamburg, Germany, but that the local police were unable to find him.

....

Friedrich Kuczynski, the Organization Schmelt official instrumental in the *selektionen* of Jews in East Upper Silesia, was arrested by US military police and extradited to Poland. At his trial, Kuczynski protested that he never sent anyone to Auschwitz, blaming the deportations on the Gestapo and Hans Dreier. Convicted of war crimes, Kuczynski was hanged in 1947.

....

Erich Walter Fritz Hoffmann, the *Kommandant* of Blechhammer when it was part of Organization Schmelt, was handed over by a German de-Nazification court to the US military, which extradited him to Poland. Among those testifying before the German court were Karl Demerer and Wolf Lajtner, my father's cousin. At Hoffmann's trial in Krakow, witness after witness testified that Hoffmann had personally beat and killed prisoners.

Convicted of war crimes and murder, Hoffmann was hanged on November 13, 1948.

....

Otto Brossman, the first SS *Lagerführer* of Blechhammer after it became part of Auschwitz, was also arrested by American military police in 1947 and extradited to Poland. Brossman was tried for war crimes at the Jaworzno (Neu Dachs) subcamp, where he was assigned after Blechhammer, but not specifically for his time at Blechhammer itself.

At this first trial, Brossmann received the standard three-year sentence Polish authorities meted out for being a member of the SS. The prosecution appealed, and Brossmann was sentenced to death. Upon further appeals by the defense, Brossmann was eventually acquitted and freed in 1950. He died in Germany in 1958, presumably of natural causes, at age sixty-nine.

....

Kurt Klipp, the second SS *Lagerführer* of Blechhammer who was in charge of the death march to Gross-Rosen, was captured by British troops and died of typhoid fever on February 2, 1945, in the Bergen-Belsen concentration camp, which had been turned into a POW camp.

....

The identity of notorious SS guard known as **Tom Mix** eluded authorities and researchers for decades. He was identified by German Federal authorities only in 1975 as Hermann Leinkenjost, an ethnic German from Romania. His fate is unclear. According to German military records, a Hermann Leinkenjost died in the battle of Breslau (now Wroclaw, Poland) in 1945. However, this Leinkenjost's birthplace is listed as Buchen, Germany, and not Romania. In any case, a body was never found.

....

The **Jozef Skopek Werke** in Strzemieszyce, where my father, his uncle, and cousins worked before the ghetto there was liquidated, was seized as property of the state by Polish authorities in November 1946. A twelve-page public notice lists sixty-nine businesses and factories subject to seizure, the owners of which overwhelmingly have German-sounding surnames. Skopek Metal Werke is number forty-one on that list. I could find nothing about Skopek himself.

....

The **Blechhammer North Synthetic Oil Refinery** became operational in May 1944 but produced only ninety-six thousand barrels of synthetic petroleum before being knocked out by the 15th Air Force.

The massive archives behind its innovative technology, however, survived.

As the Allies advanced into Germany, some two dozen members of the Technical Oil Mission, made up of American and British civilian oil experts, fanned out across Europe to still-smoldering synthetic oil refineries and offices of IG Farben. They gathered up an estimated one-hundred-seventy-five tons of technical data—plans, refinery records, blueprints, scientific reports, and other data. The most critically important documents were microfilmed—306 rolls with 1,000 frames per roll—306,000 pages of data. The balance was shipped back to the United States.

After the war, successive bureaucracies continued the work, using hundreds of German translators supervised by Allied personnel. The Bureau of Mines, later rolled into the Department of Energy, planned pilot and demonstration plants in Pennsylvania, Colorado, and Wyoming, and set up a successful pilot plant in the town of Louisiana, Missouri. It also acquired tons of sophisticated equipment taken from German synthetic refineries and laboratories, though probably none from the

Blechhammer plants as they were stripped bare by the Soviets, who occupied the region.

Interest in the innovative German technology quickly withered for the same reasons that had doomed the synthetic oil program in prewar Germany: It became obvious that oil from coal could never compete with cheap oil from Oklahoma, Texas, and the new oilfields of the Persian Gulf.

By 1948, the US Office of Technical Services reported that twenty-five hundred trunks of documents had never even been opened and were consigned to a warehouse as dead storage (cue music from *Raiders of the Lost Ark*).

On December 18, 2018, the *Wall Street Journal* reported that North Korea was stepping up efforts to convert its abundant coal reserves to gasoline as a way to ease US-imposed sanctions. The article noted that the technology had been used by Nazi Germany and pariah states like Apartheid-era South Africa.

ACKNOWLEDGMENTS

....

This book took a long time to research and much too long to write. Along the way, I've been the beneficiary of a lot of help and support.

Scott Miller and Bill Connelly, both since retired from the US Holocaust Memorial Museum (USHMM) in Washington, tracked down my father's Auschwitz registration form, which intrigued me to wonder what else might be out there. They also introduced me to researchers and made available the voluminous material in the USHMM's archives.

It was Scott who introduced me to Jeff Cymbler. Jeff is more than a walking encyclopedia about the Jewish communities of East Upper Silesia; he also has a museum's worth of artifacts— prewar phone books, business directories, genealogical records, and German documents. Moreover, he has generously shared his collection and knowledge with me and other researchers.

My first, tentative explorations into Lajtner family history were possible only with the help and encouragement of my cousins Avi Stavsky and Tamar Scheinberg. Their father is Icia, and Avi gave me copies of Icia's unpublished memoirs, which proved invaluable in filling in details and color about our family's forgotten history. Successive generations of aunts, uncles, and cousins were often named after the same grandparents, aunts, and uncles.

Keeping it all straight was beyond me, and without the help of Avi and Tamar, hopeless. Sadly, my dear cousin Avi died in May 2019 before this book was published.

Figuring out my grandfather Abram's early marriages and which child belonged to which wife would also have been impossible without the help of Stanley Diamond and the Jewish Records Indexing-Poland. Stanley has labored for years to assemble comprehensive genealogical records into a cohesive database. The database also revealed that Grandpa Abram had more children than our family in the United States knew about.

I became more serious about maintaining careful citations while taking several courses on the Holocaust with Prof. Natalia Aleksiun at Touro College in New York. It was largely because of her influence that I began rethinking the scope and approach of this book as something beyond a son's memoir about his father.

In Poland, I had the good fortune to work with several Polish individuals who went above and beyond in helping me get to the roots of my project.

Zdzislaw Les, owner of the Jarden Jewish bookstore in Krakow, became much more than a guide, translator, and driver. In the long hours spent traversing the region, Les was always an insightful and funny companion. He seemed to know everyone worth knowing to a researcher like me.

I met Edward Haduch, the Polish researcher, during a visit to Blechhammer. We began exchanging tips and insights, and it quickly became clear that his interest in the Jewish Forced Labor Camp was at least as intense as mine. Besides mounting the exhibition about Blechhammer at his local library, he also helped design a YouTube animation of Blechhammer that takes the viewer through the physical layout of the camp, pausing to show before-and-after images of key sites, like the front gate, guard towers, and the crematoria.

While the history of the US bombing campaign against the German synthetic oil refineries, including the Blechhammer

North and Blechhammer South facilities, is not the focus of this book, getting a handle on its scope proved surprisingly difficult. There is no central database listing the dates and number of attacks, the number of bombers involved, or the precise planes and airmen lost during the six-month campaign. Szymon Serwatka did much of this work, assembling and collating the data from the logs and action reports of individual air combat units into a slim volume he coauthored on the air campaign. The depth of help Szymon afforded me is not reflected in the manuscript.

During my last visit to Poland in 2015, I was fortunate to work with Jakub Czuprynski, a professional genealogist who has helped many children of survivors like me explore their roots. Jakob accompanied me to Strzemieszyce and also conducted research on my behalf on genealogical material. I will always be grateful for his drive and intellectual curiosity.

Early drafts, stories, and chapters were scrutinized by fellow writers at numerous workshops at The Writing Institute at Sarah Lawrence College. I thank my fellow writers in the struggle for their thoughtful suggestions and questions. The instructors there—Joelle Sanders, Steven Lewis, and Jimin Han, and the Institute's former director, Patricia Dunn, have been encouraging and critical readers and always helpful.

Duke Coffey, a friend and former colleague and editor at United Press International, as well as a true World War II history buff, helped clarify passages, correct mistakes, and simplify construction.

Andre Weiss, a personal friend for almost thirty years, brought his critical lawyer's eye to the manuscript, insisting on precision where I might have been satisfied with looser language.

My old J-school comrade, Louise Levathes, herself a successful author/historian, made important contributions and offered timely insights and encouragement. I also benefited from Iris Blasi's early review of the manuscript and encouragement.

As a former editor myself, I often smiled at Beverly Ehrman's gentle, subtle edits and suggestions that invariably improved the narrative and pacing. She truly understands the difference between editing and rewriting.

Thoughtful, thorough copyediting by Anne Durette helped prevent much subsequent gnashing of teeth on my part. She thoroughly vacuumed the final manuscript of inconsistencies, errors, and typos large and small, and wrestled the endnotes and bibliography into proper shape for publication. That said, any mistakes of omission or commission are strictly mine.

Chances are you would not have clicked on or opened this book had it not been for its cover. David Ter-Avanesyan, working with SparkPress Creative Director Julie Metz, created a striking book cover that captured both the mood and import of the book.

When reading these kinds of acknowledgments in other books, it's required boilerplate for the author to thank his wife and family for their help and support. In my case, this is no cliché. Throughout the years-long process, my wife and life partner, Anat, has supported and encouraged me. She has been my muse for ideas as well as frustrations. I must apologize to my daughters for putting them in the difficult position of asking them to critically read their father's manuscript. Ayelet and Elena, both excellent writers themselves, have made solid, thoughtful suggestions that are reflected in the final product. Daddy loves you and is grateful.

PARTIAL BIBLIOGRAPHY

AHRP. "Breaking the Silence About Sexual Violence Against Women During the Holocaust." November 18, 2014. http://ahrp .org/sexual-violence-against-women-during-the-holocaust/.

Avalon Project. "The Trial of German Major War Criminals: Proceedings of the International Military Tribunal Sitting at Nuremberg Germany." http://avalon.law.yale.edu/imt/12-12 -45.asp.

Baldwin, Hanson W. "Germany's Synthetic Oil; It Bulks Large in a Supply of Fuel That Apparently Meets the Enemy's Needs." *The New York Times*, January 18, 1943. http://timesmachine .nytimes.com/timesmachine/1943/01/18/85072136.html ?action=click&contentCollection=Archives&module=Article EndCTA&region=ArchiveBody&pgtype=article.

Blatman, Daniel. "The Death Marches, January–May 1945: Who Was Responsible for What?" Edited by David Silberklang. *Yad Veshem Studies* XXVIII (2000): 155–201.

Blatman, Daniel. *The Death Marches: The Final Phase of Nazi Genocide*. Translated by Chaya Galai. Translation edition. Cambridge: Belknap Press, 2011.

Blumenthal, Ralph. "A Visit to the Unfathomable Past of Auschwitz." *The New York Times*, May 8, 2019. https://www .nytimes.com/2019/05/08/arts/design/auschwitz-exhibition -review-holocaust.html.

Braasem, Joseph. "Interview With Joseph Braasem." Edited by R.C. Broek. Translated by Wijnie de Groot. 2015. State Institute for War Documentation (NIOD), August 11, 1947.

Brandt, Kersten, ed. "The Jews of Bedzin." In *Before They Perished: Photographs Found In Auschwitz*, 624. Munich: Gina Kehayoff, 2001.

Browning, Christopher R. *Nazi Policy, Jewish Workers, German Killers*. New York: Cambridge University Press, 2000.

Chatel, Vincent and Chuck Ferree. "The Forgotten Camps." https://www.jewishgen.org/ForgottenCamps/Index.html

Clary, Robert. *From the Holocaust to Hogan's Heroes: The Autobiography of Robert Clary*. Lanham: Taylor Trade Publishing, 2007.

Clary, Robert. "Interview with Robert Clary." Youngstown State University Oral History Program. Interview by Hugh Earnhard. Transcribed Interview, O.H. 436, May 21, 1986. https://jupiter.ysu.edu/record=b1548490

Corbett, Ray. *Sunday Sunrise*–Transcript. Interview by John Collis. Television broadcast, March 24, 2002. 7plus.com.au.

Czech, Danuta. *Auschwitz Chronicle: 1939–1945*. First Edition. New York: Henry Holt & Co, 1997.

Deputy Theater Judge Advocate's Office, War Crimes Branch, United States Forces, European Theater. "Information Regarding Alleged War Crime." January 2, 1946. IPN GK 184/262.

Eizenstat, Stuart. *Imperfect Justice: Looted Assets, Slave Labor, and the Unfinished Business of World War II*. New York: Public Affairs, 2004.

Epstein, Helen. *Children of the Holocaust*. Lexington: Plunkett Lake Press, 2010.

Focke, Harald, and Uwe Reimer. *Alltag der Entrechteten: Wie die Nazis mit ihren Gegnern umgingen. Originalausg* edition. Hamburg: Rowohlt Publishing House, 1980.

Formular Z32 Rentabilitätsberechnung. n.d. Photograph. DaA F 6436, 05754, 0003. Archives of Dachau Memorial.

Friedlander, Saul. *Nazi Germany and the Jews, 1939–1945: The Years of Extermination*. New York: Harper Perennial, 2008.

Friedman, Philip. *Roads to Extinction: Essays on the Holocaust*, edited by Ada June Friedman. New York: Conference on Jewish Social Studies, Jewish Publication Society of America, 1980.

Fulbrook, Mary. *A Small Town Near Auschwitz: Ordinary Nazis and the Holocaust*. Oxford, UK: Oxford University Press, 2012.

Gastfriend, Edward. *My Father's Testament: Memoir of a Jewish Teenager, 1938-1945*. Philadelphia: Temple University Press, 1999.

Glauning, Christine. "Bisingen I Places: Concentration Camp and Oil Shale-Works." Translated by Judith Rentschler, n.d. http://kzgedenkstaettenbisingen.files.wordpress.com/2008/10/bisingen-i-places-concentration-camp-and-oil-shale-works.pdf.

Grynberg, Yechiel Jean. "Central DB of Shoah Victims' Names–Record Details, Item No. 1401535." *Yad Vashem*, April 17, 1993. https://yvng.yadvashem.org/nameDetails.html?language=en&itemId=1401535&ind=1.

Gutman, Israel, and Belah Guterman, eds. *The Auschwitz Album: The Story of a Transport*. Jerusalem : Oświęcim: Yad Vashem, Auschwitz-Birkenau State Museum, 2002.

Halerie, Avram (Adolf). "Danielle and David Snegg Papers." United States Holocaust Memorial Museum Archives, 2014.230.1. https://collections.ushmm.org/search/catalog/irn86811#?rsc=186009&cv=0&c=0&m=0&s=0&xywh=-1228%2C-157%2C4473%2C3129.

Holocaust Education and Archive Research Team. "Auschwitz Concentration Camp: The Gas Chambers & Crematoria. 2012. http://www.holocaustresearchproject.org/othercamps/auschwitzgaschambers.html.

Honey, Michael. "Research Notes on the Hungarian Holocaust." July 2008. http://www.zchor.org/hungaria.

Hoppen, Cila Katriel. "A Rough Road: Skopek Strzemieszyce Pola." Translated by Lisa Newman. In *Katowice: The Rise and Decline of the Jewish Community; Memorial Book.* Tel Aviv: 1996. http://www.jewishgen.org/yizkor/katowice/kat220 .html#Page223.

Höss, Rudolf. *Death Dealer: The Memoirs of the SS Kommandant at Auschwitz.* Edited by Steven Paskuly. Translated by Andrew Pollinger. New York: Da Capo Press, 1996.

Hyde-Clark, Eddie. "A Country Boy's Story of the Death March." *East Anglian Daily Times*, February 26, 2010. http://www.eadt.co.uk/ea-life/a-country-boy-s-story-of-the -death-march-1-85756.

Iszak, Martin. USC Shoah Foundation Visual History Archive. Interview by Robert Clary. Video and Audio Tape, October 26, 1994. http://vhaonline.usc.edu.

James, George. "New York Killings Set a Record, While Other Crimes Fell in 1990." *The New York Times*, April 23, 1991. https://www.nytimes.com/1991/04/23/nyregion/new-york -killings-set-a-record-while-other-crimes-fell-in-1990.html.

Jewish Virtual Library. "Auschwitz: Number of Prisoners in Auschwitz Camps (January 17, 1945)." https://www.jewishvirtual library.org/jsource/Holocaust/austats.html.

Jewish Virtual Library. "What Are Concentration Camps?" https://www.jewishvirtuallibrary.org/what-are-concentration -camps.

Jewishgen. "Pinkas Hakehillot Polin: Dabrowa Gornicza." Dabrowa Gornicza Encyclopedia of Jewish Communities in Poland, Volume VII. http://www.jewishgen.org/yizkor/Pinkas _poland/pol7_00131.html.

Klein, Marcel. USC Shoah Foundation Visual History Archive. Video and Audio Tape, April 9, 1995. Int Code 1909. http://vhaonline.usc.edu/viewingPage?testimonyID =1948&segmentNumber=0.

Klewitz, Bernd. *Die Arbeitssklaven der Dynamit Nobel.* Schalk-smühle: Engelbrecht, 1986.

Kluger, Jeffrey. "Genetic Scars of the Holocaust: Children Suffer Too." *Time,* September 9, 2010. http://content.time.com /time/health/article/0,8599,2016824,00.html.

Kogon, Eugen. *Der SS-Staat Das System Der Deutschen Konzentrationslager.* First edition. *Frankfurter Hefte,* 1946.

Kogon, Eugen. *The Theory and Practice of Hell.* Translated by Heinze Norden. New York: Berkley Books, 1998. http://archive .org/details/EugenKogonTheTheoryAndPracticeOfHell.

Konnikova, Maria. "You Have No Idea What Happened." *The New Yorker,* February 4, 2015. https://www.newyorker.com/ science/maria-konnikova/idea-happened-memory-recollection.

Krammer, Arnold. "Technology Transfer as War Booty: The U.S. Technical Oil Mission to Europe, 1945." *Technology and Culture* 22, no. 1 (1981): 68–103. https://doi.org/10.2307/3104293.

Kutatóközpont. "Hungarian Jews in Auschwitz-Birkenau." Accessed December 31, 2018. http://konfliktuskutato.hu /index.php?option=com_content&view=article&id=288 :hungarian-jews-in-auschwitz-birkenau&catid=36:english.

Lasker, Rutka. *Rutka's Notebook: A Voice from the Holocaust.* Edited by Daniella Zaidman-Mauer and Kelly Knauer. New York: Time / Yad Vashem, 2008.

Lencner, Sabina. USC Shoah Foundation Visual History Archive. Interview by Barbara Orris. Video and Audio Tape, July 13, 1995. http://vhaonline.usc.edu/viewingPage.aspx?testimonyID =4158&segmentNumber=0.

Maclean, John. "I Watched Nazis Work Auschwitz Slaves to Death; Scots POW Witnessed Horror of the Holocaust." *Sunday Mail* (Glasgow, Scotland), January 21, 2001. https: //www.highbeam.com/doc/1G1-69361665.html.

McFadden, Robert. "TimesMachine: March 30, 1970." *NYTimes* .com. http://timesmachine.nytimes.com/timesmachine/1970 /03/30/issue.html.

Meirtchak, Benjamin. *Jews-Officers In The Polish Armed Forces, 1939-1945*. Revised edition. New Haven: Avotaynu, 2004.

Metzger, Pola. USC Shoah Foundation Visual History Archive. Interview by Barbara Orris. Video and Audio Tape, November 6, 1996. http://vhaonline.usc.edu/viewingPage.aspx?testimonyID=22872&segmentNumber=0.

Military Government Liaison Office Det. E213 SK Munich Special Branch. "Trial of Spruchkammer VII on 23 July against Dr. Hoffmann, Erich, Walter, Fritz, Born 24 June 1897 at Breslau, Residing at Nordhorn, Hauststre. 56 (English Zone)," July 24, 1947. IPN GK 164/4600.

News/Museum/Auschwitz-Birkenau. http://auschwitz.org/en/museum/news/2-million-320-thousand-visitors-at-the-ausch witz-memorial-in-2019,1400.html.

Oxford Academic (Oxford University Press). "Bedzin: A Small Town Near Auschwitz." February 13, 2014. https://www.youtube.com/watch?v=iHyRb3ctnx0.

Piper, Franciszek. "Das Nebenlager Blechhammer." *Hefte von Auschwitz* 10 (1967): 19–39.

Pressac, Jean-Claude. "Auschwitz: Technique and Operation of the Gas Chambers." 1989. https://phdn.org/archives/holocaust-history.org/auschwitz/pressac/technique-and-operation/pressac0095.shtml.

Richter, Dorshavitz, Bardah and Kolar. "Documentation from the Israel Police unit for the Investigation of Nazi Crimes." Israeli National Police, 1976 1975. Tr.11/253.1. Yad Vashem, Jerusalem.

Rodriguez, Tori. "Descendants of Holocaust Survivors Have Altered Stress Hormones." *Scientific American*, March 1, 2015. https://doi.org/10.1038/scientificamericanmind0315-10a.

Rosengarten, Israel J. *Survival: The Story of a Sixteen-Year-Old Jewish Boy*. Syracuse: Syracuse University Press, 1999.

Sacks, Oliver. "Speak, Memory." *The New York Review of Books*, February 21, 2013. https://www.nybooks.com/articles/2013/02/21/speak-memory/.

Schaufeld, Abraham. USC Shoah Foundation Visual History Archive. Interview by Ludovic Gielen. Video and Audio Tape, January 17, 1996. http://vhaonline.usc.edu/viewingPage .aspx?testimonyID=8160&segmentNumber=0.

Seema, Yasmin. "Experts Debunk Study That Found Holocaust Trauma Is Inherited." Chicagotribune.com. http://www .chicagotribune.com/lifestyles/health/ct-holocaust-trauma-not -inherited-20170609-story.html.

Serwatka, Szymon, and Michal Mucha. *From Italy to Poland.* Rumia, Poland: Biuo Uslug Komputerowych, 2002.

Shpeizman, Leib. "Jews in Zaglembie During the Second World War." Pages 60–71. http://www.jewishgen.org/yizkor/zaglembia /zag060E.html, 1972.

"ŚLĄSKO-DĄBROWSKI NR 31 KATOWICE, DNIA 20 LISTOPADA 1946." http://docplayer.pl/43257326-Slasko-dabrowski-nr-31-katowice-dnia-20-listopada-1946.html.

Smolen, Kazimierz. *Auschwitz, 1940–1945.* Albuquerque: Route 66 Pub Ltd, 1995.

Spitzer, Walter. *Deportation by Train from Strzemieszyce Wielkie 1574.Jpg.* 1945. Pen and ink drawing. http://www .infocenters.co.il/gfh/multimedia/Art/1574.jpg.

Spitzer, Walter. *Sauvé Par Le Dessin; Buchenwald.* Non Classé. Lausanne, France: Editions Favre, 2004.

Steinbacher, Sybille. "In the Shadow of Auschwitz: The Murder of the Jews of East Upper Silesia." In *National Socialist Extermination Policies: Contemporary German Perspectives and Controversies*, edited by Ulrich Herbert, 276–305. New York: Berghahn Books, 2004.

Stern, Yehiel. "And You Raised My Bones from There." Translated by Lance Ackerfeld. Pages 546–548. http://www .jewishgen.org/yizkor/zaglembia/zag541.html.

Szymaniak, Matylda. "Oral History Interview with Matylda Szymaniak–USHMM Collections Search." http://collections .ushmm.org/search/catalog/irn509214.

Transport 35 from Pithiviers, Camp, France to Auschwitz Birkenau,Extermination Camp, Poland on 21/09/1942. "Transports to Extinction: Holocaust (Shoah) Deportation Database." https://deportation.yadvashem.org/index.html?language =en&itemId=5092608.

Trundle, George. "Sound: POW's and Forced Marches." Video, n.d. https://nzhistory.govt.nz/media/sound/pows-forced-marches.

USHMM. "Oral History Interview with Matylda Szymaniak [Oral History Transcript or Notes]– USHMM Collections Search." http://collections.ushmm.org/search/catalog/att509214 _9215.

Vick, Karl. "Iran's President Calls Holocaust 'Myth' in Latest Assault on Jews." *Washington Post*, December 15, 2005. http: //www.washingtonpost.com/wp-dyn/content/article/2005 /12/14/AR2005121402403.html.

Virtual Shtetl–Museum of the History of Polish Jews Polin. "Jewish Cemetery in Będzin (Podzamcze Street)." https://sztetl .org.pl/en/towns/b/406-bedzin/114-cemeteries/6812 -jewish-cemetery-bedzin-podzamcze-street.

Wachsmann, Nikolaus. "'Annihilation through Labor': The Killing of State Prisoners in the Third Reich." *The Journal of Modern History* 71, no. 3 (1999): 624–59. https://doi.org/10.1086 /235291.

Walder, Sigmund. Fortunoff Video Archive for Holocaust Testimonies. Interview by Laurel Vlock, Dori Laub, and Eva Kantor. Video and Audio Tape, 1982. HVT-55.

Welch, Steven. "'The Annihilation of Superfluous Eaters': Nazi Plans for and Use of Famine in Eastern Europe." http: //www.isn.ethz.ch/Digital-Library/Publications/Detail /?ots591=cab359a3-9328-19cc-a1d2-8023e646b22c&lng =en&id=92170.

Widerman, Pawal. *The Blond Beast*. Munich, 1948.

Widermann, Robert. "Mémorial de la Shoah." http://ressources .memorialdelashoah.org/notice.php?q=fulltext%3A%28

widermann%29%20AND%20id_pers%3A%28%2A
%29%20AND%20survivant%3A%281%29&spec_expand
=1&start=0.

Wikipedia. "Adam Czerniaków." June 11, 2018. https://en
.wikipedia.org/w/index.php?title=Adam_Czerniak%C3
%B3w&oldid=845448214.

Wikipedia. "Crime in New York City." July 31, 2018. https://en
.wikipedia.org/w/index.php?title=Crime_in_New_York
_City&oldid=852854947.

Wikipedia. "Oradea Ghetto." June 25, 2017. https://en.wikipedia
.org/w/index.php?title=Oradea_ghetto&oldid=787431959.

Wikipedia. "Wawel Castle." December 7, 2020. https://en
.wikipedia.org/w/index.php?title=Wawel_Castle&oldid
=992860696.

Wodzinski, Marcin and Janusz Spyra. "'Walking in the Steel
Boots of Faith...': Anti-Semitic Journalism in the Voivodship of Silesia 1922-1939." In *Jews of Silesia*, 468. Cracow:
Księg. Akademicka, 2001. https://books.google.com/books?id
=3bVtAAAAMAAJ.

Women's eNews. "Holocaust Women's Rape Breaks Decades of
Taboo." Accessed November 1, 2017. http://womensenews
.org/2011/05/holocaust-womens-rape-breaks-decades-taboo/.

Y. Arad, Y. Gutman, and A. Margaliot (eds). "Memorandum by
General von Gienanth to the General Staff of the Wermacht
in Reaction to the Removal of the Jews from Industrial
Production, Sept. 18, 1942." *Documents on the Holocaust,
Selected Sources on the Destruction of the Jews.* Jerusalem:
Yad Veshem (1981): 287–88.

NOTES AND THOUGHTS

....

Documents are the raw material on which historians and investigative journalists depend. Think Pentagon Papers or, more recently, the many trails of emails that buttress both stories and investigations.

I was luckier than I could have imagined.

In all, I uncovered a paper trail of more than twenty documents bearing Josef Lajtner's name, not all of which are referenced in this book. I had also found documents with the names of other Lajtner family members, my father's friend, Charlie Feder, and "Red" Martin Izyck, the head *Kapo* of the electricians and welders at Blechhammer.

Documents, however, are useless without context. For me, that meant learning the murky history of Nazi annexation of Zaglebie, the Dabrowa Basin, renamed East Upper Silesia or the East Strip by the Germans. Among the most helpful texts were *A Small Town Near Auschwitz*, by British historian Mary Fulbrook. Professor Fulbrook also answered my follow-up questions over the years. Another important essay is *In the Shadow of Auschwitz: The Murder of the Jews of East Upper Silesia*, by German historian Sybil Steinbacher. Steinbacher, Professor of Holocaust Studies at Goethe University Frankfurt, also graciously answered my early questions.

For history about the Organization Schmelt, see Wolf Gruner's *Jewish Forced Labor Under the Nazis*, and Bella Gutterman's *A Narrow Bridge to Life*. To get the flavor of day-to-day life in Schmelt camps, *Sala's Gift* by Anne Kirshner was most helpful. For in-depth analyses of the Nazi forced labor program, Christopher Browning's *Nazi Policy, Jewish Workers, German Killers* and Michael Thad Allen's *The Business of Genocide* are key.

In describing the *Judenräte* and its controversial leader, Moniek Merin, I quoted *The Blond Beast*, by Pawal Wiedermann, published in Germany in 1957 and now out of print. (I used an unofficial English translation.) Wiedermann is also the main source about Merin cited by Isaiah Trunk in his definitive history of the Jewish Councils, *Judenrate*. Wiedermann himself described his book as a novel. He uses dialogue as a literary technique to present varying views and to move the action forward. Wiedermann repeatedly says that everything depicted in the book actually happened. What gave me (and other researchers) pause were the lengthy quotes attributed to Merin. As far as is known, no texts exist of Merin's fiery speeches. We do not know if Wiedermann had copies of Merin's speeches or, more likely, reconstructed them after the war. Precise quotes aside, Wiedermann's depiction of Merin as haughty, driven, and dismissive of opponents is supported by numerous survivor testimonies.

A must-have book for any serious researcher of Auschwitz is Danuta Czech's *The Auschwitz Chronicle*, a compendium of Nazi documents into a near-daily dairy of this notorious concentration camp. If, however, you want the definitive study of Auschwitz, especially the gas chambers and crematoria, nothing is more detailed and exhaustive than Robert Jan van Pelt's *The Case for Auschwitz: Evidence from the Irving Trial*.

While no academic history can capture the horror of the death march as do firsthand testimonials, for the big picture view, Daniel Blatman's *The Death Marches* is a must-read, though not necessarily an easy one.

Of published survivor memoirs, I found Israel J. Rosengarten's *Survival* consistently reliable in getting nitty-gritty correct. Perhaps because he is an artist, Walter Spitzer's *Sauvé par le Dessin: Buchenwald* captures nuances of color, smell, and place better than many of his contemporaries.

Unlike Erik Larson, who says he eschews the internet for research (at least in *Devil and The White City*), this book would have been impossible without the rich wealth of material found online. The most important for this period are the JewishGen. org website's extensive Shtetlinks and Yizkorbooks archive of testimonials and microhistories of disappeared Jewish communities. Many of these have been translated over the years from the original Yiddish or Hebrew by Lance Ackerfeld and a dedicated team of volunteers that included my friend Hannah Berliner Fischtell and my late cousin, Avi Stavsky.

There are two schools of historiography regarding Holocaust studies. The first, epitomized by Raul Hilberg, argues only documentary evidence should be considered because any firsthand accounts other than contemporaneous diaries are likely to become polluted with the passage of time, and the further from the event, the more unreliable the account. There is always the possibility that, as Oliver Sacks himself experienced, incidents overheard become passed on as actual experiences. Critics of this strict approach, however, argue that the story of the Holocaust is then reduced largely to the history written by the perpetrators— the Nazis.

The second school willingly incorporates personal testimonials, like Saul Friedlander did in *The Years of Extermination: Nazi Germany and the Jews, 1939–1945*, which won the Pulitzer Prize in 2008. The problem here is the risk cited above: Memory is terribly fickle, and there's a temptation to go for the colorful over the factual.

While I use documents to anchor and corroborate the narrative, I also sought out testimonies that told a colorful story.

That said, working with survivor testimonials can be incredibly frustrating. Many interviews were conducted by well-meaning volunteers who did not know enough history to intelligently question their subjects. At times, I wanted to tear my hair out and scream at the computer screen when an intriguing statement by a survivor was ignored by an interviewer more intent on asking every question on their list. Or, when an interviewer became so enthralled with a dramatic story, they were oblivious to obvious follow-up questions or failed to probe vague generalities.

Yet when multiple survivor testimonials confirm the essential facts of an event it would be a shame to discount them because they are not contemporaneous or because exact dates or times do not match up. This is true for the August 12, 1942, mass selection in East Upper Silesia, the June 23, 1943, liquidation of the Strzemieszyce ghetto, and the death marches of January 1945.

To be clear, although this is a work of nonfiction, I reconstruct my father's stories as best as I can *remember*. Everything else within quotation marks comes from interviews, diaries, published histories, memoirs, courtroom testimony, or survivor testimonials. To pin down *context* as accurately as possible, I tried to triangulate multiple sources. When they appeared to line up, I went with that. One unintended consequence was that I omitted a couple of particularly dramatic stories because I could not find any corroboration. Yet I also tried to balance allowing individual survivors to tell their stories with the journalistic rule calling for at least two independent sources to support key parts of the narrative.

All this leads to the conundrum: to footnote or not to footnote—that was a tough question. This began as a personal memoir informed by a Nazi paper trail. Initially, I copied scores of accounts and documents found online without noting their sources. As the book evolved to include the untold story of Blechhammer and that small strip of Polish territory the Nazis called East Upper Silesia, this omission cost me hours of additional work when I began adding formal citations to keep track of information sources.

The following notes are not meant to be academically comprehensive but more as a guide for anyone interested in pursuing the subjects.

ENDNOTES BY CHAPTER

CHAPTER 2

Page 9, *southeast. One website* . . . "The Forgotten Camps."

Page 11, *Corbett from Scotland* . . . Corbett, Sunday Sunrise - Transcript.

Page 11, *by Sigmund Walder* . . . Walder, Fortunoff Video Archive for Holocaust Testimonies.

Page 16, *your own needs."* . . . Walter Spitzer had told me much the same. When I voiced frustration that he couldn't tell more stories about my father, he retorted that he was too preoccupied with his own survival to care about what other prisoners were doing to live.

Page 17, *autobiography, in French25.* . . .Walter Spitzer, *Sauvé Par Le Dessin; Buchenwald*, Non Classé (Favre, 2004).

Page 22, *accept this claim* . . .Vick, "Iran's President Calls Holocaust 'Myth' in Latest Assault on Jews."

CHAPTER 4

The analysis of Hungarian deportations synthesized two lists from two sources: transport lists of trains leaving Hungarian territory and a log of arriving transports assembled by a prisoner at the Birkenau camp.

I matched up the transports leaving Oradea with those arriving at Auschwitz and concluded that my mother and grandfather likely were on Transport 40. I reviewed this analysis with

Prof. Randolf Braham, the preeminent expert on the Hungarian Holocaust, at his office at the City University of New York. (Coincidentally, I had Prof. Braham for a political science course on Communism as an undergraduate at CCNY decades earlier. Braham died on November 25, 2018.)

I became acutely aware of the fickleness of memory when writing about the candy store. I wasn't sure of the year Helen had purchased it. I spoke to the sons of Rose and Jack, and both insisted their parents had bought their candy store in 1962. So I initially went with that. Months later, I found the original lease signed by Helen. It was dated June 1, 1961. My friends admitted their memories had been faulty.

Page 41, *visitors in 2019* . . . "News/Museum/Auschwitz-Birkenau."

Page 41, *1.86 million visitors* . . ."The Mine sums up 2019 - blog - The 'Wieliczka' Salt Mine."

Page 41, *about 1.9 million* . . . "Wawel Castle."

Page 41, *study of Blechhammer* . . . Franciszek Piper, "'Das Nebenlager Blechhammer.'"

Page 41, *to 1.1 million* . . .Piper told me the initial estimates of four million killed in the Auschwitz gas chambers were made by Soviet investigators after the Red Army liberated the camp in January 1945. It was largely based on simple math: the theoretical capacity of the gas chambers multiplied by their theoretical days of operation. Piper instead analyzed logs of train transports from across Europe and other records to come up with the lower number.

Page 43, *of human hair* . . . Smolen, *Auschwitz, 1940–1945*, 33.

Page 44, *and arrival logs* . . . Michael Honey, "Research Notes on the Hungarian Holocaust," zchor.org, July 2008, http://www.zchor.org/hungaria; Also see "Oradea Ghetto," Wikipedia, June 25, 2017, https://en.wikipedia.org/w/index .php?title=Oradea_ghetto&oldid=787431959.

Page 44, *on each oven* . . . Holocaust Education and Archive Research Team, http://www.HolocaustResearchProject.Org /othercamps/auschwitzgaschambers.html.

Page 45, *than nine thousand."* . . . Höss, *Death Dealer,* 37.
Page 45, *The Auschwitz Album* . . . Gutman and Gutterman, *The Auschwitz Album.*
Page 45, *with a number* . . ."Hungarian Jews in Auschwitz -Birkenau."

CHAPTER 5

A cousin arranged a meeting with Adek's daughter in the lobby café of the Sheraton Hotel in Tel Aviv. She insisted her father had sought control of the Lajtner properties, including my grandfather's house, only to keep them out of the hands of the Communist Polish government. The lawsuit suggests otherwise. She also confirmed she still owned a number of the properties in Poland. There are family rumors that she and some of the cousins were working on a reconciliation that would include transferring or sharing some of the real estate.

CHAPTER 6

Page 62, *intact, though deteriorating* . . . "Jewish Cemetery in Będzin (Podzamcze Street) | Virtual Shtetl."
Page 67, *dropped all charges* . . . Jewishgen, "Pinkas Hakehillot Polin: Dabrowa Gornicza."
Page 68, *Illiteracy was widespread* . . . Measuring literacy depends on who was asking the question and how. Russian census takers were interested in who could read and write Russian and ignored knowledge of Yiddish or Hebrew for Jews, as well as Polish for Poles. By that criteria, in the 1897 census, illiteracy was 68.4 percent for Yiddish speakers and 73 percent for Roman Catholic Poles. When Poland became independent, its census maximized (and likely overstated) Polish language acceptance among the population, and illiteracy among Jews was put at 4.6 percent in 1921 and .4 percent in 1931, similar to the Roman Catholic Polish majority. See Corrsin, Stephen D. "Literacy Rates and Questions of Language, Faith and Ethnic Identity in Population

Censuses in the Partitioned Polish Lands and Interwar Poland (1880s-1930s)." *The Polish Review* 43, no. 2 (1998): 131-60. http://www.jstor.org/stable/25779044.

Page 69, *slander—and win* . . .Marcin Wodzinski, "'Walking in the Steel Boots of Faith . . .' Anti-Semitic Journalism in the Voivodship of Silesia 1922-1939," in *Jews of Silesia*, 1st Edition (Cracow : Wrocław : [Český Těšín]: Księg. Akademicka, 2001), 101.

CHAPTER 7

Page 76, *was Helen Epstein* . . . Helen Epstein all but created the genre about the effects of the Holocaust on the second-generation survivors. She has since followed up her original work with two more volumes, *Where She Came From: A Daughter's Search for Her Mother's History*, and *The Long Half-Lives of Love and Trauma*. In 2020, she published her mother's memoir, *Franci's War*. If my initial rection to her request comes off as harsh, it is because it reflected my feelings at the time. That is not to denigrate her groundbreaking work in any way; she was the first who tried finding answers when most of us children of survivors couldn't figure out the questions. All quotes, with permission, are from: Helen Epstein, *Children of the Holocaust* (Plunkett Lake Press, 2010).

Page 80, *A recent theory* . . . Rodriguez and Rodriguez, "Descendants of Holocaust Survivors Have Altered Stress Hormones." See also Kluger, "Genetic Scars of the Holocaust" but for an alternate view, see Yasmin, "Experts Debunk Study That Found Holocaust Trauma Is Inherited."

CHAPTER 8

Page 80, *shortly before hostilities* . . . One of the anti-Semitic tropes was that Jews did not fully participate in the defense of Poland and were not represented in the Polish military. In his seminal work, Benjamin Meirtchek, a decorated officer in the Polish army, said his research suggested some two hundred thousand Jewish soldiers served in the Polish military, and he identified by name nearly five thousand officers. See Meirtchak, *Jews-Officers In The Polish Armed Forces, 1939–1945.*

Page 84, *future national leadership* . . . For a harrowing view of this, see "Poland's Holocaust."

Page 84, *in his diary* . . . Fulbrook, *A Small Town Near Auschwitz: Ordinary Nazis and the Holocaust* and Friedlander, *Nazi Germany and the Jews, 1939–1945*, 29.

Page 85, *Einsatzgruppen ZB V* . . . Kersten Brandt, ed., "The Jews of Bedzin," in *Before They Perished: Photographs Found In Auschwitz* (Munich: Gina Kehayoff, 2001), 16, and for eyewitness accounts, see Oxford Academic (Oxford University Press), *Bedzin: A Small Town Near Auschwitz*, accessed April 7, 2018, https://www.youtube.com/watch?v=iHyRb3ctnx0.

Page 88, *boundless, nervous energy* . . . Memorial book of Zaglembie, "Zaglembie, Poland (Pages 60–71)."

Page 90, *of the war* . . . Steinbacher, "In the Shadow of Auschwitz: The Murder of the Jews of East Upper Silesia," 285.

Page 91, *to say desirable* . . . Browning, *Nazi Policy, Jewish Workers, German Killers*, 66.

Page 94, *decide the issue* . . . Most of what we know of Merin comes from a single source: Pawal Widerman, *The Blond Beast.*

Page 94, *been murdered there* . . . Czech, *Auschwitz Chronicle.*

Page 96, *chambers of Auschwitz* . . . Czech, 182–83.

Page 97, *in your hair* . . . Fulbrook, 230.

Page 97, *a corresponding rate* . . . Fulbrook, 229.

Page 98, *to his wife.* . . . "Adam Czerniaków."

Page 99, *in her diary* . . . Lasker, *Rutka's Notebook.*

Page 100, *to her mother* . . . Fulbrook, 281

Page 102, *among the Jews* . . . Fulbrook, 281

Page 102, *new Sosnowiec ghetto* . . . Friedman, *Roads to Extinction*, 361. The book does not offer any source of this quote, which also does not appear in the translation of *The Blond Beast* that is the most referenced work about Merin.

Page 102, *occupied Poland, wrote* . . . Y. Arad, Y. Gutman, and A Margaliot (eds), "Memorandum by General von Gienanth to the General Staff of the Wehrmacht in Reaction to the Removal of the Jews from Industrial Production, September 18, 1942," *Documents on the Holocaust, Selected Sources on the Destruction of the Jews* . . . Yad Veshem (1981): 287–88.

Page 103, *day to disappear* . . . Y. Arad, Y. Gutman, and A Margaliot (eds).

Page 103, *distinguished military career* . . . Browning, *Nazi Policy, Jewish Workers, German Killers*, 78.

CHAPTER 9

This chapter draws from the following:

—Testimonials by my father's cousins, Sabina Lencner and her sister, Pola Metzger, both housed in the Visual History Archive of the USC Shoah Foundation.

—Interviews with Walter Spitzer and excerpts from his autobiography, Spitzer, *Sauvé Par Le Dessin; Buchenwald*, Non Classé (Favre, 2004).

—Interview with Zieute Licheter, a distant cousin.

—Interview with Mark Beck.

—Testimonial by Matylda Szymaniak, USHMM, "Oral History Interview with Matylda Szymaniak [Oral History Transcript or Notes] - USHMM Collections Search."

—Testimonial by Cila Kateriel Hoppen, "Katowice, Poland [Pages 220-234]."

—Also see Yehiel Stern, "And You Raised My Bones From There."

All drawings by Walter Spitzer courtesy of Ghetto Fighters Museum, Nahariya, Israel.

Page 105, *the yellow star* . . . Lasker, *Rutka's Notebook*, 22.

Page 105, *neighborhood of Bedzin* . . . Before her family was relocated to the ghetto, Rutka arranged for a Polish Christian girl-friend to retrieve the diary from its hiding place under the stairs in her apartment building. That friend, Stanislawa Sapinksa, kept the diary for more than sixty years. In 2006, a nephew persuaded her to donate it to the Bedzin Municipal Museum. That same year the diary was published in Polish and the mayor of Bedzin decided the diary should be entrusted to Yad Vashem, in Jerusalem. Rutka was deported to Auschwitz during one of the *Aktionen* and was murdered there. Her father, however, survived. He eventually moved to Israel and started a new life and new family.

Page 106, *there and live* . . . Matylda Szymaniak, "Oral History Interview with Matylda Szymaniak - USHMM Collections Search."

Page 107, *recalled Sabina Krajce*r . . . Lencner, USC Shoah Foundation Visual History Archive.

Page 107, *of declining production* . . . Browning, *Nazi Policy, Jewish Workers, German Killers*, 82.

Page 108, *to her mother* . . . Fulbrook, *A Small Town Near Auschwitz: Ordinary Nazis and the Holocaust*.

Page 109, *arms and surrendered."* . . . Spitzer, *Sauvé Par Le Dessin; Buchenwald*.

Page 110, *we were downstairs."* . . . Metzger, USC Shoah Foundation Visual History Archive.

Page 110, *Walter recalled* . . . Spitzer, *Sauvé Par Le Dessin; Buchenwald*, 67.

Page 111, *irreversible has happened."* . . . Spitzer, 67.

Page 112, *their deaths anyway."* . . . Matylda Szymaniak, "Oral History Interview with Matylda Szymaniak—USHMM Collections Search."

Page 112, *connection to her."* . . . Clia Katriel Hoppen, "A Rough Road–Skopek Strzemieszyce Pola."

Page 113, *of the Aktion.* . . . All sketches by Walter Spitzer courtesy of the Ghetto Fighters Museum, Nahariya, Israel. Walter Spitzer, *Deportation by Train from Strzemiesyce Wielkie 1574.Jpg*.

Page 116, recalled in his testimonial. . . . Yehiel Stern, "And You Raised My Bones From There."

CHAPTER 10

Page 119, *24 June 1897* . . . Military Government Liason Office Det. E213 SK Munich Special Branch, "Trial of Spruchkammer VII on 23 July against Dr. Hoffmann, Erich, Walter, Fritz, Born 24 June 1897 at Breslau, Residing at Nordhorn, Hauststre. 56 (English Zone)," July 24, 1947, IPN GK 164/4600.

Page 120, *was Karl Demerer* . . . Karl Demerer testimonial, O.3/3635 found in (Richter, 077550, Yad Vashem, Jerusalem.

CHAPTER 11

Page 136, *Germany's Synthetic Fuels* . . . Hanson W. Baldwin, "Germany's Synthetic Oil; It Bulks Large in a Supply of Fuel That Apparently Meets the Enemy's Needs."

Page 137, *for eating purposes."* . . . Avalon Project, "The Trial of German Major War Criminals: Proceedings of the International Military Tribunal Sitting at Nuremberg Germany," Text, The Avalon Project: Nuremberg Trial Proceedings, accessed September 20, 2013, http://avalon.law.yale.edu/imt/12-12-45.asp .

Page 137, *extermination through work.* . . . Avalon Project.

Page 140, *at a time* . . . Jean-Claude Pressac, "Auschwitz: Technique and Operation of the Gas Chambers," 95.

Page 140, *sent to Blechhammer* . . . Schaufeld, USC Shoah Foundation Visual History Archive.

CHAPTER 12

Page 146, *by Israel Rosengarten* . . . Israel J. Rosengarten, *Survival: The Story of a Sixteen-Year-Old Jewish Boy* (Syracuse University Press, 1999), 147 and 159–160.

Page 149, *13-page testimonial* . . . Braasem, "Interview With Joseph Braasem."

Page 150, *after the war.* . . . Höss, *Death Dealer*, 230.

Page 151, *come to light.* . . See "Breaking the Silence about Sexual Violence Against Women During the Holocaust,"

AHRP (blog), November 18, 2014, http://ahrp.org/sexual
-violence-against-women-during-the-holocaust/ ; Also see "Holocaust Women's Rape Breaks Decades of Taboo," Women's
eNews, accessed November 1, 2017, http://womensenews.org
/2011/05/holocaust-womens-rape-breaks-decades-taboo/

Chapter 13

Page 157, *them got killed."* . . . Schaufeld, USC Shoah Foundation
Visual History Archive.

Page 157, *Marcel Klein from.* . . Klein, USC Shoah Foundation
Visual History Archive.

Page 160, *of the defecation."* . . . Widerman-Clary, "Mémorial
de la Shoah."

Page 160, *and posted it* . . . Clary, *From the Holocaust to
Hogan's Heroes*, 67. Clary wrote he only learned the letter had
reached its destination in 1981.

Page 166, *through July 1944.* . . "Danielle and David Snegg
Papers." Halerie's great-grandson, Marc Snegg, donated the letters to USHMM in 2014. He plans to write a book based on the
archive about the experiences of Halerie and Fernande, who was
Snegg's grandmother and died in 2009.

Page 171, *Israeli police documents* . . . From 1975 to 1976, West
German Federal Authorities launched an investigation into war
crimes committed in Blechhammer, focusing on several camp
guards. The Israeli National Police deposed a number of Blechhammer survivors and sent the affidavits, in German, to their
German Federal counterparts. As cited above, Karl Demerer's
testimony is included in these files. See Richter, Dorshavitz,
Bardah and Kolar, "Blechhammer."

CHAPTER 14

Page 174, *of superfluous eaters."* . . . Steven R. Welch, "'The
Annihilation of Superfluous Eaters': Nazi Plans for and Use of
Famine in Eastern Europe."

Page 176, *annihilation through labor* . . .For a comprehensive review of this, see Wachsmann, "'Annihilation Through Labor': The Killing of State Prisoners in the Third Reich."

Page 176, *of the exhibit* . . .Blumenthal, "A Visit to the Unfathomable Past of Auschwitz."

Page 176, *the concentration camps* . . . See Prison Labor subsection in, "What Are Concentration Camps?"

Page 176, *the SS State* . . .Eugen Kogon, *Der SS-Staat Das System Der Deutschen Konzentrationslager*, First Edition (Frankfurter Hefte, 1946).

Page 176, *Practice of Hell* . . . Eugen Kogon, *The Theory And Practice Of Hell*. See bibliography for link to download 1998 version of the book.

Page 176, *Outside interference* . . . Eugen Kogon, 302.

Page 178, *accepting my counsel."* . . .Eugen Kogon, 264.

Page 179, *taken from Schnabel* . . . *Formular Z32 Rentabilitätsberechnung*.

Page 180, *book, Imperfect Justice* . . . Stuart Eizenstat, *Imperfect Justice: Looted Assets, Slave Labor, and the Unfinished Business of World War II* (New York: Public Affairs, 2004).

Page 180, *in a German book* . . . Klewitz, *Die Arbeitssklaven der Dynamit Nobel*.

Page 180, *another German book* . . . Focke and Reimer, *Alltag der Entrechteten*.

CHAPTER 15

Page 185, *Sacks recalled* . . . Sacks, "Speak, Memory."

Page 185, *never actually experienced* . . . For a deeper discussion of how we remember, see "Why We Remember So Many Things Wrong | The New Yorker."

Page 186, *two other refineries* . . . The most comprehensive study of the numbers of missions, bombers and casualties of the air campaign I could find was carried out by Szymon Serwatka and Michal Mucha. The number of raids cited here is based on the four refineries in Silesia. Bombing raids often targeted multiple refineries. See Szymon Serwatka and Michal Mucha, *From Italy to Poland* (Biuo Uslug Komputerowych, 2002), 15.

CHAPTER 16

Page 188, *accompany the prisoners* . . . For a comprehensive study, see Daniel Blatman, "The Death Marches, January-May 1945: Who Was Responsible for What?" ed. David Silberklang, *Yad Veshem Studies* XXVIII (2000): 155–201.

Page 188, *inmates at Blechhammer* . . . Jewish Virtual Library, "Number of Prisoners in Auschwitz Camps (January 1945) | Jewish Virtual Library."

Page 188, *trembling with fear."* . . . Edward Gastfriend, *My Father's Testament: Memoir of a Jewish Teenager, 1938–1945* (Temple University Press, 1999), 139.

Page 193, *about his shoulders.".* . . Eddie Hyde-Clark, "A Country Boy's Story of the Death March."

Page 193, *Red Martin recalled* . . . Iszak, USC Shoah Foundation Visual History Archive.

Page 194, *saw them again.".* . . George Trundle, "Sound: POW's and Forced Marches."

Page 195, *by the road."* . . . John Maclean, "I Watched Nazis Work Auschwitz Slaves to Death; Scots POW Witnessed Horror of the Holocaust," *Sunday Mail* (Glasgow, Scotland), January 21, 2001, https://www.highbeam.com/doc/1G1-69361665.html.

Page 195, *supposed to go,"* . . . Höss, *Death Dealer*.

Page 195, *at Romilly, France* . . .[excerpt from Pvt. Heinrich Schaefer. . .] "Information Regarding Alleged War Crime," 1–3, Schaefer Affidavit.

Page 195, *march, Abraham Schaufeld* . . . Schaufeld, USC Shoah Foundation Visual History Archive.

Page 198, *13 August 1945.* . . [Excerpt from Pvt. Franz Ludwig] . . . "Information Regarding Alleged War Crime," 2–3, Ludwig Affidavit.

Page 198, *those thirteen days.* . .The figure of 800 killed is widely quoted and comes from Piper, see Franciszek Piper, "'Das Nebenlager Blechhammer,'" *Hefte von Auschwitz* 10 (1967): 19–39. When I asked Piper where he got the number, he allowed it was his best guess estimate. The number of days of the death march, from Blechhammer to Gross Rosen, varies from 8 to 14, depending on the account, with many survivor testimonials saying 12 or 13.

CHAPTER 17
Page 200, *Gross-Rosen Concentration Camp* . . . The route here is based on Piper's study, see Franciszek Piper.
Page 200, *ninety-seven thousand prisoners* . . . Blatman, *The Death Marches*, 97–98.
Page 200, *recalled Edward Gastfriend* . . . Gastfriend, *My Father's Testament*, 149.
Page 201, *stacks of them.* . . . Spitzer, *Sauvé Par Le Dessin ; Buchenwald*, 139.
Page 201, *Clary recalled.* . . . Clary, Robert, and Hugh G. Earnhart. "Interview with Robert Clary." Oral History Program, O.H. 436, 1986.

CHAPTER 18
Page 207, *in Grynberg's backstory* . . . Grynberg, "Central DB of Shoah Victims' Names—Record Details, Item No. 1401535" Also see Item No's: 1714073 and 1697252.
Page 207, *survived the war* . . . "Transports to Extinction: Holocaust (Shoah) Deportation Database."

CHAPTER 19
Page 215, *prisoners had died* . . . Christine Glauning, "Bisingen I Places: Concentration Camp and Oil Shale-Works."

CHAPTER 20

Page 216, *he was fading.* . . . Of all my father's stories, I had him repeat the one about his escape more than any other. It stuck with me because the story was one of the few in which he came off as truly heroic, demonstrating bravery, cunning, and grit.

CHAPTER 21

Page 223, *to 48 percent.* . . ."Crime in New York City," Wikipedia, July 31, 2018, https://en.wikipedia.org/w/index. php?title=Crime_in_New_York_City&oldid=852854947. Also, George James, "New York Killings Set a Record, While Other Crimes Fell in 1990," *The New York Times*, April 23, 1991, sec. N.Y. / Region, https://www.nytimes.com/1991/04/23/nyregion /new-york-killings-set-a-record-while-other-crimes-fell-in -1990.html.

Page 226, *Easter Sunday Blizzard* . . . Robert McFadden, "TimesMachine."

EPILOGUE

Page 247, *on that list* . . . "Śląsko-Dąbrowski Nr 31 Katowice, Dnia 20 Listopada PDF."

Page 248, *of I.G. Farbin* . . . For a more complete study, see Arnold Krammer, "Technology Transfer as War Booty: The U.S. Technical Oil Mission to Europe, 1945," *Technology and Culture* 22, no. 1 (1981): 68–103, https://doi.org/10.2307/3104293.

PHOTO AND DOCUMENT CREDITS

Drawings of camp life by Walter Spitzer, reprinted with permission of Ghetto Fighters House Museum, Nahariya, Israel.

Image of Jean Grynberg, reprinted with permission of Yad Vashem, Israel.

Excerpts from *Children of the Holocaust* by Helen Epstein, reprinted with permission of author.

Excerpts from *From the Holocaust to Hogan's Heroes: Autobiography of Robert Clary*, reprinted with permission of author.

Excerpts from oral testimonial of Sigmund W., Holocaust Testimony (T-55), reprinted with permission of Fortunoff Video Archive for Holocaust Testimonies, Yale University Library.

Excerpts from Survival, by Israel Rosengarten, reprinted with permission, Syracuse University Press.

Excerpts from *A Small Town Near Auschwitz: Ordinary Nazis and the Holocaust*, by Mary Fulbrook, reprinted with permission of author.

Images of Josef Lajtner Auschwitz registration form and diamond documents, courtesy of Auschwitz-Birkenau Memorial and Museum, Oswiecim, Poland.

Images from the Dabrowa *Judenrat* archive, courtesy of the State Archives in Katowice (Katowice, Poland).

Images from Transport Lists, courtesy of United States Holocaust Memorial Museum, Washington, DC.

ABOUT THE AUTHOR

For some two decades, Mel Laytner was a reporter and editor of hard news, much of it covering the Middle East as a foreign correspondent for NBC News and United Press International (UPI).

Mel started his full-time career with UPI, where he covered all manner of urban mayhem in New York City, his hometown. He was promoted to a bureau manager before moving to the General News and Cables (Foreign) Desks where he had final responsibility for selecting and editing the top stories of the day for UPI's four hundred afternoon newspaper clients.

Mel's first foreign posting was London. A year later, UPI assigned him to the Tel Aviv bureau. Soon after, he was named Jerusalem Correspondent. NBC News recruited Mel as its Middle East Radio Correspondent.

After seven grinding years overseas, he won a prestigious Knight-Bagehot Fellowship in Economic and Business Journalism, which included a year's residency at the Columbia Graduate School of Business.

Mel received his BA in political science at the City College of New York. He earned master's degrees from the Columbia Graduate School of Journalism, with a concentration in broadcast news, and from Columbia's School of International and Public Affairs, with a specialization in foreign policy analysis.

He and his wife, an artist, live in New York City and are the proud parents of three daughters.

Author photo © Mel Laytner

Selected Titles From SparkPress

SparkPress is an independent boutique publisher
delivering high-quality, entertaining, and engaging
content that enhances readers' lives, with a special focus
on female-driven work. www.gosparkpress.com

Behind the Red Veil: An American Inside Gorbachev's Russia,
Frank Thoms, $16.95, 978-1-68463-055-4. Frank Thoms went
to Russia seeking to understand himself—and to empathize
with Russians living in a deteriorating Communist society. In
Behind the Red Veil, he takes readers inside the culture of "the
enemy," inviting them to discover both Russia and its people
for themselves.

The Journalist: Life and Loss in America's Secret War, Jerry
A. Rose and Lucy Rose Fischer, $16.95, 978-1-68463-065-3. A
collaboration between Lucy Rose Fischer and her late brother,
The Journalist tells the story of Jerry Rose, a young journalist and
photographer who exposed the secret beginnings of America's
Vietnam War in the early 1960s. He interviewed Vietnamese
villagers, embedded himself with soldiers, and wrote the first
major article about American troops fighting in Vietnam.

*The Restless Hungarian: Modernism, Madness, and The
American Dream,* Tom Weidlinger. $16.95, 978-1-943006-
96-0. A revolutionary, a genius, and a haunted man . . . The story
of the architect-engineer Paul Weidlinger, whose colleagues called
him "The Wizard," spans the rise of modern architecture, the
Holocaust, and the Cold War. The revelation of hidden Jewish
identity propels the author to trace his father's life and adventures
across three continents.

Mission Afghanistan: An Army Doctor's Memoir, Elie Cohen,
translation by Jessica Levine. $16.95, 978-1-943006-65-6.
Decades after evading conscription as a young man, Franco-
British doctor Elie Paul Cohen is offered a deal by the French
Army: he can settle his accounts by becoming a military doctor
and serving at Camp Bastion in Afghanistan.

ABOUT SPARKPRESS

....

SparkPress is an independent, hybrid imprint focused on merging the best of the traditional publishing model with new and innovative strategies. We deliver high-quality, entertaining, and engaging content that enhances readers' lives. We are proud to bring to market a list of New York Times best-selling, award-winning, and debut authors who represent a wide array of genres, as well as our established, industry-wide reputation for creative, results-driven success in working with authors. SparkPress, a BookSparks imprint, is a division of SparkPoint Studio LLC.

Learn more at GoSparkPress.com

CPSIA information can be obtained
at www.ICGtesting.com
Printed in the USA
LVHW031135091021
699997LV00002B/6

9 781684 631032